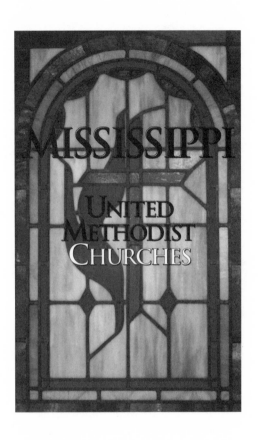

MISSISSIPPI

UNITED
METHODIST
CHURCHES

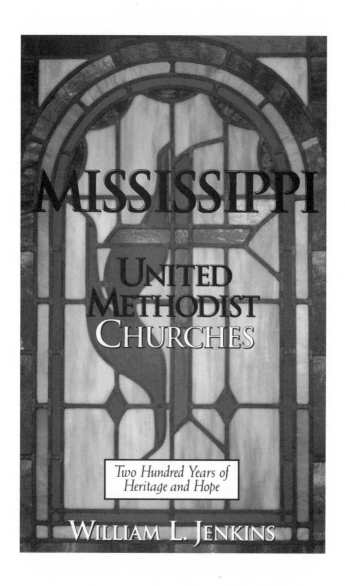

MISSISSIPPI

UNITED METHODIST CHURCHES

Two Hundred Years of
Heritage and Hope

WILLIAM L. JENKINS

PROVIDENCE HOUSE PUBLISHERS
Franklin, Tennessee

Printed in the United States of America

02   01   00   99   98   1   2   3   4   5

Library of Congress Catalog Card Number: 98-66284

ISBN: 1-57736-104-0

Cover illustration: The stained glass titled "Cross and Flame" was commissioned and donated by Walter May and hangs in the Mississippi United Methodist Conference Building, Jackson, Mississippi. Photo by Woody Woodrick.

Cover design by Gary Bozeman

Published by
PROVIDENCE HOUSE PUBLISHERS
238 Seaboard Lane • Franklin, Tennessee 37067
800-321-5692

TO

THE REVEREND AUBREY B. SMITH

The finest Methodist pastor
I ever met.

CONTENTS

PREFACE AND ACKNOWLEDGMENTS

THE BICENTENNIAL ANNIVERSARY OF METHODISM IN MISSISSIPPI WILL be celebrated in 1999. In 1799, Tobias Gibson, a twenty-seven year old circuit riding minister from the Pee Dee District of South Carolina, was appointed by Bishop Asbury to become a Methodist missionary to Natchez, Mississippi. At the first signs of Spring in 1799, Gibson departed from Anson Circuit, North Carolina, where he served the Winter quarter. He traveled through the Smoky Mountains to Nashville, a tiny new settlement in the Tennessee wilderness, where he sold his horse and bought a canoe. He floated up the Cumberland River to the Ohio River, near present day Paducah, Kentucky. There he met more experienced navigators, known as "Kaintucks," who offered him passage down the Ohio and Mississippi Rivers aboard their crudely made flatboat. The circuitous trip from the Carolinas to Natchez took weeks to complete.

Reverend Gibson arrived in Natchez around April 1799 to start his frontier mission. His nearest colleague was over 500 miles away. Despite a notorious reputation, the Natchez area offered hope that his labors would not be in vain. Natchez had already become home to some of Gibson's relatives from South Carolina. No doubt, it was in their homes that Tobias Gibson found a warm reception, and preached his first sermons.

From that humble beginning the present Mississippi Annual Conference of The United Methodist Church has grown to more than 1,200 churches with 186,000 members.

This book was prepared as a project of the Mississippi Methodist Bicentennial to celebrate "200 Years of Heritage and Hope." Due to the limitations of time and space, only active Mississippi United Methodist Churches were included.

This book does not contain all the information I sought. Appeals for local church histories were made on the floor of Annual Conferences sessions the last three years, and the Church History Form was printed in the *Advocate*. I am pleased that we collected historical information on 1,000 of the 1,200 churches.

I apologize for inevitable errors contained within. Efforts were made to verify dates, but readers will find errors. My task has been that of collector, not author. Please submit corrections and missing local church histories to the J. B. Cain Conference Archives, Millsaps College, Jackson, Mississippi. Perhaps a second edition of this book will be published with all the local church histories and more accurate data.

Sources for information included: Conference histories and Journals, Charge Conference reports, Church History Forms, published and unpublished church histories, church cornerstones, church pictorial directories, county histories, newspaper articles, letters, telephone conversations, James Brieger's *Hometown Mississippi*, and the General Board of Global Ministries database (which supplied dates of organization for 150 churches for which no other data was available).

A list of contributors appears in the appendix. However, I must say a special word of thanks to certain individuals and groups, without whose help this project would have been impossible. First and foremost, I thank my wife, Anita Cabral, who proofread the manuscript numerous times, drew two dozen or more of the church drawings, and offered encouragement and support to see the work through to completion. Debra McIntosh, Conference Archivist, was instrumental in assisting me. Bishop Marshall Meadors' encouragement enabled me to attempt this project. All the District Secretaries devoted many hours to help me, without whose help many dates would be omitted. Among them, I particularly want to thank Norma Hubbard, Janie Knight, Karen Wong, Shelby Oaks, Anne Winstead, and Jewel Jones, who worked above the call of duty. All the District Superintendents encouraged me, particularly Jack Nabors, Henderson Rasberry, and Gary Knight. I want to thank the Bicentennial Steering Committee, The Commission on Archives and History, and The Conference Historical Society for their help and support. James E. "Sam" Price, of Vicksburg, assumed the mission of locating all the church histories in the West Jackson District. Numerous county libraries supplied useful data. A special word of thanks goes to Independence United Methodist Church of Morton, for their patience, love, and understanding that allowed me time to complete this book.

The churches are listed alphabetically by name, followed by county, physical location, city, and postal code, if known. Some of the designations may seem unusual, because they come from the United States Geographic Survey map database. Those designations were used when no other physical location data was available. Many churches submitted photographs of their buildings, and some submitted drawings. A decision was made to use only drawings in this publication.

All materials collected in this project have been donated to the J. B. Cain Archives of the Mississippi Annual Conference at Millsaps College, Jackson, Mississippi, and are available for review.

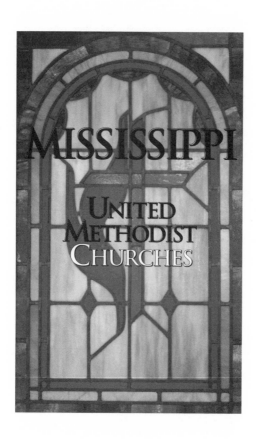

MISSISSIPPI

**UNITED
METHODIST
CHURCHES**

ABBEVILLE *(Lafatette County: Abbeville 38601)*. Abbeville community was settled in the early 1830s, burned in the Civil War, and declined when the railroad bypassed the area.

Aberdeen First United Methodist Church

ABERDEEN FIRST *(Monroe County: 300 College Place, Aberdeen 39730)*. Records show that in 1836 to 1837, a circuit in northeast Mississippi was named Aberdeen. The first pastor was J. L. Finley. During this formative period, it was in the Tuscaloosa District of the Alabama Conference, but in November 1840, it became a part of the Memphis District. Bishop Robert Paine presided when the 1848 conference met in Aberdeen. There have been four church buildings. A small wooden frame building was constructed about 1837, near the Monroe County Courthouse, and in 1840, a second wooden structure was erected on the present site. In 1859, the cornerstone was laid for the third church, and Reverend J. T. Meriwether preached the first sermon. It was a brick church, with a wide upstairs gallery for the Black members. A parsonage was built next door about 1880. In 1912, the fourth church building replaced the

third at the same location. An organization of young women called the Dorcas Band subscribed $3,000 by having bazaars. Reverend I. D. Borders preached the first sermon. This building of Gothic architecture was enlarged to include a Sunday School annex in 1955. This sanctuary is graced by stained glass murals made by the master American glass craftsman, Louis Tiffany. The windows include three biblical events, the birth of Christ, Jesus with Martha and Mary, and Christ's ascension. Bishop Paine is buried in Aberdeen.

Ackerman First United Methodist Church

ACKERMAN FIRST *(Choctaw County: 118 Church Highway, Ackerman 39735)*. This community was established in 1883. The church was organized in 1879. The oldest church register of the Ackerman United Methodist Church dates back to the year 1882, and at that time the church was in the French Camp Circuit of the former North Mississippi Conference. Other churches on this circuit were McCool, Liberty Chapel, Salem, Pisgah,

Chapel Hill, and Prospect. The Ackerman Church was organized about the time the Illinois Central Railroad was built through Choctaw County. Since there was no church building at that time, the early Methodists worshipped in the little log schoolhouse which was located somewhere in the vicinity of the Ackerman High School. The preacher was a circuit rider who rode horseback to each of the churches in his circuit, one or maybe two each Sunday, so the Ackerman Methodists had church only once each month. For a number of years the people worshipped in the schoolhouse, then they began to work toward a church. A lot was purchased on 14 December 1885, on the south side of East Church Avenue. The deed is found recorded in the Land Deed Records of Choctaw County. There is no record as to when this church was dedicated. The Ackerman Methodist Church was a circuit with four to six churches until the Conference of 1921, when it became Ackerman and Weir. In 1929, it became a station church. In 1939 it became Ackerman and South Union, and in 1950 it became a station again. It was in the Durant District from 1906 through 1919 when it was placed in the Columbus District. Since 1959 the Ackerman Church has been in the Starkville District.

ACONA *(Holmes County: Route Three Lexington 39095).* The church was organized in March 1874. The two and one-half acres on which the church was built in 1874 was bought from Mrs. A. T. Lendfair for twenty-five dollars. Some years later, J. P. Harvey deeded an additional one-half acre "for love of the church." The charter

Acona United Methodist Church

members of the church were Steven Johnson, John A. Hamilton, Benjamin H. McGee, Henry Bonner McGee, T. M. Merritt, George Weatherby, Mrs. Sara Ferrell, Mrs. A. T. Lendfair, John Wright McRae, P. M. Diggs, and J. S. Herbert. The members were assisted in building their church by the neighboring Sweetwater and Black Hawk Churches. The lumber was brought to Vaiden by rail and hauled by mule-drawn wagons. Reverend K. A. Jones was the first pastor in charge. The parsonage was purchased in 1916. The cemetery committee was organized 21 October 1899. In January 1961, Acona was recognized as one of the top ten rural churches in Mississippi.

ADAMS *(Lincoln County: 2201 Brumfield Road SW, Summit 39666).* The church was organized in 1811. It was the site of the 1815 Annual Conference and first district conference in Mississippi, in October 1822.

ADAMS CHAPEL *(Jefferson County: Martin Luther King Drive, Natchez 39120).* This church was organized 6 June 1870. The present frame structure is the original church building.

ADAMS CHAPEL *(Clarke County: Quitman 39355).* The church was organized in 1916.

ADATON *(Oktibbeha County: Reed Road, Starkville 39759).* The church was organized in 1878.

ADKINS CHAPEL *(Tippah County: 7321 County Road 700, Blue Mountain 38610).* Adkins Chapel Methodist Episcopal Church was organized on 15 July 1896, when Henry Adkins and his wife, Princy, deeded a parcel of land for the purpose of founding a church named Adkins Chapel. The church was built in 1904, with the help of Reverend E. F. Scarborough. The first church was built on a different section of the land which was located on the right side of the present Pontotoc Road in the middle of a field. The first church was destroyed by a fire in 1914, and the church was relocated on the opposite side of the road. The second church was rebuilt with the help of the General Conference. The church also served as a school for many young Black people until a school was built in the lower front southeast corner of the property. The third church, located at the present site, was first a white wood frame building with a tin roof and two doors on the front.

ALDERSGATE *(Hinds County: 655 Beasley Road, Jackson 39206).* On 5 December 1965, the first worship service was held in the neighboring structure which now houses the Saint Christopher Episcopal Church. The following Sunday, 12 December 1965, the District Superintendent, Reverend John H. Cook, led the official organizational service. Aldersgate became the name in the wish

that the same warmth that John Wesley experienced on Aldersgate Street in 1738, would always prevail in this place. For approximately eighteen months, worship services were held in the Saint Christopher building. Charter Sunday was observed on 22 May 1966. Seventy visionaries had the faith to believe that on this five acre plot would be a church. On Sunday, 29 January 1967, Bishop Edward Pendergrass led the congregation in a ground breaking service. In early May of 1967, the first unit was completed at a cost of $80,000, and on Aldersgate Sunday, 21 May 1967, the formal opening and consecration service was held. Reverend John Higginbotham, who served from 1 October 1965 through 1969, is remembered as the organizing pastor. Historical records reflect that during the latter part of the 1970s and early 1980s, the neighborhood began to change, resulting in a substantial loss in membership. By 1982, the congregation had become predominately Black. Under the leadership of Reverend Harrell, the church held a mortgage burning service on Aldersgate Sunday 1985. The Bishop, in 1987, appointed the first and only female minister to serve this church, Reverend Marjorie Walker.

ALDERSGATE *(Oktibbeha County: Evergreen Highway, Starkville 39759).* During the 1950s and 1960s, interest had been developing in the First United Methodist Church of Starkville concerning the need for another Methodist church in Starkville. A resolution was adopted by the Board of First Methodist Church declaring its intention of support for a new church. The Commission on Church Extension also pledged to provide financial and moral support. The North Mississippi Conference appointed Reverend Lonnie Johnston as the first pastor of the new church. On 26 June 1960, under the leadership of Reverend Lonnie Johnston, a small group of people gathered under pecan trees at Sudduth School. The church was completed in 1968, and consecrated 15 September 1968, by Bishop Pendergrass.

ALGOMA *(Pontotoc County: 1161 Algoma Road, Algoma 38820).* The Algoma United Methodist Church was organized in the schoolhouse of Old Algoma in 1895, with Reverend F. A. Whitson as pastor. It was part of the four-point Pontotoc Charge. At Annual Conference in 1908, Palestine Circuit was formed with Algoma, Ebenezer, Campground, and Palestine Churches being included as part of the Aberdeen District. In 1916, the circuit was changed from Palestine to Algoma, with Algoma having a membership of about thirty-five. The Methodist and Presbyterian people conducted their Sunday School services together for a number of years after the churches ceased to use the school building as a place of worship. The two denominations shared services until the Methodists built their building in 1921 on a lot purchased from E. W. Bost.

ALLENS CHAPEL *(Lee County: Highway 178, Mooreville 38857).* This church was organized in 1880.

ALTA WOODS *(Hinds County: 109 Alta Woods Boulevard, Jackson 39204).* Early in 1952, a religious census was made of the Alta Woods Community under the direction of the Board of Evangelism of the Mississippi Methodist Annual Conference. The results proved the need for a new church. Sunday, 7 July 1952, a small group attended services for the first time in the home of Mr. and Mrs. Julian Brown. Present were: Reverend Aubrey C. Walley, Mr. and Mrs. Julian Brown, Miss Virginia Brown, Mrs. Roy Brashier, Mrs. Charles Sloan Jr., Mr. and Mrs. Mims Brown, and Miss Natalie Brown. The church was officially organized 28 September 1952, in the Alta Woods Presbyterian Church. Bishop Marvin Franklin was the speaker. Doctor B. M. Hunt, District Superintendent, directed the organization. The church officially began with seventy-one members. At a meeting of the Quarterly Conference, a building committee was officially appointed. On 26 May 1953, the Quarterly Conference authorized the purchase of a parsonage on Glenn Street. Reverend Aubrey C. Walley was appointed the first full time pastor of the church in June 1953. Prior to his appointment Reverend Cecil Williamson had served as associate pastor. A large lot just west of the church property was purchased. On 29 May 1955, Bishop Marvin Franklin turned the first shovel of dirt in the ground breaking ceremonies for the new sanctuary and on 12 August 1956, Bishop Marvin A. Franklin officially opened the new sanctuary.

AMORY FIRST *(Monroe County: 107 South Third, Amory 38821).* The first congregation of Methodists in Amory was

Amory First United Methodist Church

organized in 1884, with Reverend Whitehurst as pastor, and was a part of the Smithville Charge. The majority of the people are believed to have come from Cotton Gin Port on the Tombigbee River. Methodists completed a small frame church in 1894. In 1914, the first brick church was erected. The church was made a station in 1921, and entertained Annual Conference on 16 and 17 November 1921. It was dedicated by Bishop William N. Ainsworth of Macon, Georgia, on Sunday, 5 February 1924. During this service, the death of President Wilson was announced. In 1923, a large education building was erected, joining the sanctuary, and is the only part of the first brick building now standing. This church burned on 11 January 1926, but the education building was saved. By the spring of 1927, the church was dedicated on Easter Sunday by Bishop Warren A. Candler of Atlanta, Georgia. Tragedy struck the church again in 1936. A quote in the Quarterly Conference report reads, "Our Church building and annex caught fire in the early morning of 26 February 1936 and was destroyed." The church that was built by December 1936 was a replica of the one that burned. All four churches were built on the present site.

ANDERSON *(Hinds County: 6205 Hanging Moss Road, Jackson 39206).* Anderson United Methodist Church began as a mission in 1914 under the leadership of local ministers from the Central and Pratt Methodist Episcopal Churches. One of the ministers, Reverend R. L. Pickens, pastor of Central, helped organize the Cloverleaf Methodist Episcopal Mission. During the 1920s, the first group of members met at the home of William Harper, where they worshipped until a specific location was secured. By 1928, a temporary house of worship for the Mission was obtained, an old abandoned store on Whitfield Mill Road, now Martin Luther King Drive. In 1936, a lot on Spring Street was purchased, and the first church building was constructed. It was named for Reverend R. L. Anderson, the first conference appointed minister. Reverend Anderson died in 1930. Reverend I. R. Kersh Sr. was the pastor at the time. Anderson Chapel, as it was known then, was constructed. In September 1952, under the leadership of Reverend Blackmon, a new structure was built on Page Street and given the name Anderson Memorial. In 1968, under C. P. Payne, Anderson Memorial became Anderson United Methodist Church. In 1972, during the tenure of Reverend H. C. Clay, the white and Black United Methodist conferences merged into one conference. Under the pastorate of Reverend J. A. Stallworth, the church moved to West Northside Drive. Because of its tremendous growth, Anderson relocated to Interstate 220 at Hanging Moss Road in November 1994.

ANDREW CHAPEL *(Rankin County: 113 Meadows Cove, Brandon 39042).* This church was organized between 1856 and March 1899.

ANDREWS CHAPEL *(Lauderdale County: Hillview Drive, Meridian 39305).* The church was organized in 1873.

ANDREWS CHAPEL *(Lee County: Highway 371 South, Evergreen).* This church was organized in 1872.

ANGUILLA *(Sharkey County: 601 Front Street, Anguilla 38721).* This community was once known as McKinneyville in honor of an early settler and plantation owner. With the arrival of the railroad in 1884, the village became known as Anguilla. The Methodist church was organized here between 1869 and 1888. The first church, known as Union Chapel, may have been a Union church, conducting services with other denominations.

ANTIOCH *(Choctaw County: Reform Street, Ackerman 39735).* This church was organized in 1860.

ANTIOCH *(Greene County: 154 Albert Reeves Road, Mclain 39456).* This church was organized in the 1800s.

ANTIOCH *(Jones County: 845 Lower Myrick Road, Laurel 39440).* Antioch United Methodist Church was originally organized in 1875 as Antioch Congregational Methodist Church with eleven charter members. The ministers serving the church at that time were Reverends Thomas Windham and Daniel Walters. Although the original location of the church is unknown, in August 1891, the present parcel of land was deeded by John and C. C. Hamper Lumber Company to the trustees of the church. A new frame sanctuary was built in 1902. On 12 September 1924, Antioch Congregational Methodist was accepted into the Methodist Episcopal Church, South. A conference was opened at Antioch on the third Sunday of October 1924, when thirty members presented their names as applicants to become members of the Methodist Episcopal Church, South. Sometime between 1924 and 1933, a new church was built. On 1 April 1933, this new church was dedicated. The present parsonage was

opened 22 September 1963, with Bishop Marvin A. Franklin as guest speaker. The first service was held in the present sanctuary on 24 November 1974.

ANTIOCH *(Monroe County: Smithville 38870).*

ARCOLA *(Washington County: 101 Broadway, Arcola 38722).* The church was organized between 1854 and 1866.

ARKABUTLA *(Tate County: Arkabutla 38602).* Reverend J. L. Brown purchased large tracts of land from the Indians in 1836 for five dollars an acre. He donated land for schools and churches in this area. The Methodist church was organized in 1854, and a new building erected about 1876.

ARTESIA *(Lowndes County: Front Street, Artesia 39736).* The church was organized in 1860.

ASBURY *(Forrest County: 101 Morris Street, Suite A, Petal 39465).* The church was organized in 1996.

ASBURY *(Hinds County: 210 Raymond-Bolton Road, Bolton 39041).* Asbury Church was organized in 1872. It was rebuilt in 1898 under the leadership of Reverend D. D. Goodwin. As the years passed, Asbury prospered and was remodeled in 1926. Asbury, and what was to become Kingsley Chapel United Methodist Church of Edwards, were united on the same charge. In 1972, Asbury became a United Methodist Church. Reverend Doctor Oscar Allen Rogers Jr. served for twenty-two years, the longest pastorate in the history of Asbury. In May of 1984, Doctor Rogers accepted the Presidency of Clafton College, Orangeburg, North Carolina.

ASBURY *(Itawamba County: Tremont 38876).* Asbury Church was established first at Old Jim's Creek cemetery site, about a mile east of the present building. The first sanctuary was constructed in 1840, and the first pastor was Floyd Martin. The present building was built as an academy or school, and two acres of land were given for that purpose. Around 1935, Mrs. W. D. Evans deeded the land over to the Methodist Conference when it began to be used for the Asbury Church. This church has been called Whitney, Jim's Creek, and Asbury. The parsonage for this charge was first at Asbury, which is the house presently behind the church. Reverend York was the first pastor to use it as a parsonage, probably around 1910. There were seven churches on the charge at that time.

ASBURY *(Marshall County: 60 West College Street, Holly Springs 38635).* This church was organized in June 1866. Moses Adams was the first pastor. The Upper Mississippi Conference was organized in this church on 5 February 1891. Bishop E. J. Johnson was the presiding bishop. The Mississippi Conference, before dividing, was held at Holly Springs on 29 December through 2 January 1871. Since the organization of the Upper Mississippi Conference, the Annual Conference has been held at Asbury Church six times. Rust College was organized in this church in 1866. The following persons have entered the ministry from this church: C. A. Talbert, M. L. Talbert, M. W. Lindsey, Richard Bynum, and C. F. Golden. Hiram Revels was buried here in January 1901, and his tombstone still stands. The last session of the Upper Mississippi Conference was held at Holly Springs. The Conference began here in 1891, and ended here in 1974.

ASBURY *(Noxubee County: Shuqualak 39361).* This church was organized in 1880.

ASBURY *(Prentiss County: Morgan Road, Baldwyn 38824).* Asbury was organized in 1890.

ASHLAND *(Benton County: Ashland 38603).* The church was organized in 1860. Before the Civil War, Ashland Methodist Church was part of the Salem Circuit. Salem, the county seat, was burned by the Union Army during the war. The community was established in 1870, and named for Henry Clay's home in Kentucky. In 1873, Ashland became a charge that included Salem, Union Hill, Shawnee, and Wesley Chapel. Bishop Paine appointed Hiram R. Caldwell the pastor, and the charge had 181 members. In 1876, the acre on which the church building stood was purchased. The first parsonage was built 1896 through 1897, when R. E. Duke was pastor. In the Fall of 1905, Liberty joined the Ashland Charge. Black Jack was added to the charge in 1914. It has been on and off the charge two or three times. In 1917, Shawnee, Salem, and Union Hill were discontinued, and 198 members from Shawnee and Salem went to Liberty. In 1925, Wesley Chapel burned and members transferred to Black Jack. In 1934, Harris Chapel, Lamar, Early Grove, and Rice Chapel joined the charge. Early Grove left by 1948, Lamar left in 1960, and Rice Chapel in 1961.

ATHENS *(Monroe County: Route Four, Aberdeen 39730).* The church was organized in 1879. Athens United Methodist Church was built around the late 1890s. The first pastor to serve the church was Reverend W. E. Franklin. In 1932, this building burned and worship services were held under a brush arbor until another church was built. That church was built under the leadership of Reverend N. H. Cooperwood. He served the congregation until 1962, when that building was demolished and the present building was erected under the leadership of Reverend J. P. Watson. In 1983, the present building was remodeled and a fellowship hall was added. The entire church was bricked under the leadership of Reverend Benjamin Wax.

AVON *(Washington County: Highway One South, Avon 38723)*. The Avon Methodist Church was organized in 1902 by a small group of the area's early residents. Some of the charter members were: Mrs. S. A. Branton, Mrs. W. T. Glathary, Mr. and Mrs. H. H. Key, Mr. and Mrs. J. B. Romine, and Mr. C. S. Rowe. During the early years the services were held in the one-room school building. In 1913, a frame church building was constructed on a one acre site. The building was paid for that year with a small donation from the Methodist Conference and from local contributions by different denominations. Wooden planks were used for seats until pews were purchased in 1916. In 1957, the present building was constructed. Pledges were made to cover the cost over a period of six years. The old church building was sold and was moved to Leland to be used for a church. The building was presented for dedication by Mr. W. A. Branton during a service of worship on 25 February 1962, conducted by Bishop Marvin Franklin. The parsonage was built in 1969, during the pastorate of Wallace Roberts.

BAILEY MEMORIAL *(Calhoun County: Loyd Community, Vardaman 38878)*. This church was organized prior to 1900. A new sanctuary and education building were built in 1955. The church has an adjacent cemetery.

BAKER'S CHAPEL *(DeSoto County: 965 Johnston Road, Hernando 38632)*. Reverend German and Mary Keyser Baker, and their young family, moved into the area soon after DeSoto County was formed in 1836, and established a church and a school at their home about three miles north of the present church location. German Baker is buried in the now abandoned Baker's Cemetery. The oldest marker in the cemetery is dated 1865. On 8 May 1852, land was deeded for the present church site. The church was built and dedicated in 1857, and named Baker's Chapel in honor of German Baker. In 1892, the church records list as members the families of Anderson, Chamberlin, Harris, Johnson, Laughter, Lauderdale, and Vaiden, among others. In April 1939, a tornado demolished the original building. Before the building could be replaced, World War II made any kind of building impossible. In October 1952, a new Baker's Chapel Church building was dedicated. An educational addition was made in 1962. In 1981 the entire building was refurbished and bricked. In 1994 the educational annex was enlarged, and in 1996, the sanctuary was enlarged.

BALDWIN *(Noxubee County: Cliftonville)*. This church was organized in 1903.

BALDWYN FIRST *(Prentiss County: West Street Baldwyn 38824)*. In 1848, a Methodist Church was organized about one mile northwest of Baldwyn. The first pastor was Joseph T. Talley. The church was moved to

Baldwyn in 1861, where services were held in the Baldwyn Masonic Hall until the church was built. The church was a member of the Memphis Conference before it was a member of the North Mississippi Conference. The church has been located in the Aberdeen, Verona, Iuka, Corinth, and New Albany Districts. The original wooden church structure was torn down, and the cornerstone of the new brick church building was laid in 1925. The church was heavily damaged by a tornado on 16 April 1942. A portion of the sanctuary was remodeled during the repairs made to the church building. An education building was added to the church about 1957 or 1958. The parsonage was built in 1921, by W. C. McCay. The parsonage was also heavily damaged during the 1942 tornado. Members of the Baldwyn First United Methodist Church who have entered the ministry include: John Marion McCay, who originated the Mississippi Methodist Hour; John Savoy, and Charles Boyer, ministers in the North Mississippi Conference; Mark Anderson; and Andrew Lee Henry, a minister in the Memphis Conference.

BARLOW *(Attala County: Highway 429, Sallis 39160).* The church was organized 17 April 1886. The first building was a frame structure. The second building was brick, built in 1950.

BARTON *(Marshall County).* Prior to the Civil War, this place was known as Oak Grove. When a post office opened, it had to change its name, since there was already an Oak Grove in the state.

BARWICK *(Leflore County: Minter City 38944).* The church was organized in 1976. It was once known as Walnut Grove.

Batesville First United Methodist Church

BATESVILLE FIRST *(Panola County: 19 Panola Avenue, Batesville 38606).* The church was organized between 1844 and 1872. Land was purchased 4 November 1872. The first pastor, J. W. Bates, for whom the town was named, was assigned in 1873. There were nine founding members. The trustees bought the property around 1872. The first church at Batesville was a frame building, which burned in 1879. A brick building was erected to replace the frame one, but it, too, burned in 1911. In 1913, the present building was constructed with beautiful stained glass windows. A Mohler pipe organ was purchased. Andrew Carnegie matched the funds raised by the women of the church. In 1956, the annex was erected. In 1970, the fellowship hall was built. New classrooms were added to the annex. Those who have gone into full-time Christian service are: Myrtle Pollard, George Boyles, Lonnie Magee, Edward Pruett, Allen Mothershed, and Victoria White.

BATSON *(Forrest County).* Batson began as an extension ministry of Court Street Methodist Episcopal Church, South, 18 October 1909. The first frame building, built between 1908 and 1909, was bricked in the 1940s. An educational annex was added in the 1940s.

BAY SPRINGS *(Jasper County: 11 West Fifth Avenue, Bay Springs 39422).* The community was settled about 1892. The Methodist church was organized in 1905.

BAYLIS CHAPEL *(Marion County: 15 East Baylis Chapel Road, Columbia 39429).* The church was organized in 1901.

BEASLEY (Sunflower County: 100 Union Street, Drew 38737).

BEAUMONT *(Perry County: Beaumont 39423).* Records show that Methodist services were conducted in the Beaumont community in 1904. Older members recalled that services were conducted in a building that later became a private dwelling. Another denomination held services in that same building on alternate Sundays. The present building was built between 1914 and 1915, and the first services in the new building were conducted in July 1915. Mr. Jeff Griffis and J. H. Overstreet, early settlers, furnished the materials and had the church built. Mr. Rudolph Barron, another settler, owned a woodworking shop, and made the pews, pulpit, and altar rail. A fellowship hall was added in the 1960s, and an educational unit was added in the 1970s.

BEAUREGARD *(Copiah County: 1027 North Street, Wesson 39191).* The church was organized between 1866 and 1879. In 1883, a tornado destroyed all but three homes in this town.

BEAUVOIR *(Harrison County: 2113 Pass Road, Biloxi 39531).* On Sunday, 19 February 1956, the first Church School, and the first worship service were held in a small four-room house in an area just west of Keesler Air Force Base. The building was rented on faith, the landlord giving two Sundays in which to raise the month's rent of fifty dollars. Harold Ryker, local preacher of the First Methodist Church of Biloxi, supervised the church school and preached the first sermon. The enthusiasm and attendance continued to grow so that on Sunday, 8 April 1956, Reverend D. T. Ridgeway, District Superintendent, convened a church conference, and Beauvoir Methodist Church was organized with Harold Ryker as pastor. Seventy-seven people signed the registration book as charter members, while Reverends W. A. Tyson, T. O. Prewitt, D. T. Ridgeway, and Harold Ryker looked on. With the help of the men of the church a steel quonset-type building was acquired and erected on the property and the first service was held in it 12 July 1956. On 28 October 1956, Bishop Marvin Franklin broke ground for the education building. It was completed and formally opened Sunday, 3 February 1957.

BELDEN *(Lee County: Belden 38826).* This community was founded in 1872.

BELL CHAPEL (Oktibbeha County).

BELLE HILL (Jefferson County: Union Church 39668). This church was organized in 1892.

BELLEFONTAINE *(Webster County: Bellefontaine 39737).* Bellefontaine United Methodist Church dates back to 1835, when it was known as North Union Methodist Church. The Methodists shared a schoolhouse for church purposes with the Baptists of the area on a site that is now North Union Cemetery. In 1835, they constructed a log building and enclosed the cemetery. There were five founding members. In May 1903, a new building was constructed in Bellefontaine at the present location. In the 1920s this building was destroyed by a storm and built back soon after where it now stands. The Sunday School rooms were added in 1952. In December 1950, James Price, a member of South Union Methodist Church, entered the ministry. John Douglas Pepper, another member, also entered the ministry.

BELMONT *(Tishomingo County: 400 Third Street, Belmont 38827).* The Belmont was organized as early as 1849, or as late as July 1881. The first pastor was W. A. Woods. It was known as the Valley Methodist Church, located on the flatwoods just off Bear Creek Road. The original log church was destroyed by a woods fire in November 1892. G. A. (Dick) Clark and his wife, Julia Ann, deeded the church trustees about one and one-quarter acres of land. In 1911, the Methodist congregation moved to Belmont. The church was damaged by a storm, and was rebuilt in 1933. It was here they worshiped until 1955. In 1945, the congregation began a building fund, under the pastorate of Reverend J. L. Nabors Jr. It was in 1954, under the pastorate of Reverend E. S. Furr, that they completed the present church building. It became a station church in 1967, under the leadership of Reverend Huey Wood. In 1980, a steeple was erected. This church has had four former members to enter the ministry.

BELZONI FIRST *(Humphreys County: 202 Castleman Street, Belzoni 39038).* In the early 1870s, there was a little post office and landing on the north bank of the Yazoo River north of Silver City, known as Greasy Row. This was later changed to Belzoni in honor of Count Belzoni of Italy, a close friend of Elvira Fisk who owned all the land and timber in the area. The first religious services were held here for all Christians, whenever a minister was available, in the home of J. S. Bowles. In 1879, Elvira Fisk and his wife gave the deed to the land where the present church stands to the Methodist Episcopal Church, South. The church was organized in 1884. In 1887, the first small frame church was erected and was used by all Protestants. The present sanctuary, which is the third building, was completed in 1927. An annex was added in 1960. From this church, the following have entered the ministry: Sale Lilly Jr., Wallace Blackwood, and Tommy Sorrells.

BENOIT *(Bolivar County: 301 East Preston, Benoit 38725).* In 1832, Reverend John G. Jones came to Bolivar, a tiny community just three miles from Benoit, to organize a mission. Bolivar became the county seat of Bolivar County when the county was formed in 1836. The Benoit community dates back to 1888. It was named for Gus Benoit, plantation manager of the town's land owner, James Richardson. Benoit was incorporated and the Methodist church was organized in 1901. The Benoit Church was part of a Union church with Baptists and Presbyterians.

BENTLEY CHAPEL *(Forrest County: 611 Ashford Street, Hattiesburg 39401).* This church was organized in 1912.

BENTON *(Yazoo County: 1384 Old Highway Sixteen, Benton 39039).* John Cotton was sent to Benton in 1829, when he organized the Yazoo Methodist Circuit.

In 1831, Thomas Griffin served the circuit, and in 1832, John Lane was appointed. In 1836, the Benton Church became a regular appointment with Jeptha Hughes as the preacher. Out of a Benton Methodist protracted meeting sprang the Presbyterian Church in Yazoo City. Benton probably had a stronger church than the one at nearby Yazoo City at that time. Reverend John G. Jones, Mississippi Methodists' primary historian, likely preached at Benton in 1828 when he made an historic journey to Hanan's Bluff and Manchester, later called Yazoo City. It was on this journey that historic Ebenezer Church, in what is now Holmes County, was organized.

BENTONIA *(Yazoo County: 703 Cannon Avenue, Bentonia 39040)*. The Bentonia Church is thought to have been organized by Reverend Richard Abby in December 1884. Reverend Abby served a circuit named "Stations on the Yazoo Railroad" during this year. The Yazoo Railroad was completed from Jackson to Yazoo City in 1884. The railroad company built a depot beside the track, named it Bentonia, and the village soon grew around it. The circuit named the "Stations on the Yazoo Railroad" was unusual. The railroad had opened up a whole new country. The pastors took advantage of the trains and visited the new villages and the new churches. They undoubtedly preached one Sunday per month, spent the day, and visited parishioners. The fourth Quarterly Conference of the Flora Charge was held at Bentonia in 1886. In 1889, a new charge was created named Bentonia and Dover.

BETHANY *(Simpson County: Cato Road, D'lo 39062)*. The community which later became known as Bethany was established between 1840 and 1850 by a group of Scottish immigrants. Reverend T. C. Clark, while visiting John Colquehoun (Calhoun), who was ill, learned that the community wished to organize a church. Being quite familiar with the Scriptures, he related this situation to Bethany in the Bible. Thus, Bethany Methodist Church received its name. The first site was about a mile south of the present location. Reverend Clark was the first pastor to preach in the log building after the church was formally organized in 1850. The membership increased, and the church relocated to the Gum Springs area shortly before the Civil War. Following the war, the church moved back to the Bethany community. The next site was approximately twenty-five feet west of the present location. Today's church was built in 1887, with Fielding Kendall in charge of the work. The pews, which are still being utilized, were made of longleaf yellow pine and hand planed. Reverend Dan Miller was the pastor, and Reverend B. H. Rawls of Morton preached the dedication sermon. Reverend Bob Nay's first sermon was delivered from Bethany pulpit, and he later became one of Bethany's preachers. While Bob Nay was training for the ministry, Reverend Walter Ranager came and continued from 1946 to 1949. Reverend Nay returned in 1949 and served the church for two years. George Phillips, son of Mrs. Myrtle Phillips and the late Mr. Phillips and a member of Bethany, studied for the ministry at Millsaps. He was appointed to serve Bethany as a student supply preacher from 1952 to 1955. The roof was blown off in a March 1973 tornado.

BETHANY (Yazoo County: Graball-Freerun Road, Yazoo City 39194). The church was organized in 1898.

BETHEL *(Alcorn County: County Road 410 Unit 73, Rienzi 38865)*. Bethel Church was organized in 1845.

BETHEL *(Attala County: Zemuly Community, Kosciusko 39090)*. This historic old church, located seven miles northwest of Kosciusko on the site of an old Methodist campground, may have been in existence as early as 1838. It met in an old log building. Grave markers in the cemetery give evidence of this early settlement. Old record books show that members were received as early as 1838. The present church was organized in 1871. The present building was erected in 1873. It was in this church that Bishop Charles Betts Galloway preached his first sermon at age eighteen.

BETHEL *(Benton County: Pine Grove, Hickory Flat 38633)*. In 1872, some devout men from this community asked Reverend Sweeney Carson of Holly Springs to come to their community and hold a revival if they would build a church. They finished the building in October of that year. Reverend Carson organized the church with five members, then held a revival, during which fifteen or twenty more joined. The church was admitted to the conference in December 1872. The first church was about half a mile from the present one. In 1897 another church was built at Bethel Cemetery. It burned in 1919. A third house was erected. This was used until the present building was constructed in 1947. Seven men have entered the ministry from this church.

BETHEL *(Carroll County)*. This church was organized in 1846.

BETHEL *(Clarke County: Shubuta 39360)*.

BETHEL *(Covington County)*. The church was first organized in 1852 by ten women, including Mrs. Mary F. Welch, Mrs. Jane Patten, Miss Susie Welch, Miss Polly Welch, Miss Rachel Welch, Mrs. Sallie Welch, Miss Phayby Welch, Miss Nancy Welch, Miss Judith Welch, and Miss March Welch. The first preaching was in an old house used as a schoolhouse. Mr. Jimmy Welch used slave labor and built a log house. That was a few years before the Civil War. This house served as the church until about 1889 or 1890, then the present structure was built. This house was built by Mr. C. W. Willis. The lumber was sawed near the church by J. N. Welch at his water mill. After the lumber was seasoned, J. S. Welch dressed it by hand. G. W. Wilson and W. L. Ellzy split boards for the roof from heart virgin pine timber, and this was the first house in the vicinity to be made of sawed and dressed lumber. In 1939 and 1940, the members of Bethel Methodist Church built an annex on the back of the church for school rooms. In the early days of 1954, the members of the church began to give Bethel a new look for her 100th birthday. The walls were covered with masonite boards and painted.

BETHEL *(Lauderdale County: 4328 Old 8th Street Road, Meridian 39301)*. The church was organized in 1897.

BETHEL *(Lee County: Belden 38826)*. This church was organized in 1870.

BETHEL *(Lincoln County: Heavens Way Road, Brookhaven 39601)*. The church was organized in 1875.

BETHEL *(Tallahatchie County)*. This church was organized in 1940.

BETHESDA *(Copiah County: 3160 Bethesda Road, Crystal Springs 39059)*. The church was organized in 1840.

BETHESDA *(Franklin County: Wrights Chapel Road, McCall Creek 39647)*. Goodspeed, in his Memoirs of Mississippi, says that Bethesda Church was established at Wright's Campground. While its official name is Bethesda, it has always been known as Wright's Church by those who worshipped there. The earliest official reference to Bethesda Church is found in the Quarterly Conference records of the Claiborne Circuit in 1823. It is possible the church was organized before that time. The probability is that the early members met for worship in the home of Elijah Wright, or on the campground. The first building was a half mile from the present church building, which was completed in December 1890.

BETHLEHEM *(Franklin County: Roxie 39661)*.

BETHLEHEM *(Jasper County: Lake Como)*. This church was organized between 1896 and 1910.

BETHLEHEM *(Marshall County: Highway 349, Bethlehem)*. When the Bethlehem post office opened in 1852, it was named for the Bethlehem Methodist Church, already in existence. The town incorporated in 1882.

BETHLEHEM *(Montgomery County: Winona 38967)*. Bethlehem Methodist Church was organized in August 1846, by Peter E. Green, junior preacher on the Greensboro Circuit, in the home of Mrs. Elizabeth J. (Betsy Holmes) Fisackerly, widow of John Fisackerly. She and her children constituted seven of the thirteen charter members. Apparently it was a part of the Middleton Circuit for twelve of its first fifteen years. The first church building was a log house located north of the present cemetery, and built soon after the church was organized, probably 1847. The property on which the second church was built in 1884, north of the present building, was given by J. G. Fisackerly. From the best information available, the present sanctuary was erected in 1903. Three Sunday School rooms were added in July 1949. Following the death of Maude Coleman Tyler in 1965, her children contributed funds for the start of a vestibule, which was completed in 1968. A simulated pipe reed organ was given in 1959, by Doctor Leigh Bartlen. In 1907, a parsonage was purchased. After Bethlehem was linked with Kilmichael in 1977, this parsonage was no longer needed and was sold.

BETHLEHEM *(Union County: 1560 County Road 81, New Albany 38652)*. Bethlehem was organized in the late 1860s. The first pastor was D. L. Cogdell. It was not until after the Civil War that a group organized and erected a building, naming the church Bethlehem. The original church building had two seats in the back for the freed slaves to worship. Some slaves are buried at the Bethlehem Cemetery. When enough funds were on hand, the church began constructing a new building. Reverend L. P. Wasson dedicated the building. Not long after this, some of the women of the church felt that additional space was needed for the educational program of the church. In the spring of 1956, the addition was completed. Since then another addition has been added "because the people had a mind to work."

Don Bishop entered the ministry from this church.

BETHLEHEM *(Yalobusha County: Velma)*. This church was organized in 1901.

BEVERLY *(Lafayette County: Route Two Oxford 38655)*.

BEVILL HILL *(Winston County: Bevil Hill Road, Louisville 39339)*. The Bevill community was settled about 1835. Bevill Hill United Methodist Church is an extended ministry of Louisville First United Methodist Church. Surrounded by the Noxubee Wildlife Refuge and Tombigbee National Forest, Bevill Hill provides a quiet and peaceful refuge for worship and fellowship. The church, destroyed by fire in 1987, was quickly replaced with a modern brick structure that includes a fully equipped kitchen, and fellowship hall. Most of the members, displaced by the "game area," willingly drive some distance to gather for worship and fellowship each Sunday at "The Church in the Wildwood."

BIG CREEK *(Calhoun County: Big Creek 38914)*. Chapel Hill Methodist Church at Big Creek, was organized in 1856. Reverend J. M. Hampton, who donated land for a church, lodge, and cemetery, served as its first pastor. The original building, built near the time of organization, was removed, and a chapel was dedicated 24 May 1959. The oldest tombstone in the large cemetery is dated 5 May 1858. Elis Kilgore, a native of the community, who was born the year the Chapel Hill Church was organized, became a Methodist minister and evangelist. Ben Bounds, a native of the community, entered the ministry and served as pastor of Chapel Hill

Methodist Church in 1873 to 1874. From 1856 to 1868, Chapel Hill was in the Memphis Conference. In 1870, it became a part of the newly organized North Mississippi Conference. Near the turn of the century the congregation left the original building and held services in Big Creek Presbyterian Church, a frame structure. Chapel Hill became Big Creek Methodist in 1909. The Methodists, Baptists, and Presbyterians worshipped together in the Presbyterian Church building until 1949. In 1962, the Methodists purchased the Presbyterian property, removed the old building, and built the present brick building in 1965. Big Creek Methodist Church was dedicated 28 January 1968, by Edward J. Pendergrass, Bishop; W. R. Lott, District Superintendent, and Kenneth Corley, pastor.

BIG CREEK *(Oktibbeha County: 1809 Maben-Sturgis Road, Sturgis 39769)*. The church was organized in the 1878.

BIG HILL *(Lee County: Bissell)*.

BIG OAK *(Kemper County: Mosco)*. The church was organized in 1865.

BIG POINT *(Jackson County: Big Point)*. This church was organized in 1876.

BIG ROCK *(Wayne County: Denham)*. The church was organized between 1832 and 1881.

BIGGERSVILLE *(Alcorn County: Highway Forty-five South, Biggersville)*. Biggersville United Methodist Church was organized in the home of Mr. and Mrs. W. M. Dees. Reverend G. H. Holloman, District Superintendent of the New Albany District, and Reverend H. W. Lay, pastor of the Rienzi Charge, met with twelve interested persons from Bethel Methodist

Church on 18 May 1960, and organized the new church. Reverend H. W. Lay conducted the first worship service at the Biggersville High School on 29 May 1966. On 19 June 1966, Reverend Shelby Hathorn, pastor of Trinity Church, Corinth, was appointed pastor of Biggersville Methodist Church. Preparation began soon after that when two members of the church donated a lot on which the church was to be built. 20 June 1966 was an important day for the church, when a total of thirty members were registered and plans for a church building were discussed. The ground breaking for the church was 11 June 1967, by the pastor, Shelby Hathorn. The church had their first service in December 1967, and the dedication service was held on 7 March 1971. Prior to 1973, Biggersville was on the charge with Trinity of Corinth. Biggersville and Shady Grove Churches were made a two-point charge by Reverend Roy McAlilly, District Superintendent of the New Albany District. Reverend Ann Childers was serving as pastor at that time. 1974 brought plans for a parsonage and the two churches purchased a house near the Shady Grove Church to be used as the parsonage.

BILOXI FIRST *(Harrison County: 120 Hopkins Boulevard, Biloxi 39530).* The church was organized in 1842. First Church, Biloxi, was located on Washington Street from 1851 to 1881 in a frame structure. Reverend H. W. Van Hook came from the Ocean Springs Methodist Church to Biloxi, and under his guidance a new church was planned and a building fund started. In 1904, the old Masonic Hall was torn down and construction began on the

Biloxi First United Methodist Church

new church, with Reverend Van Hook himself laying many a row of bricks. The church was completed in 1908 and for the next forty years was known as the Main Street Methodist Church. The second brick building was at Main and Washington from 1891 to 1950. The present brick building was constructed between 1949 and 1950.

BINFORD CHAPEL *(Montgomery County: 417 Martin Luther King Drive, Duck Hill 38925).* The church was organized in 1889. A new sanctuary and education building were built in 1925.

BINNSVILLE *(Kemper County: Scooba 39358).* Binnsville was once a thriving community of 500 residents, and home to Fairview College. The Methodist church was organized between 1840 and 1879.

BLACK HAWK *(Carroll County: Black Hawk)*. Named for a local Indian chief, this community dates back to 1818. Black Hawk was first placed on a circuit in 1818. The first structure completed was built of logs, the second structure was built in or about 1880, the third building, which is in use today, was built in 1904 by Mr. Smith Turner. The buildings have been built on land deeded to the trustees of the Methodist Church on 25 February 1840 by William and Elizabeth Gillespie. This lot is 160 feet long and 137 feet wide. In 1846, Mr. and Mrs. William Gillespie donated twenty acres upon which a parsonage was built. Mr. Alfred Atteneave, an Englishman, who was a member of the church, gave an organ which required two people to operate, one to play and one to pump. In 1869 and 1870, Charles Betts Galloway, who later became bishop, served this charge. On 1 October 1905, Bishop Galloway returned to Black Hawk and dedicated the church. He also taught school while here. Reverend J. I. E. Byrd served Black Hawk in 1843. Sunday School was organized in 1850. In 1846, the Black Hawk Male and Female Seminary was organized and incorporated. Eudocia College gave the town of Black Hawk some fame as an educational center. The present Sunday School rooms were added during the pastorate of Reverend T. G. Lowry in the mid-1950s.

BLESSED TRINITY *(Hinds County: 5045 Clinton Boulevard, Jackson 39209)*. This church was founded in 1990. The Trinity United Methodist Church closed their doors because the members were moving out of the community and new members were not coming into the church. This situation allowed the beginning of Blessed Trinity to establish a new United Methodist congregation. Blessed Trinity United Methodist Church was established with the leadership and guidance of Reverend Bill Watkins, pastor Henry Thornton, Michael Montgomery, Bob Steward, and Grace Fergerson. The founders of Blessed Trinity United Methodist Church were: Reverend Paul E. Luckett, his wife Rosemary, and their two sons; Paul C. Luckett and Nehemiah E. Luckett; Chestine G. Louis; Feddie Robinson; Mary Robinson; Tishea Robinson; Annie L. Williams; Jimmy Cavett; James Donald; Eric J. Donald; Jennifer A. Walker; and Reverend Cecil Jones. The dedication service was held Easter Sunday, 31 March 1991 with sixty or more people in attendance.

BLUE HILL *(Jefferson County: McBride)*. The church was organized in 1890.

BLUE MOUNTAIN *(Tippah County: Highway Fifteen, Blue Mountain 38610)*. This community was settled in the 1830s, and is best known as home to Blue Mountain College, a Baptist school. This church was organized in 1909.

BLUE RIDGE *(Jasper County: Route Fourteen, Laurel 39440)*. This church was organized in 1884.

BLUES CHAPEL *(Kemper County: Scooba 39358)*. The church was organized in 1868.

BLYTHE'S CHAPEL *(Prentiss County: Booneville 38829)*.

BOGGS CHAPEL *(Tishomingo: 177 County Road 147, Tishomingo 38873)*. Boggs Chapel was organized in 1903.

BOGUE CHITTO *(Lincoln County: 0429 South Street, Bogue Chitto 39629)*. The church was organized in 1882.

BOLTON CHAPEL *(Greene County: Third Street, Leakesville 39451).*
BOLTON CHAPEL *(Perry County: 1185 Bolton Loop Road, Beaumont 39423).*
BOND *(Stone County: Highway Forty-nine North, Wiggins 39577).* The community was named for Preston Bond Sr., who built a home here in 1878. The Bond Methodist Church was organized in 1885.
BONITA *(Lauderdale County: 641 Bonita Drive, Meridian 39301).* The Bonita community was established in 1896, although settlers arrived in the area as early as 1833. In 1926, a small group formed Bonita Methodist Church, and used as a meeting place a sister church, Oak Grove Baptist. A group of thirty-one members held the dedication service for the new one-room church, erected in 1932. During the pastorate of J. W. Courtney in 1940, the building was remodeled and enlarged, adding four schoolrooms. Again in 1947, under the leadership of Reverend T. J. O'Neal, a basement and education building were added. Among the members who have entered the ministry are: Raymond Wesson, Clifton Aston, Russell Gilbert, Waddell Roberts, Tommie Gilbert, and Lucious Crosby
BONNIE CHAPEL *(Jackson County: Wire Road, Vancleave 39565).* According to Reverend J. B. Cain, a church named Union existed before the Civil War, and was known by several names during its existence. It became known as New Chapel Methodist. In the late 1800s, there was a church, called New Prospect, located on the New Prospect campground. It burned in 1902, and was not rebuilt. A few years later, the former members began

Bonnie Chapel United Methodist Church

holding services in the Bonnie School. This church became known as Bonnie. New Chapel and Bonnie Churches on the Vancleave Charge were authorized to merge on 28 October 1928. The new church became known as Bonnie Chapel. This church had two sanctuaries. The first was constructed in 1929, and was destroyed by termites. The present sanctuary was constructed in 1948. An education building was added in 1968, and more classrooms were built in 1983.
BOONES CHAPEL *(Chickasaw County: Buena Vista).* This church was organized in 1890.
BOONEVILLE FIRST *(Prentiss County: 400 West Church, Booneville 38829).* The church was organized in 1867 by a "small band of Christians who met in a frame building, used for a schoolhouse, and orga-

nized the first Methodist Church in Booneville," according to historical information written in 1931. In the beginning, it was a part of the Rienzi Circuit. The first building was located in an old schoolhouse on Fourth Street in Booneville in 1867. In 1875, after the church-school property was sold, the Railroad Company gave the church a corner lot near the old railroad station. Efforts began in 1895 to build a new brick church, and the building was completed in 1897. This structure was at the corner of Main and East Church Street, where the Prentiss County Chancery Court building is presently located. The 1897 church was destroyed by fire in 1901, but was rebuilt. In 1928, the present building was completed. The education building was erected in 1963. The bell in

Booneville First United Methodist Church

the Bell Tower was purchased in 1904; however, the Bell Tower was constructed in 1970. Sue Robinson, daughter of one of the ministers, was a missionary in Africa.

BOVINA *(Warren County: 70 Bovina Drive, Vicksburg 39180).* The United States Post Office was established at Bovina on 30 July 1833. A Methodist Society that was to become Bovina United Methodist Church may have existed soon after the Civil War. The railroad was constructed through the area before 1840. In 1863, a new highway through the area was constructed from Vicksburg to Jackson. This new road was named "Warrior's Trail." This is the route General Grant's Army followed in 1863. The church was organized by 1873, when the South Warren Circuit was composed of Asbury, Bethel, and Bovina Churches. In 1892, the South Warren Charge consisted of Bovina, Wesley Chapel, Redbone, Flower Hill, Willis, and Asbury Churches.

BOWERS CHAPEL *(Tippah County: 22400 Highway Fifteen, Tiplersville 38674).* The church was organized in 1906. The first pastor was Reverend S. Huston. There were nine founding members. The first church, known as Neelys Chapel, was built in 1906. Mary Ella Guy received a prestigious award for writing the best history in the Upper Mississippi Conference, and was treasurer for over fifty years.

BOWLING GREEN *(Holmes County: Bowling Green Road, Durant 39063).* Spring Hill Methodist Episcopal Church was established in the early 1840s. A log building with a fireplace in one end was built by Reverend Thomas C. Rayner, his slaves, and neighbors, for use as a school, a community house, and church. By 1853, the people wanted a place for worship alone. Reverend Rayner sold ten acres of land for one dollar to the trustees. A church was built. In 1883, members of the church voted to move to Bowling Green, a growing town about five miles away. They bought a lot from J. T. Tate for ten dollars, and S. J. Siddon built a church on the bank of Little Black Creek. This place finally became too wet. In 1905, the trustees bought two adjoining lots from Mr. Almond and Doctor Doty. A new building was built, completely of cypress lumber, and "store bought pews" purchased. The same building is in use today, and its name was changed to Bowling Green. On 15 August 1984, the church was moved to its present location. The church is set among trees and high above the water. Buford Ellington entered the ministry from this church. He later became Governor of Tennessee.

BOX CHAPEL *(Alcorn County: 3310 County Road 100, Corinth 38834).* The church was organized about 1851. It is believed to be the oldest of the early Methodist churches in this area. The first building was made of logs, and is believed to have been burned by Union soldiers when they destroyed the town of Farmington. Some years later, a small boxed building was erected, and a third building was erected on the same lot thirty or thirty-five years later. This was a frame building. In 1930, when the Marvin congregation merged with the Box Chapel, both of the old buildings were torn down, and the present Box Chapel building was erected. The present building is a brick veneer structure. A fellowship hall and

additional Sunday School classes were added in 1979. During the past fifteen or twenty years, several stained glass windows have been installed in the sanctuary, and a steeple was added as a memorial. The land on which Box Chapel now stands was deeded to the trustees of the church by W. W. Steger on 20 October 1874. The land for the cemetery was donated by James Box, from whom the church got its name. Among the first converts and additions to the church was S. B. Surratt, who later was licensed to preach, and preached his first sermon here. After a long itinerary, he died in Memphis, while serving as the pastor of the First Methodist Church. Charter members were: J. M. Surratt and wife, Matthew J. Babb and wife, and James Box. The late Reverend Dan Wesley Babb was also among the early converts. He was licensed to preach in 1868, and preached his first sermon here. After fifty-four years of active ministry, he superannuated. Reverend Dan Wesley Babb had two brothers who were preachers and members of this church. Their names were Joseph Green Babb and James A. Babb. Other ministers who have gone out from this church are: Jewel G. Babb Jr., W. V. Kemp, and Barney Whitehurst. Reverend Walter Jones and Reverend Lee Merritt Jones were from the Marvin congregation.

BOYD CHAPEL *(Oktibbeha County: Louisville and Sturgis Road, Sturgis 39769).* In 1866, Liberty Methodist Church was organized with ten members. The first pastor was S. D. Hudson. The first place of worship was a brush arbor. The new church prospered, and a frame house was built on the Houston and Louisville Road. In the latter part of 1892, the church was moved onto a hill, where it stands today. The name was changed to Liberty Hill. In June 1967, the Liberty Hill Head Start Program began. In 1970, Liberty Hill and Spring Hill were united. The name of the church was changed to Boyd Chapel United Methodist Church. The church was named for Reverend Walter Boyd, who was pastor at that time. In 1979, the church was remodeled on the inside, and in 1981, the church was bricked on the outside.

BOYLE *(Bolivar County: 207 Highway 446, Boyle 38730).* This community was named for L. V. Boyle, who established a sawmill here in 1872. The church was organized in 1895. The first minister of Boyle Methodist Church was Reverend H. S. Spraggins, in December 1895. The presiding elder was Reverend J. A. Randolph. At first, services were held in the depot and store buildings. Then a Methodist Church was built east of the bayou, and a congregation was organized by Reverend J. J. Brooks. In 1907, a brick church was erected, the first brick church in Bolivar County. In May 1919, a parsonage was built at Boyle. In 1953 or 1954, the education building was built, during the time Reverend J. L. Nabors was minister. In 1969, the first brick church was torn down and removed. Reverend M. L. Prewitt was pastor at the time. The bricks were cleaned and sold. In 1970, work began to build the present building. After discussion, the church decided they wanted the brick from the old church to be used on the present building. In the present building the altar rail, church pews, altar furniture, and pulpit are from the old

church. Reverend Louis Caddell was minister. The wooden cross on the wall behind the pulpit was made by Grady Blue. This building was completed in January 1971. The first meeting in the new church was a funeral for Webster Lee Ray on 3 January 1971. The parsonage was in need of much repairs. More property was purchased from T. M. "Pinky" Jones, and in April 1974, the present parsonage was completed. The first minister to live in the new parsonage was Reverend Harry Davis. The old parsonage was torn down, and the lot cleared for the parking lot on the west side of the church. In early 1996, Tommy Patterson was licensed to be a United Methodist minister. In June 1997, he was appointed to the Rosedale-Gunnison Charge. On 3 June 1997, the Boyle United Methodist Church was honored at the Small Membership Banquet representing the Greenwood District.

BOYLES CHAPEL *(Wayne County: Whistler).* The church was organized in the year 1900 to 1901.

BRADLEY CHAPEL *(Warren County: 11031 Oak Ridge Road, Vicksburg 39180).* Bradley's Chapel had its origin as Bell Hill Church. It was located on the plantation of W. T. Bell Sr., in "The Valley," near the Yazoo River, approximately eight miles westward of its present location. Bell Hill Church was erected by the congregation; the benches, pulpit, even the blackboard were homemade. Probably after the Civil War, the church moved to a place four miles northward from its present location. Mrs. Susan Webster denoted three acres of land at the present location, and the structure was transported on logs that were rolled underneath to a new location, then known as the Vicksburg Benton Road, and nick-named the Wire Road, because telegraph wire was strung along this road in 1838. The church membership increased, and a larger building became necessary. An arbor was constructed on the lawn and church held outside when the weather was nice. In 1888, the new building was constructed and dedicated. The lumber had been hauled from Bovina by ox teams. Reverend Ralph Bradley was the first pastor in the new structure, and the church's name was changed from Bell Hill to Bradley's Chapel in his honor.

BRANDON BAY *(Walthall County: Kokomo 39643).*

Brandon First United Methodist Church

BRANDON FIRST *(Rankin County: 205 Mary Ann Drive, Brandon 39042).* It was in the first Rankin County Courthouse that the Brandon Methodist Fellowship met on 12 June 1836. At that meeting Reverend John G. Jones, presiding elder of the district, officially organized the Brandon Methodist Church. On 13 October 1834, the Methodist Episcopal Church, South, executed a deed with Alexander McDonnell for three-fourths of an acre of land in

Brandon. This plot was located approxi-mately behind where the Presbyterian Church stands today. A two-story wooden church building was erected. During the Civil War, the church building was used as a hospital. It survived the invasion of General Sherman's Union Army in 1862. But, in July 1863, General Steele's Union troops marched through Brandon and burned the church building. The bell was all that was saved. Services were then held at Brandon Female College, located on the site of the present high school. The present church site was purchased in 1864. Judge Alonzo Mayers donated the bricks to the church. Construction began in 1867, and was completed in 1873. The steeple held the bell from the first church building. Dedication was held on 26 July 1873. In 1948, an educational annex was erected at the north-eastern corner of the sanctuary, being ready for use in October. It was dedicated on 2 March 1952. On 4 April 1960, fire destroyed the education building. Rebuilding began immediately, with a better building ready for use in early 1961. When the second sanc-tuary building was demolished, Mr. Tom Berry salvaged the old bell. In 1975, a bell tower was erected on the church lawn, and the bell was home once again. In 1978, a lot and two-story building adjoining the north property line was purchased.

BRANDYWINE *(Claiborne County: Barlow).* The community of Brandywine was established in 1832. The church was organized in 1846. The church takes its name from Brandywine Creek, which flows nearby. There are some interesting stories about the origin of the name. One is that travelers in early days tasted its waters; one of them said that it tasted like wine, another that it tasted like brandy, and the two words were combined into a single name. There is a possibility that early settlers in southwest Mississippi, many of whom came from Pennsylvania and New Jersey, brought with them memories of Brandywine Creek, famous for a battle in the Revolutionary War. Brandywine Church is a successor church to an older church named Lebanon, situated some distance southwest, and established in the early days of Mississippi Methodism. This older church was still in existence in July 1857, when the funeral sermon for Reverend James Griffing, one of the first two local preachers in Mississippi Methodism, was preached by Reverend B. M. Drake at Lebanon Church shortly after his death. During the year that followed, the Lebanon Church was torn down and much of the material used in building the new church some distance away, which took the name of Brandywine. At least four ministers have come from this church. Among them was Reverend A. J. Leggett. One of his sons, Frank Leggett, served as pastor of Centenary Church, Nashville, for a number of years. The first service at Brandywine was a revival meeting held 25 through 31 October 1858. In 1885 the name of the circuit was changed to Bowerton, and in 1894 to Barlow, which included such historic churches as Rehoboth, organized in 1839, and Pleasant Valley, home church of the Millsaps family, including Major R. W. Millsaps.

BRAXTON *(Simpson County: 107 West Main Street, Braxton 39044)*. The church was organized on 10 May 1901. The church was

first known as Gum Springs Methodist Episcopal Church, South, which was merged into the new Braxton Church. There have been two frame buildings. The first frame building was destroyed by a tornado 21 April 1921. The second and present building was constructed in 1921, and an education building was added in 1961.

BREWER *(Lee County: Route Two, Shannon 38868)*. Early records date back to 1903. The church began when W. H. and Marietta Davis sold one-half acre of land to Brewer Church trustees. The property was located due west, across the road from the present church site. The church was previously located about one and one-half miles north of the present site, and was called Bethel and later Cedar Grove. The pastor was J. W. Ramsey. There were twenty founding members. The present church site was purchased in 1921. When the material was purchased to build the present church, twelve wagons with some fifteen men went to the Evans sawmill about fifteen miles from Brewer. While the church was being built, the congregation met in the school building. The first Rural Community Development Council in Lee County was organized in the Methodist Church in 1947. Felix Sutphin, a former member, went into the ministry, and served as President of Wood College. Ministers from Brewer Church include: Wilmer Stokes, Felix Sutphin, John Sutphin, Joe Young, Dennis Johnson, and William McDole. Brewer was recognized twice as Rural Church of the Year in the North Mississippi Conference.

BRIARWOOD *(Hinds County: 320 Briarwood Drive, Jackson 39206)*. Briarwood was organized in June 1956 in the rapidly

Briarwood United Methodist Church

growing area of northeast Jackson. A chapel and a youth center were constructed in September 1956. The chapel was expanded in 1959 to become the church sanctuary. An education building was constructed in 1970. Between 1980 and 1981, a major renovation of the church was completed. The notes on the church were burned on 4 November 1990.

BROADACRES *(Lowndes County: 618 Thirty-First Avenue, North, Columbus 39701).* This church was organized in 1961.

BROADMEADOW *(Hinds County: 4419 Broadmeadow Drive, Jackson 39206).* In December 1949, eight Methodists, including Bishop Marvin Franklin, met in the home of Mr. and Mrs. P. D. Wilkerson to discuss plans for organizing a church in North Jackson. During the first several months, the church met in the Wilkerson home, and then in the Pepsi Cola plant on Meadowbrook Road. In March 1950, a store building on Northview Drive was secured as a meeting place. The first permanent unit was constructed in 1951. This building served all functions of the church until the sanctuary, classroom, and office space were erected and formally opened on 9 January 1955. Several years later, an

educational annex, parking facilities and a new parsonage on Brook Drive were added.

BROOKHAVEN FIRST *(Lincoln County: 215 West Cherokee Street, Brookhaven 39601).* In the early 1800s, Samuel Jayne settled on the banks of the Bogue Chitto River and founded "Ole Brook." Methodist circuit riders brought Methodism down this major trade route

Brookhaven First United Methodist Church

from Natchez to Brookhaven. In 1843, the first Methodist church was built in the area. Jayne, along with Samuel Watt, deeded six acres of land a few miles north of Ole Brook for this purpose. First United Methodist Church of Brookhaven was born in 1857 in the newly located city of Brookhaven. The church occupied its first building in 1858 on the land donated by Milton J. Whitworth. In 1859, the Brookhaven District of Mississippi was formed. By 1904 a second building was constructed. First Methodist grew so fast in the period between 1904 and 1916, that yet another building was needed. The present home for the church was built in 1917. Brookhaven was home to Whitworth College, a Methodist female school.

BROOKLYN *(Forrest County: Burborne and Fourth Streets, Brooklyn 39425).* A ferry once operated from Brooklyn to Mississippi City by way of Black Creek. The church was organized in 1900.

BROOKSVILLE *(Noxubee County: Main Street, Brooksville 39739).* The community, named for Jarred Brooks, was settled as early as 1833, but the present village came into existence with the coming of the railroad in 1857. The church was organized in 1929.

BROWNFIELD *(Tippah County: County Road 126, Walnut 38683).* Brownfield Methodist Church, first called Brown's Chapel, was founded in 1895 with fourteen members. William H. (Captain Billy) Brown gave an acre of land, a beautiful wooded area east of the railroad. The white frame building, built in 1895, with a gabled roof at each end, faced north with two separate wooden doors on the north and one door at the south side. Three rows of pews faced the pulpit located at the south end, with two oak chairs and an organ. Atop the church, center front, was a belfry with a long rope. Captain Brown made the fire and rang the church bell each Sunday morning. Reverend J. E. Stevens was pastor here in 1910, when this church was on the old Jonesborough Circuit. He and his wife were the first to live in the Brownfield parsonage, built about 1909. In 1943, the decision was made to replace the frame church building with a brick structure. The old church building that had served for almost fifty years was torn down. In 1944, work began on the new building on the same site, and the building was completed in 1945. The new brick veneer church was dedicated on 30 September 1951. A large congregation gathered to hear Bishop Marvin A. Franklin bring the dedication message. The annex, a kitchen, and a fellowship hall were added to the church building in 1960.

BROWNLEE *(Lowndes County: 6540 Wolfe Road, Columbus 39701).* The church was organized in 1887.

BRUCE *(Calhoun County: Bruce 38915).* The community was established in 1927, when E. L. Bruce Lumber Company purchased a large acreage in this area. The Methodist church here was organized in 1924.

BUCKATUNNA *(Wayne County: 36 Church Street, Buckatunna 39322).* William Powe and his family were the first settlers of this area, who arrived in 1811 from Georgia, and settled one mile from Buckatunna. The Methodist church here was organized in 1885.

BUDE *(Franklin County: Main Street, Bude 39630).* This community was founded in 1912. The Methodist church was organized in 1917.

BUELAH GROVE (Pontotoc County: Northwest Pontotoc).

BUENA VISTA *(Chickasaw County: Buena Vista).* Buena Vista community dates back to 1836 with the arrival of the Pulliam family from Georgia. It was named for the famous battle in the Mexican War. A post office was established in 1847. Buena Vista Normal College opened in 1884, but was later discontinued. The Methodist church here was organized in 1887.

BUFFALO *(Attala County: Kosciusko 39090).* Around 1871, a small group of emancipated slaves met in a log cabin owned by Mr. Jack Presley, and organized the Buffalo Church. Robert Hayes was the first pastor. They used the cabin for a church until Mr. Presley sold them the property in 1881. In 1882, they cut trees, made lumber and built a one-room frame building which was used for a church and schoolhouse. This building was destroyed by fire in 1926. A second frame building was built in 1927, and still stands. It is used as a multipurpose building for the church and community. Both of these early facilities were heated by wood stoves and lighted by kerosene lamps. The men of the church made the pews and tables for the buildings. In 1976, a modern brick building was completed with central heat and air conditioning. Since its organization, the church has been a member of the Kosciusko Circuit, the Buffalo Charge, the Kosciusko Wesley Charge and the Buffalo Circuit.

BUFORD *(Lafayette County: County Road 198, Oxford 38655).* This church was organized 14 December 1898. The church was once located on Coontown Road. There have been four sanctuaries: a brush arbor, two frame buildings, and the present brick building.

BURNS *(Lafayette County: Fifty-Seven County Road 198, Oxford 38655).* This church was organized in 1872.

BURNS *(Smithe County: Highway 481, Raleigh 39153).* About 1904, a group of twelve people met in the old one-room schoolhouse at Burns to hold church and Sunday School services. After a few months and a good deal of interest, the decision was made to erect a Methodist church. The building was erected by volunteer labor, with the help and advice of the principal of

the school, Mr. Compere. Mr. Compere also built and donated the pews for the new church. A lot on which to build a church was donated by Mr. T. B. Winstead, who later entered the ministry and served as pastor of this church, which he had helped to establish. The first service ever held in a Methodist Church at Burns was on 14 February 1906. C. C. Griffin was pastor, J. M. Morse was presiding elder, and Charles B. Galloway, a native son of Mississippi, was the Bishop. The charter members and organizers of this church were: C. C. Griffin, pastor; Mr. and Mrs. T. B. Winstead; Mrs. Myra Kelly Baker; Mr. and Mrs. Page Windham; Monroe Muckelrath; Mr. and Mrs. W. H. Robinson; Mrs. W. H McWhorter; and Sam Clark. The church remained on the Trenton Charge until 1920, when it became a part of the Raleigh Charge, with seven other churches. In 1949, the Burns Charge was formed by placing Gasque, Trenton, Trinity, and Burns Churches together. This necessitated the building of a parsonage in the Burns community. The parsonage was dedicated on Friday, 7 April 1950, by Bishop Marvin Franklin. Mr. Cromer Smith donated one-third acre of land to the existing church lot. The foundation of a new church was dug 21 November 1956. Between December 1956 and January 1957, services were held in the Burns Baptist Church. Reverend Harold Miller preached the first sermon in the new building on 10 March 1957.

BURNSVILLE *(Tishomingo County: 118 Front Street, Burnsville 38833).* The railroad was completed to this area in 1857, which greatly aided the community's development.

BURTON MEMORIAL *(Harrison County: 2419 Twenty-Second Avenue, Gulfport 39501).* In 1903, a church was started in North Gulfport. The services were held under a brush arbor by Reverend J. L Sells. Later, to accommodate the worshippers, a white frame building was erected, known as North Gulfport Methodist Episcopal Church, South. In 1921, this building was destroyed by a windstorm. The building was not restored, and the members scattered. In April 1928, Reverend J. L. Sells, presiding elder of the Seashore District, saw the need for a Methodist Church in this area of Gulfport. He invited Reverend Charles Asaaf to conduct a three weeks' revival. It was held at Twenty-first Avenue and Twenty-fourth Street under a tent. At the close of the meeting, a call for membership was given and the Second Methodist Episcopal Church, South, was organized with fifty charter members. By December 1928, a white frame building was erected. The church remained at this location until 1936. The city purchased the church lots for the purpose of erecting North Central Ward School. The church then purchased four lots on the corner of Twenty-second Avenue and Twenty-fifth Street and moved the building to that site, where it now stands. At the last Quarterly Conference of 1936, it was decided that the name of the church be changed to Burton Memorial. Reverend M. L. Burton, who had been presiding elder when the original North Gulfport Church was organized, labored faithfully to make this second venture a success. After his retirement, Reverend Burton patiently steered the church

through difficult times. Being unable to stand in the pulpit, he sat in a chair and preached. His chair occupied a sacred place in the church building long after he departed.

Byhalia United Methodist Church

BYHALIA *(Marshall County: Church Street, Byhalia 38611).* Reverend M. P. Myers purchased the land for a new Methodist church in 1842. He and dedicated members constructed a crude church building made from notched logs, with mud sealing the cracks. It was composed of two rooms, and on one side was a long fireplace that could handle a log three yards long. This building probably had a bare floor. In 1855, a two-story frame building was erected on the site of the present Methodist church. The second story of the church was used for the Masonic Lodge meetings. This new church was dedicated by Bishop Pierce. At that time, the church was in the Memphis Conference. This building was torn down in 1906, and a new church was erected. In the cemetery, one of the oldest tombstones marks the grave of Lemiel Absolum Myers, dated 1845.

Byrd's Chapel United Methodist Church

BYRD'S CHAPEL *(Pearl River County: 26 Byrd's Chapel Road, Carriere 39426).* The Byrd family (Sherrod, and his wife, Zelfa Rouse) settled in the swamp in the early 1800s. An early circuit rider was Reverend John Ira Ellis Byrd, a relative of Sherrod. Worship began regularly, and the chapel fittingly bears his name. The church was organized in 1820. The first sanctuary was across the present Route Forty-three, near the "roundtop house" on property belonging to Peter Harvey. About 1855, a two-story building was erected on the current site. It served as church, school, lodge, and courthouse for Pearl County in 1872. A fire of suspicious origins destroyed everything in 1877, and the county was

abandoned for financial reasons. A northern syndicate bought the pine forests, and the railroad was built. The county was established again in 1890, with its seat in Poplarville. The county was renamed Pearl River. The third building, which was partially destroyed by a tornado in 1934, was located east of the present one, on the old Gainesville-Columbia Road. The present building replaced the third one, and was built from timbers recovered from the old church by labor donated by the worshippers and faithful members of the community. The first Sunday School rooms, the annex, an enlarged kitchen, and the all-purpose room, were later added separately. The cemetery is the oldest in the county.

CAILE *(Sunflower County: 151 Highway Forty-Nine, Caile 38753).* Caile community was established in 1888. The church was organized in 1896.

CALEDONIA *(Lowndes County: 811 Main, Caledonia 39740).* In the years 1908 to 1909, the organization of a Methodist Church in the town of Caledonia was suggested to several Methodist families living in the surrounding area. The Christian Church had an active congregation and building in Caledonia. This congregation invited Methodists to hold their meetings there. Evangelist Len Egger of the Texas Conference was invited to hold a revival. Members were received into the Methodist faith, and members of other Methodist churches agreed to move their membership to Caledonia. They planned to build a church. The lot for the church was purchased from Will Gaston across from the

Caledonia Public School. In 1910, the first Methodist church in Caledonia was completed under leadership of Reverend Goudelock. The church grew, and a new building was completed 2 March 1936. The church was completely renovated in 1962.

CALVARY *(Union County: Highway Fifteen, North, New Albany 38652)*. The New Albany Circuit was formed at the first session of the North Mississippi Annual Conference at Water Valley in 1870 and placed on the Verona District. Two of the seven churches on the circuit were Lebanon and Locust Grove. A deed for land for Lebanon Church was dated 1858. Minutes exist of a third Quarterly Conference at Locust Grove Church in 1860. A deed shows that Lebanon and Locust Grove Churches combined in 1896, to become Union Hill Church. A building was constructed on Union Hill Road, which was used until the present building was constructed and occupied in 1951. Union Hill was still a part of the New Albany Circuit when this building was erected, and for ten years afterward. The church became a station in 1961, when land was purchased to enlarge the building. The church's name was changed from Union Hill to Calvary in 1961. A fellowship hall was completed in the spring of 1988.

CALVIN *(Marshall County: Waterford 38685)*.

CAMBRIDGE *(Lafayette County: 640 County Road 202, Abbeville 38601)*. This church was organized in the 1800s.

CAMDEN *(Madison County: Highwy Sevemteen, Camden 39045)*. Camden community was settled in the 1830s, and

Camden United Methodist Church

named for the Revolutionary War battle at Camden, South Carolina. The Methodist church was organized in 1831, just one year after the advent of Methodism in Madison County. Detailed records of the Camden Methodist Church are almost nonexistent, although a Mrs. Purviance is known to have been its first member. A brief history of the church in the *Banner County Outlook* of 3 November 1950 said, "This church stood and prospered until 7 April 1890, when it was blown away by a great wind." At the time of that catastrophe, Reverend C. F. Edgar was Camden Methodist's pastor. The newspaper continued, "The church site was moved about five years later. Another faithful band of Christians built the second Methodist church of Camden, of which they were equally proud." That building, though, suffered a similar fate. About 1917, the second Camden Methodist building was destroyed by fire. "Even with fire and winds, they were not discouraged and ready to quit, but they worked hard and built a bigger and better place to worship their Creator. The present church site was bought from the Baptists in 1920 and, under the direction of Reverend C. H.

Ellis, a church was built." The church recently received national attention when it was used in *A Time to Kill,* a motion picture based upon the book by the Mississippi author, John Grisham.

CAMPGROUND *(Tippah County: 1711 County Road 203, Walnut 38683).* The church was organized in 1853.

CAMPGROUND *(Tishomingo County: Junction of County Road 303 and 256, Iuka 38852).* Campground was organized in 1857.

CAMPGROUND *(Winston County: 940 Campground Road, Louisville 39339).* The church was originally organized in 1844 as a Presbyterian Church. Campground became a Methodist Church in 1864. In the early years, there were cabins on the church grounds for old fashioned camp meetings. The original log church was located across the road from the present church. That building was torn down and replaced by a "boxed church." In the early 1920s, the church was used as a one-teacher school. The present brick church structure was begun in December 1955, and dedicated in August 1956. A fellowship hall was added in 1981.

CANE RIDGE *(Jefferson County: Lorman 39096).* The oldest Methodist Church in Jefferson County is Cane Ridge, organized in 1817. There was a Cane Hills in 1818, and the following year the name was changed to Cane Ridge, which it has retained ever since. The first Cane Ridge Church building stood to the north and west of the present location until 1846, when a new church was built at the present Cane Ridge cemetery. This church was burned in 1864 by enemy soldiers, leaving the congregation without a house of

worship until 1867, when the Pleasant Grove Church was moved to Cane Ridge. This church stood until 1916, when the present church was built during the pastorate of J. T. McVey. During the pastorate of W. F. Baggett, an annex was added to the church building.

CANTON *(Madison County: Canton 39046).* The church was created by a merger of four churches, including historic Asbury Church.

Canton First United Methodist Church

CANTON FIRST *(Madison County: 3301 South Liberty, Canton 39046).* The church was organized in 1836 and was Canton's first church. Services were held in the Union Church building which was built by the citizens of this newly formed settlement, and was located on the north side of North Street, just one block off the present Court Square. In that year, the Methodists of Canton built their first church, which was located on the southwest corner of Peace and Lyon Streets. This church was used until 1847, when present church property was purchased. A new brick church was constructed on this property, and used for a period of thirty years, and then torn down. In 1878, a new wooden church was built and used until

1923, when it was torn down, and the present church constructed. The beautiful memorial windows in the present sanctuary came out of the old church. In 1872, the first parsonage was built on the lot just to the north of the present church, which is now a church parking lot. It was used until 1903, when it was torn down. The new parsonage burned in 1915, and narrowly avoided the destruction of the stained glass windows on the north side of the church. The Garner Smith home on South Union was purchased for a parsonage, and was used until 1947. It was sold and a new parsonage built on Academy Street. That was sold in 1994 and a new parsonage constructed on Sunset Drive.

CAROLINA *(Itawamba County: 3384 Carolina Road, Nettleton 38858).* Settlers from the Carolinas arrived here in the 1840s, and named the community for their former home. They soon built a school and church.

CAROLINA *(Prentiss County: 2000 Ninth Street, Booneville 38829).* The church was organized on 15 June 1858. The first pastor was W. R. Williams. Carolina was, at the time of its origin, known as the Carolina Methodist Episcopal Church, South. It was part of the Booneville Circuit until 1920 when it became a part of the new circuit with J. D. Boggs as pastor. In 1949, it became a station church, and in 1952, it rejoined the Booneville Circuit. In 1961, it became a part of the West Prentiss Parish, which dissolved in 1984, and Carolina became a part of the Carolina-Pisgah Charge. In 1952, the members of the church planted a "Lord's Acre" and raised

cotton to make money to add four classrooms, have the building bricked, and put in a new heating system. In 1984, new stained glass windows were installed. In the cemetery, there are tombstones dating back to 1858. The original small cemetery was on the opposite side of the road.

Carpenter United Methodist Church

CARPENTER *(Copiah County: Hurricane Road, Utica 39175).* There was no village at Carpenter before the railroad arrived about 1880. The community was named for J. N. Carpenter, railroad president. Mr. and Mrs. W. W. Brashears gave the church lot to the trustees of Carpenter United Methodist Church on 5 December 1900. Carpenter Methodist Church was organized on 1 September 1901, and is on the National Register of Historic Places. The charter pastor was Robert F. Witt of Hermanville. On preaching Sundays, he rode the train from Hermanville in the morning and returned on the afternoon train. Charter members were the W. A. Price family, consisting of Charner and Luther Emmette Price, and Miss Eliza Jane and Ollie Price, W. H. Ritchey, Mrs. Mary Tillman, Mrs. Louise Brashears, and Harry H. Coleman. Mr. W. A. Price was the owner of a sawmill, and wanted only perfect lumber in his church. Mr. Price later served as District Lay Leader. Carpenter United Methodist Church was on Hermanville and Rocky Springs Charges, and has been on the Utica Charge since 1922. Under Reverend J. R. Cameron's urging, Sunday School rooms were added in 1947. During the pastorate of Hollis H. Youngblood, 1977 to 1978, a storm dislodged the church steeple, which was replaced with a smaller steeple.

CARR *(Scott County: Highway 501, South, Forest 39074)*. The church was organized in 1830. The original frame building, built in 1838, still serves the church.

CARROLLTON *(Carroll County: 501 Green Street, Carrollton 38917)*. The town of Carrollton was founded in 1836. The Methodist church was organized about 1834 as a mission. The first pastor was Milton H. Jones. The first sanctuary was constructed in the 1840s. Early records of the church were lost, but in 1871, at the time of reorganization, there were thirty-seven members. Carrollton's first place of worship occupied Lot Ninety-seven. Some think the building was torn down just preceding the Civil War; others say the materials were on the ground, but a building was never constructed. During the

early years, the members shared the Presbyterian Church, and from the minutes of the Baptist Church, we know their house of worship was often used by the Methodists. About 1870, the Methodists bought the lower story of the Masonic Temple, which was then located on the south side of Lot Ninety-six. There the congregation worshipped until the arrival of Reverend H. E. Smith in 1884, who inspired the membership to build the present structure in 1885. On the first Sunday in January 1886, the building was dedicated by Reverend Charles B. Galloway. During the years 1832 to 1886, the Carrollton Church was a part of numerous charges. In 1832, the area was a part of the Big Sand Mission. Later it was part of the Tallahatchie Mission, then the Yalobusha Mission, then Carroll Circuit, then Carrollton Circuit, and during the Civil War years, Carrollton was affiliated with the Black Hawk Circuit. In 1870, it was placed with the Winona Circuit. In 1879, Carrollton Circuit was again established.

CARSON *(Jefferson Davis County: North Carson Road Off Highway Forty-Two, Carson 39427)*. The church was organized in 1903.

CARTHAGE FIRST *(Leake County: 201 East Franklin Street, Carthage 39051)*. The Carthage United Methodist Church traces its beginning to a circuit rider revival in 1846, when Mrs. Joseph D. Eads became a member by vows. Hers is the first name appearing on the earliest membership roll. The church came into being between 1848 and 1850, when W. W. Wadsworth was assigned to Carthage by the Annual

Carthage First United Methodist Church

Conference, presumably for the purpose of organizing a church. In the early years, Carthage was part of a large circuit with the minister coming from Forest or Walnut Grove. Church records in the decade from 1880 to 1890 reveal the evangelistic appeal of the early pastors. Records show large numbers joining the church then. The church has occupied five buildings during its existence. The present brick structure was built in 1927 with extensive renovations in 1989. Other property has been acquired through the years, such as, three different parsonages, a chapel and education building, a large fellowship hall, a van, a parking lot, and a lot for recreation.

CASWELL SPRINGS *(Jackson County: 18601 Highway Sixty-three, Pascagoula 39581).* The church was organized in 1875.

CAYUGA *(Hinds County: 3118 Old Port Gibson Road, Utica 39175).* The church was organized in 1828 on Cayuga Road, where a Baptist church is now located. The first building was constructed in 1828, and the present building was erected in the 1920s.

CEDAR BLUFF *(Clay County: Cedar Bluff).* The church was organized in 1850.

CEDAR GROVE *(Amite County: Liberty 39645).* This church was organized in 1890.

CEDAR GROVE *(Smith County: Route Two, Highway 501, Raleigh 39153).* This church was founded in the 1890s.

CEDAR LAKE *(Harrison County: 12332 Cedar Lake Road, Biloxi 39532).* The church was organized in 1906.

Centenary United Methodist Church

CENTENARY *(Pike County: Delaware at Fifth Street, McComb 39648).* From 1873 to 1876, a small group of Methodists in McComb worshipped in the second story of a blacksmith shop at the corner of Front and Canal Streets. In 1876, the congregation gathered in the Presbyterian Church for services twice a month. When the Methodists of McComb authorized the construction of their first building in 1884, they named the church Centenary in commemoration of the one hundredth anniversary of Methodism in America celebrated that year. The first services were held 19 April 1885 in the new wood frame building erected on the present site of First Bank's main office. In 1906, a brick building replaced the wooden one. This building was enhanced by the first pipe organ in McComb. The third church building, the present structure, was completed in 1926.

CENTER RIDGE *(Kemper County).*

CENTER RIDGE *(Winston County: Shiloh Road, Louisville 39339).* This church was founded in 1859.

CENTERPOINT *(Copiah County: Hazlehurst 39083).*

Central United Methodist Church, Jackson

CENTRAL *(Hinds County: 500 North Farish Street, Jackson 39202).* Central Church was organized in September 1889 as an outgrowth of the Jackson Mission, organized in 1866, and First Church, organized 1876. The mission was located in the area of today's Millsaps College, and the former First Church was at the corner of Lamar and Fortification Streets. The first sanctuary was a brick structure constructed in 1892. This building served the congregation until the mid-1900s. Ground breaking for the present building was held 28 March 1965, and the brick sanctuary was completed in 1966. James Lynch had close

ties to the development of the mission that became Central. He served as presiding elder, and was Mississippi's Secretary of State during Reconstruction.

Central United Methodist Church, Meridian

CENTRAL *(Lauderdale County: Twenty-Third Avenue at Tenth, Meridian 39301).* The present building on Twenty-third Avenue is the fourth structure to house Central Methodist. The first building in 1852 was a log cabin on A Street between Ninth and Eleventh Avenues, often known as Dearman Chapel. The next was a log and frame church constructed in 1860 on the corner of Eleventh Street and Twenty-seventh Avenue where Central had its first appointed pastor. In 1873, continued growth led the congregation to purchase four lots on the corner of Eighth Street and Twenty-third Avenue and move the building by ox teams to the new location. In 1885, the church completed a new brick and stone building, and moved the old log and frame building by oxen along Fifth Street to Fortieth Avenue where it became Fifth Street Methodist Church. The new downtown church with its tall steeple burned in 1913, and the congregation met in the courthouse until 1919 when the present building was opened. The dedication was in 1923, and the pipe organ was installed in 1924. Central added the three-story education building in 1951, and did extensive remodeling to the main building in 1959 and 1960. They completed the new family life activities center in 1982. In 1993, a belfry, steeple, and new entrance foyer with handicap access to the sanctuary and education building, were completed.

CENTRAL *(Lowndes County: 1201 College Highway, Columbus 39701).* Central was the outgrowth of a cottage prayer meeting instituted by Mrs. A. P. Leech, the wife of superannuated Reverend A. P. Leech. In 1899, she noticed a large number of children playing in the streets near her residence on North Third Street. She called her daughter, Mrs. J. S. Boucher, to assist her in organizing a Sunday afternoon meeting for them. Her pastor, J. A. Bowman of First Methodist Church, suggested forming a Sunday School under Reverend Leech's direction. The Sunday School grew to over 100 members, and moved to a store on Fifth Avenue, South. Reverends E. P. Craddock and Leech organized a church with thirteen members in 1902. A lot on Bell Avenue was secured behind the College for Women, and a frame building was erected in 1903, called Second Methodist Church. In 1913, a lot was purchased near the entrance to the college, and in 1921 a beautiful brick church building was erected. The name of the church was changed to Central Methodist.

CENTREVILLE *(Wilkinson County: 258 Howard Street, Centreville 39631).* The Midway Methodist Church was organized in Wilkinson County about 1811 as a brush arbor, near the present town of Centreville. Two of the principal founders of the church were Reverend Matthew Bowman,

a Methodist local preacher from South Carolina, and Colonel John Gauldin Richardson from the same state. Several other Methodist families came from the Carolinas together and added their influence to the young and growing church, which took its name from its position halfway between the settlements on the Mississippi and those on the Pearl River. In 1817, Midway Church entertained the fifth session of the Mississippi Conference, Bishop William McKendree presiding and John Menefee serving as secretary. The eighth conference session was also held at Midway in November 1820. Reverend Ashley Hewitt was the presiding officer. At this time Reverend William Winans of Pennsylvania had settled in the neighborhood, where he made his home until his death on 31 August 1857. The second Midway Church was built some years after the first and served the local congregation until some years after the Civil War. The building of a new railroad through the county in 1885 resulted in the establishment of the present town of Centreville, and the removal of the church to that place, the third home of old Midway Church. The beautiful old church was destroyed by fire in 1924. The fourth brick structure was dedicated by Bishop Collins Denny on 14 September 1930. The Great Depression caused the church to delay construction of a planned education unit, which was finally dedicated by Bishop Franklin 26 February 1950. A parsonage was added in 1952.

CHAPEL HILL *(Attala County: French Camp 39745).* Poplar Springs school, a small one-teacher building built before 1879, served the educational and religious needs of this Attala County community.

The Methodists organized and built a frame church building in 1880, known as Chapel Hill, which served as both church and school. A separate school was built later. When the church building burned, the church again met at the school until they could build a new church in 1910.

Charleston First United Methodist Church

Chapel Hill United Methodist Church, Sandersville

CHAPEL HILL *(Jones County: 304 Lindsey Street, Sandersville 39477).* The church was organized in 1893. There have been four structures. The first two were frame buildings. One was made of blocks. The present building, constructed in 1978, was a brick structure.

CHAPEL HILL *(Kemper County: Oak Grove).* The church was organized in 1874.

CHAPEL HILL *(Panola County: Courtland 38620).* This church was organized in 1860.

CHAPEL HILL *(Webster County: Bellefontaine 39737).* The church was organized in 1865.

CHAPEL OF THE CROSS *(Marion County: 1639 Highway Ninety-Eight East, Columbia 39429).* The church was organized in 1977.

CHARLESTON FIRST *(Tallahatchie County: Cossar Road at Sabine Street, Charleston 38921).* Methodism in

Charleston dates back to 1846 when the first Methodist church was organized. It was not until 1855 that the first church building was constructed on lots deeded by John S. Topp and Alexander Davidson. By 1873, the church was in such bad state of repair that it was abandoned. The Methodists joined with other denominations of Charleston in moving the Old Wellington Church to a lot owned by the school and formed a Union church. In 1889, B. F. and Mary Saunders deeded a lot on the corner of Church and Gay Streets to the Methodist trustees. A church building was erected that year under the pastorate of J. B. Porter. In 1918, a new church and parsonage were constructed at the corner of Main and Sabin Streets. The North Mississippi Conference met in this building. Charleston Methodists again felt their building was inadequate. In 1954, another building program began on the eastern half of the block, just in front of the old building between Main and Walnut Streets. Pastor G. W. Curtis conducted the ground breaking on 28 June 1954, and Bishop Marvin A. Franklin laid the cornerstone on 16 January 1955. The first services in the new building were held on 10 April 1955, exactly 100 years after the first Methodist church was constructed in Charleston.

CHRIST *(Alcorn County: 3161 Shiloh Road, Corinth 38834).* The first church, named Southside, was organized in the home of W. L. Madden in May 1906, with fifteen charter members. John D. Simpson was the first pastor. Soon a building was erected on property given by Mr. Madden on the corner of Meigg and Pierce Streets. Reverend J. D. Simpson was pastor. By 1907, the debt had been retired, and, due to the illness of Bishop Wilson, Reverend B. P. Jaco, presiding elder, preached the dedication sermon. Reverend L. M. James Sr. entered the ministry from this church. The second sanctuary was built in 1948, at the corner of Tate and Madison Streets, and was known as Trinity. On 24 April 1949, Reverend S. M. Butts, pastor, invited Bishop Marvin A. Franklin to dedicate Trinity and its contents. Two young men entered the ministry from this church, Zelfred Smith Jr. and Frank L. Madden. The third church building was completed early in 1975 and the first service was held on Palm Sunday, 23 March 1975, conducted by the pastor, Reverend Claude L. Fleming Jr. The note burning took place on 12 February 1984.

CHRIST *(Clay County: Churchill at Eshman, West Point 39773).* The church was organized 10 July 1960. The first worship services were conducted in the Clay County Courthouse. The present brick building was constructed in 1962.

CHRIST *(Harrison County: 6121 Beatline Road, Long Beach 39560).* In 1983, a group of lay persons and clergy came together to form the Seashore District New Church

Christ United Methodist Church, Long Beach

Development and Revitalization Committee. In June of that year, Clint Gill was district superintendent. Prior to Reverend Gill's arrival, the Mississippi Conference had been engaged in a comprehensive study of each district to ascertaining the need for new churches, merging existing churches, etc. After careful study, one of the three top areas in which a new church was needed was the area of Long Beach on Beatline Road in the northern section of the city. The problem of funding had to be resolved, since neither the district nor the conference had the resources to underwrite such a project. As a result of the task force's work, the concept of the "Kingdom Builder's Club" came into being. By 1 June 1986, two new churches had started: the first at Ocean Springs, and the second in North Biloxi or D'Iberville. The committee then turned its attention to Long Beach and the search for land. With approval being given, the land was purchased. In June of 1986, the Bishop and cabinet appointed Reverend Glenn Seefeld to the yet unnamed church. A parsonage was secured for the Seefeld family and the significant history of the Beatline Road church was fully underway.

CHRIST *(Hinds County: 5301 Old Canton Road, Jackson 39211).* On a hot July Sunday in 1961, in the living room of the original parsonage, twenty-three people stepped

Christ United Methodist Church, Jackson

forward to be received as the first members of the city's newest Methodist church. From those humble beginnings Christ United Methodist Church emerged, and is now listed among the top twenty-five United Methodist churches in the nation with over 4,500 members. Only four have served as senior pastor: J. Willard Leggett, III (1961 to 1970), Seth W. Granberry (1970 to 1972), David A. McIntosh Sr. (1972 to 1983), and John M. Case (1983 to present). The present three acre site was purchased, and in 1962, the first sanctuary was dedicated. It would seat 200. A study on church growth in 1981 predicted that the church had reached its potential and would probably no longer experience growth. Three thousand members later, it is obvious that report was wrong. The church has grown, and ministries have expanded. Christ Church is active in twenty-eight mission projects. It has received national recognition for the Urban Ministry in North Midtown, Jackson. The Week Day Preschool, under the direction of Julia Bishop, was the first preschool in Mississippi to receive national accreditation. Other ministries which have received national attention are small group ministries, singles, youth, music, and evangelism.

CHRIST *(Lafayette County: 182 Highway Thirty East, Oxford 38655).* This church was organized in 1960.

CHRIST *(Prentiss County: 138 County Road 7200, Booneville 38829).* Christ Church was organized in 1968.

CHRIST *(Sunflower County: 801 North Sunflower Avenue, Indianola 38751).* The dream for a second Methodist Church in Indianola began with Reverend E. Allen Bailey and the first members in 1962, when they purchased the land. On 22 June 1975, thirty-seven charter members met for the first church school and worship service under the leadership of Reverend Larry M. Goodpaster, the first pastor. Members chose Christ for the name in July. Ground breaking for the first church building was 11 January 1976. On 14 November 1976, the first services in the new Christ building were held. In October 1977, ground was broken for the second phase of the building. In January 1985, the church moved into the third phase of the building: additional classrooms, and offices.

CHRIST *(Tippah County: 313 Park Lane, Ripley 38663).* On 20 September 1963, a group of Methodists met for their first services in an empty dwelling house that had been rented for that purpose, until a church building could be erected. Forty-four people became the charter members of a new congregation, later to be named Christ United Methodist Church. The first pastor was Faban Clark. On 19 April 1964, the ground breaking was held. On 4 July 1964, the members carried baskets of food for their lunches, and worked all day to be ready for services the following Sunday for the first time in the new sanctuary, even hough the furniture was not yet ready. Kim Akins, daughter of Lavaughn and Ruth Akins, was baptized. This church has been a part of three charges since their beginning: Lowry Charge, Falkner Charge and Tippah Circuit, which was at first the Ripley Circuit. A new parsonage was finished, and the present charge consists of three churches, Christ, Jacob Chapel, and New Hope. A Christain life center was constructed in 1992.

CHRISTIAN BANNER *(Scott County: 17 Martin Luther King Drive, Morton 39117).* Christian Banner of Morton, at its inception in 1896, was a mission with an adult membership of twenty-five and a total of sixty-five worshippers. The property deed was dated 1896. The earliest other document is a 1907 Journal of the Mississippi Annual Conference of the Methodist Episcopal Church. Two pastors are listed for that year: E. H. Langston and Andrew Reid, supported by the Freedom Aid Society and Southern Educational Society. The Church was in the Meridian District. The 1910 Journal listed Reverend R. B. Anderson as Morton's pastor. The church was assigned then to the Jackson District. Reverend P.W. Baldwin served the church of less than a hundred members from 1912. The present building was erected in 1963. The original building faced Tullos Drive and the B. C. Rogers plant. The church provided land for street improvement and built on this site facing the street now named Martin Luther King Drive. In the fall of 1994, the people of Christian Banner saw the need to restore their building. Christian Banner was selected the 1995 Small Membership

Church of the Year in the East Jackson District.

CHRISTIAN REST *(Lafayette County: 183 County Road 255, Etta 38627).*

CHUNKY *(Newton County: Chunky 39323).* The church was organized in 1888.

CHURCH HILL *(Jefferson County: Church Hill 39055).* Church Hill was one of the earliest settlements in the county. The present Methodist church was organized in 1890.

CLARA *(Wayne County: Clara 39324).* The church was organized in 1903.

CLARK'S CHAPEL *(Sharkey County: Carey 39054).* The church was organized in 1914.

CLARKES CHAPEL *(Kemper County: Lynville).* This church was organized in 1914.

Clarksdale First United Methodist Church

CLARKSDALE FIRST *(Coahoma County: 405 East Second Street, Clarksdale 38614).* This community was established by John Clark in the mid-1800s. Because of its susceptibility to floods, and poor transportation in the swamps, the community did not begin to grow until the late 1800s. The town incorporated in 1892. The

history of First United Methodist Church
dates back to 1846, when the Mississippi
Delta Mission was formed. Reverend
Copeland was appointed to this ministry,
and at the end of the year, there were 189
members. It was in 1851 that Reverend
James E. Scott came by horseback to the
banks of the Sunflower River and found
John Clark clearing land. Services of
worship were held in the Clark home until
an arbor was constructed on a large Indian
mound near the Sunflower River. After
using the arbor for eighteen years, the
congregation built a log church on the
mound and called it Mount Moriah. In
1878, a frame church was erected on the
mound. Soon after, Reverend J. T. Murrah
was appointed in 1896. A frame building
was erected on the lot and used until 1915.
The building was sold and moved. The
present building was completed in 1917, by
a congregation of 350 members. Bishop H.
M. Dubose dedicated this building on 31
October 1937, when Doctor J. E. Stephens
served as pastor. In 1948, a lot for the
education building was purchased and
construction was begun in 1953. Bishop
Marvin A. Franklin conducted the opening
service for the new building on 29 March
1959. In 1974, the church sanctuary was
remodeled, a new organ was installed, and a
grand piano was purchased.

CLERMONT HARBOR *(Hancock
County: Ioor Street at Clermont Boulevard,
Clermont Harbor 39551).* Mrs. Elizabeth
Jenkins and Mrs. Eugene Mogabgab orga-
nized a Bible School on 17 December
1933. It was held in the schoolhouse for a
while, and later in the Clermont Harbor
Hotel. Reverends J. E. Gray, and A. J.

Clermont Harbor United Methodist Church

Boyles, held services regularly for some
time. In April 1935, the Bible Schoo.
disbanded. A survey was made in this
vicinity early in 1944, and found thirty-five
Protestant families. In May 1944, the first
preaching service was held in the home of
Mrs. Eva Ladner, with Reverend E. E.
Samples of the Bay Saint Louis Church,
officiating. During the first part of June
1944, Doctor T. Restin Heath, a retired
minister of the Kansas Conference, living at
Kiln, was appointed as associate for
Clermont Harbor and Lakeshore
Churches. On 25 June 1944, Doctor Heath
held his first service in Clermont Harbor in
the home of Mrs. Eva Ladner. At this very
first meeting, six dollars were set aside to
start a building fund for a new church. On
8 August 1944, Myrtle Musser was
baptized, and her mother, Mrs. W. H.
Musser, was received as the first member of
the church. On 15 October 1944, Doctor
Neill established the Clermont Harbor-
Lakeshore Charge, and at the next Annual
Conference, Doctor Heath was appointed
pastor. The building was started 9 February

1947, and occupied by year's end. Hurricane Camille, in 1969, blew the Clermont Harbor building off its foundation.

Cleveland First United Methodist Church

CLEVELAND FIRST *(Bolivar County: 318 South Court, Cleveland 38732).* This community was settled about 1869 by B. C. Simms, who named the community in honor of President Grover Cleveland. The Cleveland Methodist Church was organized in the year 1870, with six members. Sylvester Cade Beevers and Elizabeth C. Beevers, were among the charter members. Preachers were assigned to the Jones Bayou Circuit (progenitor of the present church) beginning in December 1877, with the appointment of A. W. Gibson. About 1873, they built a one-room log house for a schoolhouse, and the minister preached in it. About 1879, they built a church where the log cabin stood, a one-room building made of lumber. They used that for many years. In 1887, a frame building was constructed at the intersection of Sunflower Road and Jones Bayou. The building was dedicated in 1888, by Bishop

Charles Betts Galloway. In 1917, ground was broken for the present church. The facade features four Corinthian columns topped by acanthus leaves. Six large and six smaller art noveau or Tiffany-style stained glass windows are a significant part of the sanctuary's decoration. The Cleveland Church was host for the 1939 unification service for the North Mississippi Conference. In June 1972, a newly constructed education building was formally opened.

CLINTON FIRST *(Hinds County: Mount Salus Road at Highway Eighty, Clinton 39056).* About 1823, Judge, and later Governor, Walter Leake bought land near an ancient Indian settlement near Jackson known as Mount Dexter. He built a home, and called it Mount Salus. A settlement began to emerge, and in 1828, the name was changed again to Clinton. The Methodist church here was organized in 1831. The first building served the church from 1831 to 1857, and was located at the corner of East and College Streets. The second building, erected in 1857, was located on East Street at Main Street. A third brick structure, located at West Main and Monroe, was erected in 1925. The fourth building was constructed in 1965 on Mount Salus Road at Highway Eighty. The present sanctuary was completed in 1992. The former building continues to serve as a Sunday School classroom building with a fellowship hall. A separate family life building was completed in 1978. The church has a brick from the original 1831 building, and a bell from the first train to run from Vicksburg to Clinton, one of two bells in the bell tower.

COALVILLE *(Harrison County: Gulfport 39505).* Coalville community was settled about 1840, and got its name from the charcoal burning industry that developed here. The church was organized in 1852.
COCKRUM *(DeSoto County).* The church was organized in 1835.

Coffeeville United Methodist Church

COFFEEVILLE *(Yalobusha County: Coffeeville 38922).* This community was settled prior to the 1830s, and became the county seat in 1834. It was named for one of Andrew Jackson's friends, General John Coffee. The Methodist church was organized in 1828. The foundation for Coffeeville United Methodist Church was laid by Methodist circuit riders who traveled the early wilderness trails to organize scattered believers into Societies. There were few ordained ministers. The first lay preacher in Coffeeville was William Gwin. On 7 December 1828, the Society for this county was formed. In 1831, Reverend Thomas P. Davidson, pastor of the Methodist Church in the little village of Memphis, asked to be transferred from the Tennessee Conference to serve the Coffeeville and Grenada churches in 1836 and 1837. In 1847, a small, one-room

Methodist Church was built. In 1873, it was decided that this church had become too dilapidated and that a new one would be built. At the December 1873, North Mississippi Conference at Batesville, Captain J. S. Collins invited the Conference to meet at Coffeeville the next year. A one-room white frame house was built. This house served until 1915, when, under the leadership of Reverend W. L. Storment, the membership grew and two Sunday School rooms were added. When Reverend H. G. Wallace was pastor, he and his wife aroused interest for a new church building with more adequate facilities for the young people. The present red brick building was completed in 1953 on a lot given by Miss Clyde Beadles next to her home. The first service was held 10 May 1953. Doctor Roy Beadles and Ruth Bailey were the first members to be married in the church on 11 July 1953. The church was dedicated by Bishop Marvin A. Franklin on 11 September 1955. In 1980, when Reverend Tom Hawks was pastor, a beautiful new parsonage was built on Morrison Street and was dedicated by Bishop Minnick.
COKERS CHAPEL *(Lauderdale County: 3042 Jeff Davis School Road, Meridian 39301).* The church was organized in 1840.
COKE'S CHAPEL *(Clarke County: Hale).*
COLDSPRINGS *(Panola County: Sardis 38666).* The inspiration to build a church came on 6 August 1893, as the result of a revival meeting held under a brush arbor, when thirty-eight people accepted Jesus Christ as their savior. On 6 November 1893, the land for the church site was

deeded by J. H. Carter, and the first church was erected in 1894. The church was dedicated by Reverend T. G. Weir, presiding elder, and the first sermon was preached by Reverend J. A. Braswell, the first pastor. In the summer of 1950, with a membership of one hundred and fifty, the people saw the inadequacy of the old church. Erection of the present church was begun in the early months of 1954, under the leadership of Reverend Harold Vaughn, who preached the first sermon in the new church in May of the same year. In June 1954, the Annual Conference changed charge lines, and along with Mount Olivet formed the Panola Circuit. Two years later Terza Church was added.

COLDWATER *(Tate County: Central Avenue, Coldwater 38618).* The town of Coldwater was founded in 1856, but it was not until 1866 that the first church was built. It was the Methodist church, which was a small building. The first pastor was Reverend Sage. The first lights in the church were candles. Later they were replaced by chandeliers. There were two entrances in the front. The men entered through the one on the left side, and the ladies on the right side. There was no organ or piano in the church for some time, so Mr. Baker led the singing with the aid of a tuning fork. In 1883, Reverend J. W. Wyan, the pastor at that time, organized the first Missionary Society with seven members. Mrs. P. T. Callicott was the first president, and Mrs. F. F. Veazey the vice-president. In 1889, a new church was built on the lot just west of the parsonage. In 1915, the church was remodeled. In 1942, the government forced the whole town of Coldwater to move from the old site to the present site. The church building was rolled from old Coldwater to new Coldwater. The bricks had to be removed but were replaced after it was moved to its present location. In 1976, a fellowship hall was added to the church

Collins United Methodist Church

COLLINS *(Covington County: 602 South Second Street, Collins 39428).* Collins emerged because the railroad located here in 1899. The county seat was moved from Williamsburg to Collins in 1906. The town was named for Fred Collins, a United States Marshall. Collins Methodist Church was organized in the early part of 1901. Reverend J. L. Jordan was the first pastor. The original building was erected about 1902, when Reverend J. S. Rainer was pastor. The parsonage was built in 1904. The first church building was destroyed in a cyclone in 1924, and the church constructed a second building. Ground breaking was held 7 August 1950 for the third building, and the first worship service was conducted 18 March 1951. The old church bell, which had been used for forty years before that time, was reinstated in the new belfry. A lighted cross topped the church steeple.

COLLINSVILLE *(Lauderdale County: 9126 Church Street, Collinsville 39325).* Collinsville was settled by and named for Nathaniel Monroe Collins about 1867. His grandson, Ross Collins, became a United States Congressman. The church was organized in 1910.

COLUMBIA VALLEY *(Marion County: 1118 West Avenue, Columbia 39429).* The church was organized in 1960.

Columbia First United Methodist Church

COLUMBIA FIRST *(Marion County: 411 Church Street, Columbia 39429).* Columbia was settled about 1800, and became county seat for Marion County in 1818. It also served as a temporary State Capital in 1821. It is probable that the Columbia Methodist church was organized in 1822, though the first mention of the congregation here was in 1823 when William Winans, presiding elder, preached in the State House. The Conference Historical Society has used 1823 as the official beginning of Methodism in Columbia. Miles Harper was pastor that year. The Annual Conference meeting at Natchez on Christmas Day 1823, took the

Columbia and Monticello Churches from the Pearl River Circuit and made them into a separate pastoral charge, called the Monticello and Columbia Charge. Miles Harper was assigned as pastor of the new charge, so he remained pastor of the Columbia Church. The two churches reported only thirty white, and six Black members at the 1824 Annual Conference, and were reabsorbed into the Pearl River Circuit with Peter James and John P. Haney as joint pastors of the large circuit. For a number of years, two ministers served the Pearl River Circuit. For the next thirty years, the Columbia Church continued as part of the Pearl River Circuit, until the Fall of 1854, when the name of the charge was changed to Columbia. The Columbia Circuit probably included Union Academy and Byrd's Chapel on the east side of the Pearl River. The entire membership on the charge when Henry P. Lewis became pastor was composed of ninety-eight white, and fifty Black members. Reverend J. W. McLaurin, reported to the *New Orleans Advocate* that the new church at Columbia was dedicated on the third Sunday, 15 June 1884. At the close of that year, there were six churches on the charge, with a total membership of 543, of whom 145 had been received during the year.

COLUMBIANA *(Montgomery County: Highway 407 East, Winona 38967).* The land on which the church now stands was purchased on 25 October 1886, from Robert and Caroline McNutt. The two acres of land were purchased for forty dollars. On 24 November 1896, the trustees of Columbiana Colored Methodist Episcopal Church, sold to the trustees of the Montgomery County School Board one-fourth acre of this same property for the sum of four dollars to build a public schoolhouse. The school and church burned. The school was never rebuilt. The members of the church started rebuilding on the same site. Reconstruction was underway when a windstorm destroyed the foundation. However, it was completed in 1948. In 1975, under the leadership of Reverend B. J. Cameron, the members of Columbiana United Methodist Church prayed about building a new church. The new brick building was completed in June 1978. The dedication service was held on 14 February 1988. In the spring of 1994, a plan was set in motion for an addition to the church, which included extension of the sanctuary and fellowship hall. The new addition was completed in August 1994. The church was recognized as one of the outstanding small membership churches at the Annual Conference in June 1996.

COLUMBUS FIRST *(Lowndes County: 601 Main Street, Columbus 39703).* Columbus' history dates back to 1540, when Hernando DeSoto crossed this area. But it was not until 1817 that a permanent white settlement was established here, known as Possum Town. In 1821, the village was renamed in honor of Christopher Columbus, and incorporated in 1822. The church was organized in 1823. The first pastor was Wiley Ledbetter. There were nine founding members. For ten years the congregation worshipped in the old Franklin Academy building. The group erected a frame building in 1831. The large brick building, which it erected in 1844, is now the Jewish Temple. The present large structure was begun in 1858 and was completed in 1870. During the

Columbus First United Methodist Church

bitter Civil War, construction of the building was halted, the roof was removed to make canteens for the soldiers, and the structure was used as a hospital for the sick and wounded. While the men in the congregation were involved with construction of the building, the women of First Methodist organized the first Woman's Foreign Missionary Society in the North Mississippi Conference on 24 April 1879. The first Memorial Day Service, for Confederate and Federal dead, was held here in 1866. In 1914 an annex was built, and in 1940 an education building added. First Church, Columbus, is the oldest church in the former North Mississippi conference, and was selected a "Church of

Historical Significance" in 1984. In June of 1971, a momentous event took place in this church. At the 102nd Session of the North Mississippi Annual Conference held at this church, the merger of the white and Black conferences in the northern half of the state took place. According to the Commercial Dispatch, "the cabinet called upon the delegates to make a decision according to what is right in the eyes of God, and not according to previous social customs." Many sat in the original slave balcony and watched this event of history unfold.

COMMUNITY *(Jefferson County: Route One, Fayette 39069).* The church was organized in 1950.

COMO *(Panola County: Main Street at Oak Avenue, Como 38619).* The Como United Methodist Church had its beginning in 1841, with seven founding members. The first church, built in 1841, was a log building, serving as church and school, and was located about three miles southeast of the present town. Reverend Obidiah E. Ragland was the first pastor. In 1847, a new church was built and stood until 1869, when it was moved and placed on the present site in the town of Como. The present church was built in 1912, with the first service held on 17 March 1913. Reverend J. B. Randolph was the pastor. Through the years the Como Methodist Church has been on several different circuits. The membership began with seven members in 1841, and had 232 in 1985. In 1960, an annex was added to the church and was dedicated 15 May 1960. In December 1966, during an evening worship service, lightning struck the church's dome, causing extensive damage due to fire and water, but no one was injured. In 1983, the front of the church was redesigned and renovated. The present parsonage was built and dedicated in 1954.

CONCORD *(Clarke County: Enterprise 39330).* This church was organized in 1870.

CONEHATTA *(Newton County: 8975 Highway 489, Conehatta 39057).* Conehatta was an Indian village and was settled in the 1830s. The Methodist church was organized in 1870.

CONWAY *(Leake County: 210 East Franklin Street, Carthage 39051).* The community was settled in 1848 by settlers from Conway, Arkansas. The Methodist church was organized in 1900.

COOKS CHAPEL *(Neshoba County: Route Two, Philadelphia 39350).* Pilgrim Rest was organized in 1847. The name of this church was changed from Pilgrim's Rest to Cook's Chapel in 1874, when the church relocated to the Forestdale Road, east of Philadelphia.

Cooksville United Methodist Church

COOKSVILLE *(Noxubee County: Cooksville Community, Macon 39341).* Reliable records show the Cooksville Methodist Church was organized in 1834, and that the present structure was under construction in 1846. In the Alabama Conference until 1862, the church was

ormed under the guidance of Reverend
acob Mathews, who was appointed to the
Choctaw mission. Reverend Mathews was
ssisted by Reverend Robert Lewis
Lennon and Reverend William Wier, who
erved as junior preachers. In 1876 the
Presbyterian church was dissolved, because
: had become nearly extinct, and the
emaining members were directed by the
Presbytery of Tombeckbee, to unite with
he Centerpoint Church (listed as
Centrepoint on the records). Thus the
Methodists of Cooksville became the sole
wners of the building in 1876. The struc-
ure remained much the same until two
unday School rooms and a vestibule were
ncorporated into the building in the early
950s. Adjoining the lawn is the cemetery
n which some of the earlier graves are
hose of Rosanna Prewitt, 1783 to 1844;
ohn Prewitt, 1780 to 1851; Lewis
parkman, 1800 to 1858; and Frances T.
cott, 1801 to 1885. On 8 June 1969 the
Cooksville Methodist Church held special
ervices to commemorate the extensive
enovations which were begun in the Spring
f 1968. Continuing the improvements and
eautification of the church building, two
tained glass panels were designed and
nstalled in 1981. The church was in the
Mobile Conference from 1862 to 1870.

COOPER'S CHAPEL *(Clarke County:*
131 Highway 511, Quitman 39355). The
hurch was organized in 1916.

CORINTH FIRST *(Alcorn County: 901*
illmore Street at Bunch Street, Corinth
8834). Corinth was founded in 1857. The
te had been known as Cross City, because
: formed the juncture for two early rail-
oads. The Methodists of Corinth soon set
bout to organize a church. The church was

Corinth First United Methodist Church

organized in 1857 with fourteen members.
The first pastor was John H. Garrett. The
first sanctuary built in 1858, was used
during the Civil War as a hospital and as a
prison, and burned in 1868. It was replaced
by a second frame structure. In 1892, a brick
church was erected. Enlarged in 1905, it
served the congregation until 1960, when
the decision was made to build the present
complex. The chapel, formerly the Fillmore
Street Presbyterian Church, was purchased
in 1976. Since 1949, ten parishioners of the
church entered the ministry and one
became a deaconess. In 1984, the church
was named the New Albany District
Historical Church of the Year.

CORNERSVILLE *(Marshall County:*
Highway 349, Cornersville). Settled between
1830 and 1836, the community incorporated in 1872. It gets its name because it is
located near the borders of three counties.
Cornersville Methodist Church was organized in 1874.

COUPARLE *(Yazoo County: 1901 Rocky Hill Road, Camden 39045).*

Court Street United Methodist Church

COURT STREET *(Forrest County: 609 Southern Avenue, Hattiesburg 39401).* The church was organized in April 1900, in a private school on Walnut Street. In 1901, the church moved to the corner of Court Street and Elizabeth Avenue, and constructed a frame building. A fire on 6 November 1922 destroyed this building. In 1922, the church moved again, to its present location at the corner of Court Street and Southern Avenue, and built a brick church. This building was also destroyed by fire on 18 February 1960. The new chapel, recreation hall, and classrooms were occupied 25 June 1961. On 16 September 1962, the church conducted the first service in its beautiful new sanctuary. Court Street Methodist Church was host to the 1925 and 1937 Annual Conference sessions.

COURTLAND *(Panola County: Courtland 38620).* This railroad community incorporated in 1871.

COY *(Kemper County: 108 Coy Church Road, Preston 39354).* Located northeast of Philadelphia near the Kemper-Neshob county line, Coy United Methodis Church first began meeting in a one-roor structure between 1902 and 1903. In 192C Baptists built a small church near th Methodist one, but were unable to financ a full-time pastor, so the Methodists wer invited to share use of the building. Eac denomination held services, one servic each month. In the 1950s, a new locatio across the road in Kemper County wa acquired.

CRANDALL *(Clarke County: Crandall,* The Crandall community came into exis tence when Long-Bell Lumber Compan moved here in 1907. It was named for Fre Crandall, who operated a pine lumber mil The Methodist church was organized i 1921.

CRAWFORD *(Lowndes County: Ma Street, Crawford 39743).* The church wa organized in 1850. The town incorporate in 1854, and was named for Reveren Peter Crawford, a Baptist minister.

CRAWFORD STREET *(Warre County: Crawford and Cherry, Vicksbur 39180).* The church was organized i 1834. In the yard of this church is the grav and monument of Tobias Gibson, firs Methodist circuit rider to come t Mississippi. He originally was buried in remote spot four miles to the southeast o Vicksburg. In 1805, Newett Vick and hi family moved from Virginia to th Mississippi Territory, stopping for sever: years in Jefferson County near the presen location of Fayette. It was at his home tha the first Methodist Conference of the Ol Southwest was held in 1812, with te members. Learning of better lands, in 181

rawford Street United Methodist Church

e came to Warren County and moved into
ie neighborhood of "Open Woods."
iefore his plans could be carried out, both
e and his wife died from yellow fever in
819. Their graves can be seen on Oak
idge Road. The small church at
)penwood was the forerunner of the
1ethodist Church in Vicksburg. After the
eath of Newett Vick, a long court battle
illowed which finally resulted in practi-
illy all the land on which Vicksburg is
tuated being given to his son, John Wesley
ick; who sold a lot on the northeast
orner of Cherry and Grove Streets to
dgar M. Lane. Several years later, this lot
ind part of the adjoining lot were deeded
) the trustees of the Methodist Episcopal
.hurch, South. Mr. Lane gave much of the
imber, collected money, in fact did nearly
verything necessary to erect a church on
ie site. Perhaps because of a need to

expand, several years later this church was
given to the Black members of the church.
They worshipped there for twelve years,
then the church burned and was never
rebuilt. The slaves then worshipped in the
first Crawford Street Methodist Church.
Preaching was begun within the city limits
of Vicksburg in 1820 by Reverend Lane,
who also in that year married Sally C. Vick.
He had transferred to the Mississippi
Conference from the South Carolina
Conference and Warren County was on his
circuit. He held religious services in
Vicksburg in a blacksmith shop, in his
home, and in a hotel dining room, where
preaching ran second to eating. Later,
Vicksburg became a station and services
were held in the courthouse. On 7 April
1841, J. W. Vick and his wife Catherine
Ann, sold to the trustees of the Methodist
Episcopal Church, South, the land on
which the present church stands. Plans
were immediately projected for a church
building for the site. The building was dedicated in 1850. This church withstood the
Civil War, and in 1863 no preacher was
assigned to it, as the Federals were in
possession. This church stood until 1899
when it was razed and a much more
pretentious building was erected. The lot
on Grove and Cherry Streets was sold to
John McInerney. The second church to
occupy this lot was a very lovely church.
On Palm Sunday, 5 April 1925, the congregation stood with tears streaming down
their faces and watched their church and
the new organ burn. Of the original plant,
only the Annex and the present office were
left. Services were held at the Synagogue
and the gym at the YMCA, and it was here

that the members learned of the decision to unite the three branches of the Methodist Church into the mighty Methodist Church, dropping the name "Episcopal." Under the pastorate of George H. Thompson, plans went forward immediately for a new building. In 1955, during the pastorate of Seth Granberry, a portion of the old Mercy Hospital adjacent to the church was purchased. This included the house known as the Adolph Rose Home next door to the church on Cherry Street. It houses a small chapel, the Youth Department and several Sunday School rooms. In July of 1935, the remains of Tobias Gibson, one of the founders of Methodism in Mississippi were moved from south of Vicksburg to the yard of the church on the Crawford Street side. Some members who became ministers from this church include: Cecil Jones, who became a District Superintendent, George Currey, and Warren Coile. As an outgrowth from this church, two churches were started: Hawkins Church, and Northview Church.

Crenshaw United Methodist Church

CRENSHAW *(Panola County: Terry Avenue, Crenshaw 38621).* When the railroad was built in this area in 1902, Doctor H. W. Crenshaw gave the right of way. The community that emerged incorporated in 1906 was named for him. Methodism in Crenshaw began with the organization of the Crenshaw United Methodist Church in 1906. The first sanctuary for Crenshaw Methodists was a frame structure that was destroyed by fire on 21 September 1968. The present building was constructed between 1969 and 1970, with the first services conducted 31 January 1971.

Crossgates United Methodist Church

CROSSGATES *(Rankin County: 2 Crossgates Drive, Brandon 39042).* Crossgates United Methodist Church was established 6 May 1973. The church began services in the club room of the Rankin County Livestock Pavilion. On 10 June 1973, an organizational meeting was held by District Superintendent, Robert Matheny. At this time, sixteen families were accepted as members and Sunday School classes began. Ground breaking ceremonies for the initial portion of the church building were held on 21 September 1975. Additional spaces for adult Sunday School needs were met through an arrangement with Kindergate

Day Care, and soon the church acquired a parsonage at Quail Lane. The first services for the new building were held Palm Sunday, 11 April 1975. In 1976 the Mississippi Annual Conference named Crossgates UMC "Church of the Year of East Jackson for Outstanding Achievement." In 1979, an education building with six classrooms was added, and in 1982, an additional building with fellowship hall, kitchen, and six more classrooms was completed. A larger parsonage was purchased in 1981. The original sixteen families in 1973 grew to a membership of 969. 1991 saw the completion of a new 500-seat sanctuary and five new classrooms. In December 1991, the church purchased nearly two acres of land and three buildings. In 1996 the church membership voted to purchase six acres of adjacent property for future expansion.

CROSSROADS *(George County: Merrill).* The church was organized in 1826. This church was struck by lightning and burned 3 July 1996.

Cross Roads United Methodist Church, Moselle

CROSS ROADS *(Jones County: 217 Phillips Road and Church Look, Moselle 39456).* The church was organized in

1910. It was a Methodist Protestant Church. There have been three former buildings constructed in 1910, 1936, and 1979. The first two were frame buildings, and the third was made of concrete block. On 23 January 1990, the church suffered major damage by fire, suspected to have been caused by vandalism. The fourth building was begun in 1990. The former structure was across the road from the present building.

CROSS ROADS *(Prentiss County: 229 County Road 8311, Rienzi 38865).* Crossroads Methodist Church was organized sometime around 1840. Doctor M. S. Pannell designated some of the land, and sometime later the Board of Supervisors gave approximately one-half acre of land to the church. People say that Crossroads was first a Presbyterian Church located across the road from where the building now stands. In 1897, Sim Windham was pastor. It was under the leadership of Brother Sim, that the patriotic Fourth of July celebrations were held annually. These events strengthened the love of America that Simeon Windham so much treasured. Also during this time, school was held in the old plank church building. In 1904, Crossroads and Jumpertown were organized as a charge to share preachers. The present church building was constructed in 1968. The small congregation decided to replace the old plank white building with a more modern facility. Reverend Huey Woods was the pastor at the time. The new facility was paid for and dedicated in 1976. In 1983, a fellowship hall was built.

CROWN POINT *(Jefferson County: Gin Branch).*

CRUMP CHAPEL *(Lincoln County: 1504 Zetus Road NW, Brookhaven 39602).* The church was organized in 1902.

Crystal Springs United Methodist Church

CRYSTAL SPRINGS *(Copiah County: 306 West Georgetown Street, Crystal Springs 39059).* This old community was established by a Methodist minister, Elisha Lott of Hancock County who moved here and built a grist mill and sawmill in 1823. Old Crystal Springs Methodist Church was created about 1820, though Methodist history claims 1824 as the actual date. An 1829 article stated: "A strong Methodist settlement had formed midway between Big Black and Pearl River, near the northwestern corner of Copiah County. At a place rich in pure spring water, they built a church and campground which became noted as the headquarters of Methodism in that region." They called the church and campground Crystal Spring (singular). Because it was an important point on Big Black Circuit, the name of the circuit was changed to Crystal Spring. The Old Crystal Springs Church was situated south of the Crystal Springs Cemetery. Reverend Scott, of Trenton, New Jersey, helped establish the

church in the new Crystal Springs. Before the sanctuary was built, the Methodists worshipped in the depot. In 1864, the Mississippi Annual Conference convened in the new sanctuary that had been begun in 1860. Located on the site of the present church, the old building was a frame building, painted white. Four times, this small church was host to Annual Conference: 1864, with Bishop Paine; 1870, with Bishop Doggett; 1882, with Bishop Wilson; and 1889, with Bishop Galloway. It was at the 1870 Conference that Crystal Springs became a Station. A new building was constructed in 1919.

D **'LO** *(Simpson County: Maple Street, D'lo 39062).* The church was organized in 1900.

DALEVILLE *(Lauderdale County: Highway Thirty-Nine North, Daleville 39326).* The church was organized in 1889.

DANTZLER MEMORIAL *(Jackson County: 4912 Weems Street, Moss Point 39562).* The church was organized in 1853.

DAVIS CHAPEL *(Jackson County: 16143 Kelly Church Road, Three Rivers, Pascagoula 39581).* This church was organized in 1870. Mrs. Lucy Davis, recognized as the founder of the church, and for whom it was named, donated the land upon which the first wooden structure was built in 1870. Mr. Paul Wells later donated another parcel of land where the present block building was built.

DAVIS CHAPEL *(Panola County: Sardis 38666).* The church was organized in the 1850s. The original building, with gallery, still stands.

DECATUR *(Newton County: 268 West Broad Street, Decatur 39327).* In 1838, just two years after the formation of Newton

Decatur United Methodist Church

County and after considerable campground activity in the area, pioneer families came together and organized a Methodist church four miles from Decatur at a place called Lily Dale. Thomas Benn, a minister, received and accepted an appointment to this church. Because the congregation at Lily Dale would later form the membership of the Decatur Methodist Church, the present Decatur United Methodist Church claims the distinction of being one of the oldest Methodist churches in the Meridian District. After the railroad came through Decatur in 1854, the town of Decatur doubled in size, and the Methodists organized and built a church in 1855. The church served as the center of worship until February 1864 when General Sherman and his army burned the building. This church was located in the vicinity of the present Decatur Cemetery. At the close of the Civil War, the church acquired three and one-half acres near the center of town and erected a new sanctuary. This church was constructed in 1886. Lacking a permanent home, the congregation had, since the close of the war, been meeting in homes. This structure stood until 1926 when a concrete block building

was erected. Until the 1940s, services were held only once a month. The church became a full time charge in 1942. During the ministry of Reverend James Grisham, the present sanctuary was begun, and this structure was completed in 1953. Under the leadership of Reverend James Benson in the 1960s, a new fellowship hall and education complex was built and an existing facility renovated. An additional building was purchased from Newton County and added to the church complex in 1996 while Reverend Rick Brooks was minister. There were Methodists living and meeting in Newton County before the county was organized and before Mississippi became a state.

DECELL *(Leflore County: 312 Green Street, Greenwood 38930).* Decell Church was organized in 1948 with eight members, under the leadership of Reverend Amos Holmes. Reverend Holmes was pastor of Wesley Methodist Church, which was before the merger. Reverend Holmes felt that since this area of Greenwood had begun to grow, a church in this area was needed. The land was purchased by the Methodist Conference and the present building was moved from the Greenwood Air Base in 1948. This was one of the base chapels which was used during World War II, the base being a training site. The air base had closed and most of the buildings were being sold. Reverend Holmes was pastor for two years and Reverend M. J. Stalling for six years. Since then the church has had six pastors. The church was named after Bishop J. Lloyd Decell, whose family lived in Yazoo County. John Spann was called to the ministry during the administration of

Reverend Stalling. In 1967, while Reverend Stalling was pastor, an educational annex was added to the building.

DECELL MEMORIAL *(Copiah County: Highway Fifty-One, South, Wesson 38680).* The Wesson Methodist Church started in 1867, largely through the efforts of Colonel Wesson, who was in charge of the famous Wesson Mills, and for whom the town was named. Wesson and Beauregard Churches were served in 1867 and 1868 by Reverend Benjamin F. Jones. The first church building was on the corner of Main and Church Streets. In May 1885, the church burned. The lot on which the first church stood was sold, and another lot was bought from Wesson Mills on South Beach Street just to the rear of the present building. The new church was finished the latter part of the same year. In January 1886, this frame building, was dedicated by Bishop Charles B. Galloway. About 1912, eight Sunday School rooms were added. The second church building was dismantled in the Fall of 1944 to furnish material for the construction of the present building. Reverend W. S. Cameron was pastor. The cornerstone was laid 21 January 1945, by Bishop Lloyd Decell. The congregation worshipped in the new sanctuary for the first time on 8 July 1945. The church was dedicated 1 September 1946. The name, Decell Memorial Methodist Church, was given to honor the memory of Bishop Decell who spent his early life in Wesson, and was baptized and joined this church on 20 July 1902. Bishop Decell died 10 January of the year the new church was dedicated. Wesson Methodist congregation has sent into the full-time service the following:

Miss Florence Williams, a missionary to China, Bishop J. Loyd Decell, H. S Westbrook, F. J. Jones, S. N. Young, W. A Hays, W. E. Dickens, Will Hogg, Hervic Mellard, W. J. Ferguson, Seth Granberry, W L. Youngblood, and Graham Hodges.

DEKALB *(Kemper County: 210 Churcl Street, Dekalb 39328).* The church wa organized in 1835.

DENNIS *(Tishomingo County: Highwa] Twenty-Five North, Dennis 38838).* The Dennis Methodist Church was organizec in the year 1908 with twenty members, ii an old store building owned by N. S. Davis Worship services were held in that building until 1909, when the original churcl building was erected. It was organized by the pastor of the Belmont Charge, Reverenc J. N. Flynn, assisted by J. A. Byram, who wa at that time a local Methodist preacher. The Dennis Methodist Church was originall] connected to the Belmont Charge (1908 tc 1816), the Golden Charge (1916 to 1922) the Belmont Charge (1922 to 1940), the Tishomingo Charge (1940 to 1967), and i now the Belmont-Dennis Charge. In 1952 plans were begun to completely remode the original church building. These plam were almost completed for the dedicatio1 service which was held 7 March 1954 with Bishop Marvin A. Franklin presiding W. L. Robinson, District Superintendent assisted. W. F. Appleby was the pastor. I1 1966, plans were begun to construct a nev building at a new location on Highwa Twenty-five. The first service was held i1 the new building on 28 May 1967.

DERMA *(Calhoun County: Derma 38839)* This church was organized in 1890. A nev sanctuary and education building wer completed in 1943.

DESOTO *(Clarke County: DeSoto).* Named for famed explorer, Hernando DeSoto, this community was settled as early as 1830, and was on a major east west Indian trace to Savannah, Georgia, and the gulf coast. The church was organized in 1872.

DIAMONDHEAD *(Hancock County: Diamondhead 39325).* The church was organized in 1992 under the pastorate of William L. Jenkins. This congregation began meeting in a computer training building on 16 August 1992, with eleven people present. The congregation soon moved to the Community Center to hold early Sunday services, and met in the home of Mrs. Penny Zahn for weekday Bible study. On 20 December 1992, Diamondhead was organized with twenty-two charter members; Mrs. Jack (Florence) Holt being the first member. In 1996, The Southeastern Jurisdiction United Methodist Men selected Diamondhead as their seventh church building assistance program. Diamondhead United Methodist purchased seven acres of land and, with the assistance of the United Methodist Men and Volunteers in Mission, built a modern two million dollar structure in 1997, under the leadership of Reverend Jeff Pruett. The church building was consecrated in December 1997 by Bishop Marshall Meadors.

DIXIE *(Forrest County: 136 Dixie Church Road, Hattiesburg 39401).* Dixie Church first appeared in the appointments in 1956.

DRAKE HILL *(Noxubee County: Cliftonville).* This church was organized in 1855.

DRAKES *(Rankin County: Flowood Drive, Flowood 39208).* Originally known as Drakes Chapel, this church was established 20 April 1858 on four acres of land donated by Doctor and Mrs. Oscar Hamilton. The present church is the third structure. An historic marker was placed on the church grounds by the Mississippi Department of Archives.

Drew United Methodist Church

DREW *(Sunflower County: 101 South Church Street, Drew 38737).* In 1882, Mr. Andrew Jackson Daniel moved to an area that is now known as West Drew. This area was served by the old Lehrton Circuit. When Mr. Daniel's youngest daughter, Drew, died of malaria, he named the new community "Drew" in her memory. On 23 September 1899, Governor Anselm J. McLaurin issued a charter, officially incorporating Drew. One Sunday morning in December, 1898, Reverend J. M. Davenport, who preached at the McLemore School near Drew, rode over to Drew on his mule and announced that he was going to preach that day. His first sermon was preached under a sawmill shed near the site of the present church. A Sunday School was organized that afternoon. During 1899 and 1900, Reverend Davenport held regular services in Drew and started the collection of funds for the building of a church. Services were held in stores, under sheds, or out in the open. Reverend J. J. Garner, 1901 to 1903, completed the organization of the Methodist Church, and to him is given the honor of being the first pastor of the first church building erected in Drew. This church was a union church used by both Methodists and Baptists in 1901 and 1902. In 1901, the Baptist Mission sent Reverend Donald Allen to Drew to assist Reverend Garner in union services. In 1902, the Drew Baptist Church was formed, and union services ended. The church became the Drew Methodist Episcopal Church, South. Drew Circuit was composed of Drew, Ruleville, Sandy Bayou, Rome, and Parchman. The parsonage was at Ruleville. In 1913, Drew was separated from the circuit and became an independent charge. A spacious brick church with beautiful stained glass windows and all modern conveniences was erected in 1914. Wallace Chapel joined Drew to form a two-point charge. Reverend Felix Sutphin, later President of Wood College, was sent to be pastor in 1951. During this time, the educational annex was completed, and Bishop Franklin preached the dedication sermon. While Reverend C. B. Burt was pastor, 1959 to 1964, Rome, Wallace Chapel, and Drew, combined to form the Drew Methodist Parish. During the tenure of Reverend A. L. Meadows, 1975 to 1978, the Anderson house joining the church property was purchased. In 1982, a Bell Tower was built in honor of all pastors of Drew United Methodist Church.

DRUID HILLS *(Lauderdale County: 3309 Fifty-Fourth Place, Meridian 39307).* The church was organized in 1957.

DUBLIN *(Coahoma County: Dublin 38739).* The first Methodist church in the area now known as Dublin, was called Cherry Hill, because it was located on a ridge with a growth of cherry trees. Under Reverend George B. Allen's pastoral leadership, the church was organized as early as 1858, possibly in 1857, when the Nichols, Lawler, and Hilliard families settled in the area on Hopson Bayou. The first building, constructed in 1858, was a log structure. B. W. Lawler gave some three acres of land for a church building and cemetery. In 1874, the spot was recognized as a community and named "Dublin" after Dublin, Ireland, perhaps in recognition of Irishman Patrick Murphy who was the first postmaster. In 1878, B. W. Lawler increased the church land to nine acres and in 1880, a new church and parsonage were built across the road from the log church. With the coming of the railroad, the center of the community shifted some two miles northeast. In the list of pastoral appointments taken from conference minutes, the church appears as "Cherry Hill" from 1873 until 1887. Prior to that time the church was on a scattered circuit in the "Mississippi Bottom" District, perhaps served by a circuit rider from Friars Point. Since 1888, the church has appeared in the appointments as "Dublin," but until about 1931, when a brick structure was built in the town of Dublin, the congregation continued to worship in the frame building at Cherry Hill, some two miles south of town.

DUCK HILL *(Montgomery County: Duck Hill 38925).* In about 1850, when this church was organized, it was known as Mount Zion. The first pastor was Reverend

Z. M. Rodgers. In July 1885, the deed for the present location of the Duck Hill Church was for an acre of ground given by J. R. Binford to G. P. Lake, W. H. Sykes and G. W. Sledge, trustees of the Methodist Episcopal Church, South, and acknowledged by T. J. Binford, Mayor of Duck Hill. The present building was constructed during the year of 1885, of old field pine trees from the Lake, Tyler, and Sledge farms east of Duck Hill on the Providence Road. Four Sunday School rooms were added in 1922. The oldest graves in the cemetery are Sledge, Sykes, and Tyler.

DUDLEY CHAPEL *(Jones County: Laurel 39440).*

DUMAS *(Tippah County: 3491 Highway 370 South, Dumas 38625).* Dumas Methodist was organized 8 April 1888, with four members, on land deeded by D. A. Tigrett. The first building to occupy this site, built in 1888, was razed in 1929, to make way for a new building, which is the present structure. The building was completed in 1930, during the depression. A formal dedication of the present structure was held 30 June 1940. Bishop Hoyt M. Dobbs was the presiding bishop of the area. Reverend W. R. Lott Jr. was the District Superintendent who officiated and preached at the dedication service. Reverend T. A. Filgo was the pastor and Reverend H. E. Finger Jr. was associate pastor. Reverend Finger became a Bishop of The United Methodist Church. In June 1985, Dumas Church was placed on the Lowry Charge.

DUMAS CHAPEL *(Webster County: Highway Nine North, Bellefontaine 39737).*

DUNCAN *(Bolivar County: 112 West Main Street, Duncan 38740).* This community was settled in the 1850s. Soon after its settlement, a church was erected. The Methodist church was organized in 1890. A 1929 tornado killed twenty-two people and destroyed every building in town.

DURANT FIRST *(Holmes County: 212 West Madison, Durant 39063).* The Methodists located in Durant in 1871. The first pastor was J. G. Carlisle, and the pastor at the time the first little church was built was Reverend George W. Brown. The cornerstone was laid in 1871, and the church was completed in 1872. Before this time, the Methodists of the community had worshipped at old Wesley Chapel, just west of Castalian Springs and nearby they found a convenient hillside for a cemetery. In 1914, the congregation felt that a new church building was imperative. In the early part of 1915, the cornerstone was laid. The building was completed in the early part of 1916 and was dedicated in June 1919, by Bishop J. C. Kilgo. Reverend J. Nash Broyles was pastor. The education building was built in 1982. The ground breaking ceremony was 7 March 1982. The Davis Hall building was completed in June of 1982.

EAGLE LAKE *(Warren County: 16720 Highway 465, Vicksburg 39180).* In late 1948, a Sunday School was started in an abandoned school building at the Yazoo River near Eagle Lake by some laity from Crawford Street Church in Vicksburg. Shortly after its organization, Reverend T. O. Prewitt, presiding elder, sent a preacher, Reverend Geilsman, to hold services on Sunday afternoons at the new church. Reverend Geilsman was followed by Peyton Moore, a ministerial student, and Reverend Bill Dement, pastor of the Redwood Charge. Under Reverend Dement's ministry, a drive began to build a new church by remodeling and enlarging the school building. However, the congregation decided to build the new church in the Eagle Lake community. A member of another denomination donated land, and by early 1951, ground was broken for the new building. Bishop Marvin Franklin dedicated the building on 22 March 1953, assisted by Reverend T. O. Prewitt and Reverend Seth Granberry.

EARLY GROVE *(Marshall County)*. This church was organized in 1860.

EAST END *(Lauderdale County: 1501 Sixteenth Avenue, Meridian 39301)*. East End Methodist Church, Meridian, was organized 4 January 1891, with twelve members in a store building on Sixteenth Avenue, between Fifteenth and Sixteenth Streets, by Reverend Harry C. Brown. Following the organization, the use of the East End School was obtained and services were held there until the church building on the Southwest corner of Fourteenth Avenue and Fifteenth Street was ready for use. This building, a frame structure, was erected during the pastorate of Reverend Harry C. Brown, and was dedicated in 1893, during the pastorate of Reverend B. F. Lewis. The church enjoyed a steady growth, and in January 1903, thirty-nine members transferred at one time to form Seventh Avenue (Wesley) Church. By 1915, need for a larger building with improved facilities became evident, and steps were taken to meet the situation. The lot on which the present building stands was acquired, but it was not until 1920,

during the pastorate of Reverend J. L. Sells, that work on the new building was begun. The cornerstone was laid 26 September 1920, by Bishop W. F. McMurray. The main auditorium was formally occupied the first Sunday in February 1921.

EASTLAWN *(Jackson County: 2502 Ingalls Avenue, Pascagoula 39567)*. The church was organized in 1943.

EBENEZER *(Carroll County)*.

EBENEZER *(Franklin County: Route Two, McCall Creek 39647)*. The church was organized in 1827, about one mile west of the present building. There have been three sanctuaries, and the present sanctuary was built in 1896. The first church was built of hand-hewn logs and covered with boards. It contained sections made for the Black members, who were slaves. The first building was used for worship until about 1860 or 1862. In 1835, the Micajah Pickett family donated the present church site and another building was erected on the site. The frame building had no ceiling and the pulpit was in the end of the building facing the road. In 1896, the second building was torn down and a new building was erected on the same site. The same framework was used in this building. The church has a roll book dating back to 1855.

EBENEZER *(Holmes County: Lexington 39095)*. Ebenezer is perhaps the second oldest church in the former North Mississippi Annual Conference, with an organizational date verified in September of 1828. Doctor John G. Jones, in his *A Complete History of Methodism*, related: "Early in the fall we penetrated the upper part of Yazoo County and held a two days meeting in the home of Brother Thomas

Rule, organized a class and appointed Burwell Scott class leader. The settlement was on the waters of Cypress Creek, and his society was the nucleus of the famous old Ebenezer membership and good camp meetings. The early charter members were Thomas Rule and his wife, Anna Christian James) Rule; Brittain Smith and his wife, Elizabeth (Zeigler) Smith; Charles J. Hoover and his wife Nancy (Mary) Hoover; and Burwell Scott and his wife." The church was in the Choctaw Indian country, which was called "The Wilderness." In 1829 Doctor Tally was made Superintendent of the Yazoo Circuit. He held several meetings for the Choctaws in Ebenezer and was assisted by an interpreter, Mose Perry, who had married a Choctaw Indian, and was adopted by the tribe. Greenwood Leflore, the Choctaw Chief, attended services at the Ebenezer Church several times. The first building was a log structure that served as both church and schoolhouse. This building burned, and was replaced by another in 1851.

EBENEZER *(Pontotoc County: 1411 Highway 342, Pontotoc 38863).* Ebenezer gets its name from the Biblical name of Ebenezer, which means "stone" or "rock of help." Ebenezer got its start from the Old Campground Methodist Church. Ebenezer was organized in 1894 with seventeen members, and the first pastor was F. A. Whitson. In the path of a cyclone which struck most of the county in 1913, the church building was blown partly from its foundation. Church members put the building back in shape. In 1968, Ebenezer Church bought adjoining property and renovated the existing building into a six-

room parsonage; with Ebenezer being the headquarters for the Ebenezer Charge. Ebenezer is now on the Algoma Charge with Algoma and Palestine United Methodist Church. In 1974 to 1975, a new education building was built.

EBENEZER *(Scott County: Blossom Hill Road, Morton 39117).*

EBENEZER *(Tippah County: 50 County Road 224, Walnut 38683).* The name of the church from its inception has been Ebenezer. The church was organized in approximately 1836, and the first pastor was Benjamin Watson. The first structure, built in 1836, was a brush arbor building. Split logs were used as pews and the building also served as a schoolhouse. Some "white men" and their families settled in Hatchie Bottom while the area was still inhabited by Indians. The exact date is not known and no set time for services was known, circuit riders might preach there any day of the week. The earliest written membership record is 1843. The record of the male membership was lost but two ladies who were with Reverend Watson are the earliest recorded. The second structure was facing north and south with two doors: one for the men and one for women and children. It was built sometime between 1836 and 1900. The third structure was built in 1910, a white frame building. The present structure, a brick building, was dedicated in 1964.

EBENEZER *(Union County: County Road One, Hickory Flat 38633).*

ECRU *(Pontotoc County: Ecru 38841).* The church was organized in 1908. The first sanctuary was constructed in 1911.

EDEN *(Yazoo County: Eden).*

EDWARDS *(Hinds County: 211 Magnolia, Edwards 39066).* The church was organized in 1828, and was located at the present Edwards Cemetery. It was once known as Liberty Methodist. There have been four buildings. The first was a log building, built in 1828. The second building was frame, built in 1874. A third building, also frame, was built in 1876, and burned 22 February 1938. The present brick building was erected in 1939. A fellowship hall was added in 1962.

EGYPT *(Chickasaw County: Egypt).* This community dates back to 1842. It was once known as Pikeville. It was named for a type of corn grown in the area. The Methodist church was organized in 1882.

ELIZABETH *(Lauderdale County: Kewanee).*

ELLISON *(Yazoo County: 36 Brown Road, Vaughan 39179).* This church, located about a mile west of Deasonville, was first known as New Hope Church, and was organized in 1842. The original building was donated by Moses Ellison and his wife Mary. This became the site of Ellison United Methodist Church. This site is located near Vaughan, Yazoo County. Methodists in the Vaughan area continue to worship at this site. Prior to this, church members had met at a Community Union Meeting House named "Blackjack." The Baptists continued to use "Blackjack" after the Methodists built their church. The Methodists soon erected a log building on the site. It was not long before the log house had been outgrown and another building constructed. Like the old log building, there were two front doors, the men entered and sat on one side, and the women entered the other door and sat on the other side. War came in 1862 and the

people and church suffered greatly. In 1899, Ellison was moved from the Benton Charge to form a new charge, Ellison, Vaughan, and Union. At this time, a new charge conference was established, and a new parsonage constructed at Ellison.

Ellisville United Methodist Church

ELLISVILLE *(Jones County: 202 Church Street, Ellisville 39437).* Ellisville was founded around 1800 by Powhatan Ellis, on the banks of Tallahala Creek, called "Old Town." Jones County was established in 1826 and the Methodist circuit riders traveled through this area long before that. In 1857 the Leaf River Circuit must have included the major portion of Jones County, Perry County and parts of Forrest and Lamar Counties. There were only two settlements of any note at that time in the entire circuit; Old Ellisville, county seat of Jones County, and Old Augusta, county seat of Perry County. The Ellisville First United Methodist Church had its beginning in "Old Town" in 1857, on the Tallahala Charge. Reverend F.W. Sharbrough was the first minister. The Ellisville Methodist Church was known for many years as Ellisville Mission and out of it grew Laurel and Hattiesburg Charges.

EMINENCE *(Covington County: Highway 535, Seminary 39479).* This church was organized in 1890.

EMMANUEL *(Hinds County: 100 Shands Street, Jackson 39212).* The church was organized in 1932. It was known previously as the Bessie Shands Mission and Shands Memorial Methodist Church. The church first met in a home. The first building for the Bessie Shands Mission was erected in 1939. The church was located at the corner of Beatty Street and South West Street until 1953. In that year, the church moved to its present location. The present sanctuary was constructed in 1963. The church suffered major damage by vandalism in 1985.

EMORY *(Holmes County: Emory Road, Lexington 39095).* The church was organized in 1848.

ENON *(Carroll County: Coila 38923).* The church was organized in 1858.

ENTERPRISE *(Clarke County: Enterprise 39330).* This community was settled in 1728 when Father Beaudoin, a French Jesuit priest, arrived for a seven year ministry to the Choctaw Indians. In 1735, a trading post was established. The present town was platted in 1837, and incorporated in 1846. The Enterprise Methodist Church has been in existence since the 1830s, as part of the Alabama Conference until 1862. The *New Orleans Christian Advocate* recorded a visit here by Bishop Andrew on 22 June 1857, when he dedicated a new church building. The citizens of Mobile donated an 800-pound church bell. In 1862 the church became part of the Mobile Conference until 1870. The first Methodist parsonage was located in front of the church building on a lot donated by Charles F. Mayerhoff in 1830.

EPWORTH *(Harrison County: 684 Walker, Biloxi 39530).*

EPWORTH *(Hinds County: 1315 West McDowell Road, Jackson 39204).* Early in 1954, the Board of Missions of the Methodist Church recognized the need for a mission type church in a growing rural area on West McDowell Road. When Conference met, District Superintendent Doctor M. L. McCormick made known plans for the purchase of the home of the W. A. Clements family. Reverend Ben Fairchild was appointed the first pastor. The first service was held on 18 July 1954. Those attending this service were James Champion, Freddie Hines, and Frank Johnson families. The next Sunday, the Joe Groover family began attending. Epworth was formally organized as a church on 9 October 1954. Doctor M. L. McCormick, with the help of Reverend Bob Matheny and his associate, Reverend T. B. Winstead, officiated at the birth of Epworth Methodist Church. Nineteen charter members were in attendance. The worship services were held in the living room of the "White" house and Sunday School classes met in two adjoining rooms. In January 1955, prayer meetings were begun. At Conference in June 1955. Reverend Hilman Wolfe, a student at Emory University was appointed minister. By this time the Clements family had moved, leaving the entire house for the church's use. Remodeling was done which gave living quarters to Reverend Wolfe and his new wife. Reverend Wolfe commuted from Atlanta every weekend. Epworth was growing. It was through the efforts of Blanche Watkins that the first Methodist Youth Fellowship group was started. In the summer of 1955, the first Bible School was held. The congregation was growing so rapidly that it outgrew the facilities; so plans were made and ground was broken for a Chapel on 3 March 1957. Bishop Marvin Franklin and Doctor McCormick led an impressive ceremony. The building was ready for use during that winter. In 1959, a parsonage was built on Theresa Drive. Reverend Ed Deweese was appointed minister. There was a great need for an education building. On 1 July 1961 the building was completed. The parsonage had foundation problems, so a new parsonage was built in 1963, the year Reverend Harold Fleming became minister.

EPWORTH *(Holmes County: 319 Yazoo Street, Lexington 39095)*. The Epworth United Methodist Church began in a house in a part of town known as the Schoolhouse Bottom in 1883 with about fifteen members. The first pastor was Peter H. Hill. A building was constructed in the early 1920s in its present location within the city of Lexington, south of the court square. The church was used as a head start center in the middle 1960s and early 1970s. In 1980 a new church was built.

ESCATAWPA *(Jackson County: 6414 Elder Ferry Road, Escatawpa 39552)*. The deeds of property date back to 1858 when John Newton conveyed a piece of land to the Methodist Church. Those were trying times, the Civil War, typhoid fever, malaria, and yellow fever, all affected this area. In June 1879, a parcel of land was given to the Southern Church and Society by Charles and Sarah Ehlers. Earliest records indicate that in 1895, Escatawpa Methodist was a part of Escatawpa Circuit, which encompassed the area of Escatawpa, Wade, and Big Point. In November 1905, Charles Ehlers deeded to the Escatawpa Circuit of the Methodist Episcopal Church, South, in the

Seashore District, a piece of land to be used for a church. The pastor's pocket record, published in New Orleans in 1895, listed the Escatawpa Church. In 1906, the church was destroyed by a hurricane. After one year, the new church was completed in 1907. The current church and fellowship hall was built in 1968. The parsonage was built in 1972. The upstairs part of the fellowship hall was added in 1986, after Hurricane Elena heavily damaged the building in 1985.

ETHEL *(Attala County: Ethel 39067)*. Originally known as Stonewall, an official of the Illinois Central Railroad named this community, which came into existence in 1883, for his daughter. The Methodists soon organized a church in 1884. They added a new sanctuary in 1950.

EUDORA *(DeSoto County: Eudora)*. This church was organized in 1860.

EUPORA FIRST *(Webster County: 201 West Fox Avenue, Eupora 39744)*. In 1850, the first Methodist meetings were held under brush arbors located on the east side of Highway Nine South. Services were held for a week or longer with the people camping near the arbor until the close of the revivals. This went on until the services were moved to the log cabin used as the school. In 1873, Eupora Methodist Church was organized in a log cabin used as the school during the week and church on Sunday. William S. Lagrone was the first preacher. The log cabin was located where the present Eupora Cemetery is now located. In 1889, at the fourth Quarterly Conference of that year, a Sunday School was organized. In 1890 the church was moved to the second story of a two-story brick building on Roane Avenue. In 1891, the name was changed from Early Grove to Eupora Methodist Church, and was moved to a frame building where the present Post Office is. On 13 May 1917, the lot adjoining the frame church building was added, and a new brick church was built on the same location and dedicated by Bishop J. H. McCoy of Birmingham. In February 1943, the present brick church was completed. The church underwent remodeling, including new stained glass windows, in 1962.

EUREKA *(Panola County: Route One, Courtland 38620)*. The church was organized in 1857. The building erected that year is still in use.

EVANS CHAPEL *(Humphreys County: 812 Central Street, Belzoni 39038)*. The church was organized in 1902.

EVERGREEN *(Itawamba County: 5100 Highway 371, Nettleton 38858)*.

EVERGREEN *(Rankin County: Tickham Bridge Road, Brandon 39042)*. This church was organized in 1869.

FAIRFIELD *(Jones County: Highway Twenty-Nine South, Ellisville 39437)*. This church was organized in 1900.

FAIRVIEW *(Pontotoc County: Route Five, Pontotoc 38863)* Unable to reach the Palestine Methodist Church due to impassable roads, and realizing the need for a church in the center of the community to further the programs of Methodism, part of the Palestine congregation began a campaign in the fall of 1945 to secure funds for the construction of a new church building in their own community. They were assisted by Reverend L. A. Comfort, the pastor of the Algoma Methodist

Charge. The Discipline of the Methodist Church approved the project and construction began in February 1947. On Easter Sunday, 6 April 1947, the first service was held, with Reverend L. A. Comfort bringing the message. Approximately 100 persons attended that first service and sat on planks which had been quickly arranged to provide seating. In 1969, a large two-story brick structure was built. Bishop Mack B. Stokes dedicated it on 28 September 1975. A large activities building was added to the education building in 1976. Fairview Methodist Church became a station church in June 1980. The first pastor of Fairview, as a station church, was Reverend Robert Welch.

FAITH *(DeSoto County: Southaven 38671)*. This church was organized in 1978.

FAITH *(Jackson County: 4005 Chicot Road, Pascagoula 39581)*. This church may hold the Conference record for name changes. It was a mission in 1957, and organized as Bayou Casotte Methodist in 1958. In October 1959, its name was changed to Lakeside Methodist. On 1 May 1960, the church became known as Becky Bacot United Methodist Church. In 1990, the church received its present name, Faith United Methodist Church. Before moving to its present site, it was located on Martin Road in Pascagoula. The first block building was constructed in 1959 and 1960, and was later razed for being unsafe. The present building was constructed in 1990. The education building was built in 1962 and 1963, and the parsonage was added in 1962.

FALKNER *(Tippah County: County Road 559, Falkner 38629)* This church was organized in 1854.

FANNIN (*Rankin County: 2815 Highway 471, Brandon 39042*). The church was organized in 1871.

FARR'S CHAPEL (*Chickasaw County: Houston 38851*).

FAYETTE (*Jefferson County: Highway Sixty-One South, Fayette 39069*) The church was organized in 1827. The first Methodist parsonage in Mississippi was acquired in 1827, used as a church, converted to a parsonage in 1835, and was used more than seventy years.

FELDER (*Pike County: 1030 Highway 570 North Extension, Summit 39666*). The church was organized in 1843. About 1810 or 1811 a camp meeting was held about one mile east of the present town of Magnolia by members of pioneer families from the older states. About 1822 a new campground was established on the Bogue Chitto River, probably just north of Quin's Bridge on the east side of the stream. In 1842 or 1843, among the gentlemen who joined in the establishment of a campground was John Felder, who was born in South Carolina, 8 May 1793, and came to Mississippi in 1810. He was converted at the first camp meeting held near Magnolia in 1811, and to the end of his life he was related to the Methodist Church and an active supporter of camp meetings. He moved to Topisaw Creek in 1839. He died on 20 December 1875, and his funeral sermon was preached at Topisaw by President Harvey F. Johnson of Whitworth College. There have been three buildings serving Felder Church and campground. The first log building was destroyed by the Union Army in the Civil War. The second was a frame building. The third, and present, building was erected in 1955.

FERNWOOD (*Pike County: Cherry at Oak Street, Fernwood 39635*). This church was organized in 1898.

FIFTH STREET (*Lauderdale County: 4000 Fifth Street, Meridian 39307*). The history of Fifth Street Methodist Church began with a wooden structure, built of hewn logs, and mortised together. In 1866, the church moved to what is now Eighth Street and Twenty-third Avenue, where it served as both a church and school. It was in this building that the East Mississippi Female College was organized. In 1885, the old building was put on rollers and drawn by twelve oxen to West End, and a mission church built in its stead. When a new church was needed, the site of Forty-first Avenue and Fifth Street was selected. The church was badly damaged by fire 16 October 1919, and was completely destroyed by fire on 13 June 1925, along with the parsonage. On 15 May 1928, ground was broken for the new church. Dedication services were conducted at the new church 23 October 1945 by Bishop J. Lloyd Decell.

FLETCHER'S CHAPEL (*Yazoo County: 5675 Fletcher's Chapel Road, Yazoo City 39194*). The church was organized in 1849 and named for John Fletcher, a close friend of John Wesley. The wood frame building that served as a house of worship for the community was razed in 1964 and replaced with a brick structure. The old building, built with slave labor during the pastorate of Francis M. Featherstun, had stood through the Civil War with several bullet holes as reminders of the skirmishes that swirled around it in 1863 and 1864.

FLINT HILL (*Lowndes County: Caledonia 39740*). Flint Hill was organized 4 June

1868, and was originally named Union Chapel. A log building was constructed after William Hudson and Elisha Lawrence deeded five acres of land to the trustees and their successors. Mr. D. H. Grier was one of the trustees at that time. The present building was constructed in 1889, using some timber that was blown down in a storm. At that time, the name was changed to Flint Hill. The first organ was purchased through donations by Mr. Henry Barrentine and Mr. John Darnell. Flint Hill has been the site of a two-room school, and for many years, a singing school was a regular event. The annual homecoming began in 1954.

FLORA (*Madison County: 149 Carter Street, Flora 39071*). The town of Vernon was located north of Flora. Vernon was a river port on the Big Black River. The United States Post Office at Vernon was established 2 December 1828. The Vernon United Methodist Church was organized in 1830. In December, 1834, the church was assigned its first full time pastor. In 1884, the railroad was constructed nearby. A depot was built beside the track, and the new village of Flora was established. The town of Vernon began to decline. This same year, both the congregation and the building moved from Vernon to Flora. The name changed to Flora United Methodist Church. Vernon soon became a ghost town. The new church soon became the head of a brand new circuit, Flora Charge. A small house was built for a parsonage. Soon the church had outgrown the building and, in 1904, a new one was constructed. The old church, that had been moved from Vernon, was sold and became a

residence. Soon, another new building was needed and was started in 1937. Because of the Depression and World War II, the new church was not dedicated until 1 November 1942.

FLOWER RIDGE (*Winston County: 4562 Highway Fifteen South, Louisville 39339*). The church was organized in the 1860s. Before 1914, Flower Ridge was a Union church with the Baptists and Presbyterians. There have been three buildings. One was built after organization; the second was built in 1894; and the present building was constructed in 1947. An education wing was added in 1957. The church was recognized in 1979 as "Church of the Year," and as the church with the most new members in the Conference in 1982.

FLOWOOD (*Rankin County: 1600 Oak Street, Flowood 39208*). The church was organized between 1933 and 1948. It was known as Pearl City Church. Before the church building was constructed, the members met at the Knox Glass Pavilion. The wood frame building was constructed in 1949, and was bricked in 1978. Classrooms were added in 1950, and a kitchen was built in 1988.

FOREST (*Scott County: East Third Street, Forest 39074*). It was in 1861 that the first Forest Methodists became one of the churches of the Hillsboro Charge; James Walton was the presiding elder and Harvey Copeland was pastor of the circuit. On 18 October 1871, a plot of land was purchased by the Methodists for the sum of twenty-five dollars. The first Methodist church was built on this plot, comprising four lots. The church was finished by the Spring of 1872,

Forest United Methodist Church

and was host to the Brandon District Conference. As the town grew, it became apparent that the small church building was inadequate. In 1910 the membership purchased a plot of ground from Ward G. Jackson and his wife, Mary Belle. With Reverend A. M. Broadfoot as pastor, work was immediately begun on a new church. This church was dedicated on 19 August 1917 by Bishop W. B. Murrah of Memphis during the pastorate of Brother James G. Galloway, a brother of Bishop Charles Betts Galloway. The membership increased steadily and in 1923, when Reverend J. H. Moore was pastor, an education building was added. On 5 November 1950, with Reverend Aubrey Smith pastor, the Forest Methodists observed "Brick Sunday," an initial drive for funds to erect a new brick church. On 12 June 1955 Reverend Kelly preached the last sermon in the church, which served over forty years. The formal opening of the present church was conducted on 5 May 1957 with Reverend Kelly in charge. Bishop Marvin A. Franklin led the Acceptance Service and delivered the sermon. Doctor Brunner Hunt was pastor when, on 18 July 1965, the church was dedicated by Bishop Edward J. Pendergrass.

FOREST GROVE (*Leake County: 2532 Forest Grove Road, Carthage 39051*). The church was organized in 1876. There have been two sanctuaries. The present sanctuary was built approximately in 1938.

FOREST HILL (*Hinds County: 2504 Raymond Road, Jackson 39212*). On a hill located about a day's journey from Jackson, a place of worship was erected for a growing population. Property for a new church was purchased from Toliver and Laura Lenoir with the deed being recorded on 22 September 1857. On the property that currently stands near the entrance to the Forest Hill High School Gym, Forest Hill Methodist Episcopal Church, South, was erected. It was a wooden building which was originally painted pink. In 1921, a second church building was erected which stood directly in front of the School Superintendent's home. Some of the lumber from the original church was used in its construction. This building served the congregation of Forest Hill Methodist Church for twenty-seven years. During its earlier years, the church served as a part of the Terry Circuit which was composed of Terry, Forest Hill, Byram, and Spring Ridge Churches. On 18 April 1948, Doctor B. M. Hunt, District Superintendent of the Jackson District, officially opened the new Forest Hill Methodist Church for worship.

FOSTERS CHAPEL (*Chickasaw County*). This church was organized in 1887.

FOUNTAIN HEAD (*DeSoto County: Lewisburg*). The church was organized in 1871.

FOXWORTH (*Marion County: Columbia 39429*). The church was organized in 1909.

FRANKLIN (*Holmes County: 536 Cutoff Franklin Road, Lexington 39095*).
FRANKLIN (*Jones County: 805 Northview Drive, Laurel 39440*). This church was organized in 1957.
FREDONIA (*Panola County: Fredonia*). This church was organized in 1856.
FREE SPRINGS (*Lafayette County: Tyro*).
FREENY (*Leake County: 3417 Freeny Road, Carthage 39051*). In the early 1900s, the Freeny community was without a church. In 1904 or 1905, Reverend White was pastor of the Walnut Grove Circuit, and the nearest Methodist church was two miles away at Pleasant Hill. A pioneer of the Freeny community, J. A. Snuggs, joined the Pleasant Hill Church. Upon Reverend Whites' visit, he became aware of the prospects in Freeny, and set about to hold afternoon services in Bluff Springs School. Following revivals held in 1904 and 1905, the members from Freeny who had been attending Pleasant Hill resolved to build a church in their community. By this time there were approximately twenty Methodist church members in the community. Many of the members who had been going to the Pleasant Hill Church transferred to the new Freeny Church. It was a square structure with three classrooms in the rear and a pulpit in the center of the sanctuary. In the year 1906, some fifteen or twenty more joined. Two members entered the ministry: L. C. Freeny and W. N. Ware. On 10 February 1957, the first services were held in the new church. Bishop Pendergrass dedicated the new parsonage 23 April 1967. In 1964, Freeny Methodist was selected Conference "Church of the Year."

FRIARS POINT (*Coahoma County: Friars Point 38631*). The community was named for Robert Friar. This church was organized in 1836.
FRIENDSHIP (*Attala County*). Reverend John Curtis was probably the earliest settler of this community. A native of Ireland, he came to this area before 1860 from Virginia. The church was organized in 1853. Originally, the school and church were located in Montgomery County. Both the school and church were moved closer to the Attala County line.
FRIENDSHIP (*Clarke County: Highway Eleven South, Enterprise 39330*).
FRIENDSHIP (*Itawamba County: 4435 Peppertown Road, Mantachie 38855*). In 1890, the Moore Hill Church in Itawamba County was the first place of worship for the church later named the Friendship Methodist Episcopal Church. Later, it moved to a school building near the same site on the John Nanney place. The pastor was Reverend John Shelby. In 1892, P. O. Stovall deeded the land for a sanctuary to be built where the church now stands. In 1971, a larger church was built. During the year 1928, a wing was added on the east and west side of the church for Sunday School space. In 1950, the church now standing was built, with three Sunday School rooms. The cemetery was also established during the year 1950. W. B. Stovall was the first to be buried in 1950. During the year 1962, three Sunday School rooms, and a fellowship hall were added. Members who have gone out from Friendship as ministers are: Wesley York; Edgar Isabel; Marcus Gurley; Paul York; Bobby Hankins; and William Strange.

FRIENDSHIP (*Tippah County: Highway 370, Falkner 38629*).

FRIENDSHIP (*Union County: 1536 Highway Thirty West, Myrtle 38650*). Friendship Methodist Church had its beginnings sometime around 1860, when a small band of Christians met to worship in a schoolhouse, named Friendship School, in what is now Union County. In the early 1880s, a building was erected for a place of worship and in 1883, this building and two acres of land were deeded to the Methodist Conference and Friendship Church was accepted into the conference. It was on the Old Myrtle Charge along with Old Myrtle, Cornersville, Union Hill, Bethel, Gerizim, and Ebenezer. Friendship Church has been transferred from charge to charge and district to district. From its beginning on the Old Myrtle Charge it was changed to the Cornersville Charge, Holly Springs District in 1893, and then to the Myrtle Charge, Corinth District in 1903. In 1924, it became part of the Aberdeen District and was made the Salem-Friendship Charge including Liberty Hill, Sand Springs, and Christian Rest. In 1952, the Salem-Friendship Charge was placed in the New Albany District and later changed to become the Salem-Friendship-Union Hill Charge which it is today. In 1953, a new building was completed about one and one-half miles east of the old church. It consisted of a sanctuary and three Sunday School rooms. During the years, four members of Friendship Church have been called to serve as ministers. They are: Stanley Maxey, Seaman Rhea, George Baker, and Will Baker. The oldest tombstone in the church cemetery is of Cynthia Power Gilliam, wife of John Gilliam, born in 1803, died in 1883. A steeple was added to the church in 1980, and a bell installed in it.

FULTON (*Itawamba County: 301 East Main Street, Fulton 38843*). The Methodist Church in Fulton is about as old as the town. A deed for fifty acres of land, given by the Board of Police, was dated 17 July 1837, but was not recorded until June 1838. There was a "Bull Mountain Mission" located north of Smithville in 1838. This probably included the new town of Fulton. In succeeding years records indicated that "Bull Mountain Mission" became "Fulton Circuit" in the Aberdeen District of the Memphis Conference. In 1878 or 1880, Mr. Malachi C. (Mack) Cummings built a large frame building on Block Ten in the town of Fulton and deeded it to the Methodist Church on 10 August 1880. On that same date, the trustees of the church deeded to Mr. Cummings, Block One, and that was evidently the property on which an original log cabin Methodist Church stood. This building was used by all denominations until the Missionary Baptists organized their Sunday School in a separate place in 1917, and the church of Christ built their church in 1923. In April 1930, the wooden building was torn down and a brick veneer building was built in the same location. The congregation worshipped in the grammar school building while the church was being built. The first sermon preached in the new brick building was the last Sunday in August 1930. This church was dedicated on the first Sunday in September 1935. Ground breaking services for a new sanctuary and additional Sunday School space were held 10 July 1966. The first services were held in the new sanctuary on Sunday, 16 April 1967.

GAINES CHAPEL *(Alcorn County: Highway Seventy-Two West, Corinth 38834).* Gaines Chapel is one of the oldest organized churches in the area. Reverend James Gaines organized the church in 1854 with fourteen members. According to records, Corinth Circuit and Gaines Chapel were served from Jacinto, Mississippi. The first pastor, for whom the church was named, was one of the leading ministers of old Tishomingo County, and although a resident of the county for only fourteen years, his acquaintance included every settlement. The first deed recorded shows that "William H. Kilpatrick in consideration of the love for the Cause of Christ and his Church convey unto Peter W. Nash, James Hughes, William H. Mop, John Hughes, and John Jordan, trustees for Gaines Chapel on Corinth Circuit." In 1854, the first building was erected and made with hand-hewn sleepers of white oak and poplar. From 1912 through 1914, it was decided that more efficient work could be done if the church were more centrally located, so a modest one-room frame building was erected on a lot adjacent to a school. Following a storm, which struck the community in 1924 and blew the church off its foundation, it was decided to build a larger building with separate rooms for religious education. Realizing that horse and buggy days were swiftly coming to an end, it was decided to locate on a gravel road. On 13 September 1924, an acre of ground was purchased by

the ladies of the church under the leadership of Mrs. L. S. Dalton. This is the site on which Gaines Chapel stands today.

GALATIA *(Jefferson County).* The church was organized in 1859.

GALILEE TREDWELL *(Holmes County: Lexington 39095).*

GALLATIN *(Copiah County).* The church was organized in 1870.

GALLMAN *(Copiah County: Gallman 39077).* The church was organized in 1885.

Galloway Memorial United Methodist Church

GALLOWAY MEMORIAL *(Hinds County: 305 North Congress, Jackson 39201).* Methodism started in Mississippi's capital city in 1836, under the pastorate of Thomas Ford, son of Reverend John Ford. The church was known as First Methodist until 1917. Galloway is Jackson's oldest church, having been founded in 1836, fourteen years after the city was chartered. One man and four women organized a "Methodist Society" from which the present Galloway congregation has evolved. The Methodist congregation originally met in Mississippi's first State House with Reverend Thomas Ford preaching twice a month. By an act of the Legislature approved 13 May 1837, Lot Number Thirteen North was set aside for religious purposes and divided into four squares to be sold by the Auditor. In 1838, the Methodists proceeded to purchase the southeast corner and build their first church. The church building faced south toward Smith Park; Galloway is the only church which still stands on the original land set aside by the Legislature. By the mid-1850s, the Black membership of First Church had outgrown the gallery which had been provided for them. For that reason, a brick church was built next door for the Black membership. This was the first church for Blacks ever built in Jackson. In 1854, James William Lambuth went out from this church after preaching his farewell sermon prior to going to serve as a missionary to China. The erection of the second church upon this site had its beginnings during the 1880s under the second pastoral term of Charles Betts Galloway. By 1890, the Baptists had outgrown their building, and in 1896, the Methodists purchased their property. Referred to as Epworth Hall, the building was used as a sanctuary, education classrooms, and church offices when the third church building was under construction. The present church was begun in 1913 under the pastorate of A. F. Smith, brought to completion in 1915 under the pastorate of W. G. Henry, and dedicated to the memory of Bishop Charles B. Galloway in 1917. The largest contributor was Major R. W. Millsaps, a devoted friend of Bishop Galloway. The Messina Culley home was purchased for the Galloway parsonage in 1949. In 1952, an education building was constructed, a chapel added, and the sanctuary renovated; with the addition of a church fellowship hall and stage. The 1960s were turbulent times when many churches had a closed door policy to persons of other races. Members against the United Methodist approval of integration and civil rights opted to leave Galloway to begin other independent churches in Jackson. Other members changed denomination, claiming the church was either too liberal or too conservative. The 1970s brought new growth to Jackson, and the facilities were remodeled in 1973. Clay F. Lee was elected Bishop in 1988, becoming Galloway's fourth pastor to be selected for the episcopacy. The others were Bishops Galloway, DuBose, and Decell.

GARLANDSVILLE (*Jasper County: County Road Fifty-Eight and Highway 504, Garlandsville 39345*). The church was organized in 1835. A marker was placed here by the Mississippi Historical Society in 1935.

GASQUE CHAPEL (*Smith County: Lorena and Burns Road, Raleigh 39153*). The church was organized in 1882.

GATEWAY (*Harrison County: 16020 South Swan Drive at Highway Forty-Nine, Gulfport 39503*).

GAUTIER (*Jackson County: 2717 U.S. Highway Ninety, Gautier 39553*). This church was organized in 1950.

GEORGETOWN (*Copiah County: 1002 Lane Avenue, Georgetown 39075*). The church was organized in 1895.

GEORGEVILLE (*Holmes County: Owens Wells*). The church was organized in 1904.

GETWELL ROAD (*DeSoto County: 7875 Getwell Road, Olive Branch 38654*). This community experienced rapid growth when the metropolitan Memphis area began to expand into northwestern

Getwell Road United Methodist Church

Mississippi. The church was organized 7 September 1986, and met in the Shrine Hall until 22 May 1988, when the sanctuary was completed. Nine families comprised the charter members. An education building was constructed in 1991. A family life center was constructed in 1996 through 1997.

GIBSON MEMORIAL (*Warren County: 2200 Washington Street, Vicksburg 39180*). Gibson Memorial was started when the use of a room in the old Marine Hospital on Shorter Mulberry was granted to a band of Crawford Street Methodist Church and South Vicksburg workers for the purpose of organizing an afternoon Sunday School in 1889. The land was the property of T. H.

Gibson Memorial United Methodist Church

and Mary Ann Rigby, who deeded it to their daughter, Mary Ella. Those undertaking this city missionary work were Miss Alice Shannon, Mrs. Lizzie McCutcheon, Mrs. T. H. Allen (nee Fanny Cook), and Miss Mary Lou Paxton. On 9 May 1887, during the pastorate of R. J. Jones, the trustees of Crawford Street bought a lot on the east side of Shorter Mulberry, (Oak Street) where they built a little church. When the South Vicksburg Church was organized, the property was deeded by the trustees of the Crawford Street Church to the trustees of the South Vicksburg Church. The Mississippi Annual Conference was held in Vicksburg in December 1888. In 1902 the South Vicksburg Church and lot were sold and a church built on Washington Street. It was known as the Washington Street Church of Vicksburg and was located where the Saint George Antiochian Orthodox Church. This church was under the pastorate of H. P. Lewis Jr. and Reverend George P. McKeown. About 1911 to 1913, under the pastorate of W. H. Saunders, the plan was launched for a new church. The Washington Street Methodist Church was sold to the Greek Orthodox Church and under the pastorate of L. L. Roberts, a new church was built in 1914 on Washington Street. This church was named the Gibson Memorial Methodist Church in honor of Reverend Tobias Gibson who organized the first Methodist church in Mississippi. In 1936 to 1938, plans were launched for expansion under the pastorate of J. V. Bennett. In 1963 to 1965, while Brother Wesson was pastor, plans were made for a new building program. In 1965, the old parsonage was removed and a new building added to the south side of the church. In 1964 the parsonage on Washington Street was sold and a new one purchased. Under the pastorate of David Harrison, the congregation voted in 1995 to make plans for a new location. A building committee was appointed and land was purchased on Bowie Road in 1996. The plans for a new church have been approved, consisting of three buildings: a fellowship hall, adminis-tration, education, day care, and sanctuary. Plans are made to begin work in 1998 on the first phase, the fellowship hall, educa-tion, administration, and day care building.

GILMORE CHAPEL (*Itawamba County: Gilmore Chapel Road*).

GITANO (*Jones County: Highway Twenty-Eight North, Gitano Community*). This church was organized in 1959.

GLADE (*Jones County: Laurel 39440*). The church was organized in 1958.

GLEN ALLEN (*Washington County: Lake Washington Road, Glen Allen 38744*). In 1839, this church had a growing member-ship consisting of more slaves than free men. Soon after the Civil War, the building was given to the former slaves and an all-Black church was established at Point Worthington. The church has a pre-Civil War community cemetery. Glen Allen Methodists, Baptists, Presbyterians, and Episcopalians formed a Union church in 1890, which first met in the S. M. Spencer home and later was built on land donated by Mr. Spencer. In 1900, a parsonage was bought. In 1921, the Union church burned and services were held in the new school auditorium. After a soul-stirring revival in 1923, the building site for the present

church structure was purchased. The building was dedicated in 1924. When news of the impending flood of 1927 reached Glen Allen, the pastor, Reverend N. J. Golding, Mr. W. H. Brown Jr., and Doctor W. T. Duke began building boats at the church. Services continued during the flood with worshippers arriving by boat. During the pastorate of Reverend N. L. Threat, the church annex was built. The earliest church archives show Bolivar and Glen Allen as a charge in 1899. From 1901 through 1951, Glen Allen was changed repeatedly on charges, mainly with Benoit, Winterville, or Avon. At this time these churches were in the Greenville District. From 1952 until 1969, Glen Allen was a station church. Since 1953, the church has been in the Cleveland District. The present church alignment was drawn in 1969, making Avon and Glen Allen a charge for the third time in its history. Stylon A. (Tony) Proctor entered the ministry from this church.

GLENDALE (*Forrest County: 2211 Glendale Avenue, Hattiesburg 39401*). This church was organized in 1948.

GLENDORA (*Tallahatchie County: Glendora 38928*).

GLENFIELD (*Union County: 102 N. Glenfield Road, New Albany 38652*). Glenfield Church was organized in 1884. The first church was called Valley Church. Baxter Taylor gave the land for the church. The Taylor home was headquarters for the preachers of summer revivals. The building was a modest little church. The Methodists and Baptists of the area would build brush arbors for summer revivals together. They also used the Valley Church together, each preaching once a month and having Sunday School together. Eventually the Baptist group built a church. The people of Glenfield needed a school. W. H. Jones and Mrs. M. P. A. Jones gave permission for a schoolhouse to be built south of where the present church stands. Later the school was moved to a larger building across the railroad. They also, for the sum of one dollar, deeded to G. W. Spencer, H. M. Tate, and W. H. Jones, trustees of Lynnwood (later Glenfield) Methodist Episcopal Church, South, and their successors in office, one acre more or less. The deed contained a trust clause stating: "Said premise shall be used, kept, maintained and disposed of as a place of divine worship for the use of the ministry and membership of the Methodist Episcopal Church, South." A one-room church, considerably larger than the Valley Church, was built and remained in use until the new one was begun in 1948.

GLOSTER (*Amite County: 309 South First Street, Gloster 39638*). The town of Gloster was laid out in 1883, and named for a railroad surveying engineer. Sharon Methodist Church, located two miles north of the new town, organized as early as 1840, was moved into the community to accommodate the growing populace. It was reorganized to form the Gloster Church in 1893.

GOLDEN CHAPEL (*Tishomingo County: Highway 366, Golden 38847*). The Golden Methodist Episcopal Church, South, was organized shortly after Dave Bass, an evangelist, held a tent meeting on Court Square. Reverend Bass encouraged the people to build a church in Golden. The first church building was erected in 1915 to 1916. Golden Chapel was formed when members of Golden and Patterson Chapel United Methodist Church, founded 1884, agreed to join together to mutually strengthen their services to the community. The merged new church was organized in November 1967, with sixty-eight members. The first pastor of the new church was Ruth Wood. It was agreed that the new church would be called Golden Chapel and that the money from the sale of both former church buildings would be applied to the building of the new church. The first worship services were held on 17 November 1968.

GOLDEN HILL (*Tippah County: County Road 522, Falkner 38629*).

GOOD HOPE (*Carroll County: Carrollton 38917*). The church was organized in 1883.

GOOD HOPE (*Jefferson Davis County: Lake Mike Conner*). This church was organized in 1880.

Goodman Memorial United Methodist Church

GOODMAN MEMORIAL (*Sharkey County: Highway Sixty-One, Cary 39054*). In 1884, Doctor W. L. C. Hunneycutt, presiding elder at Vicksburg, heard that a lot had been deeded for a church in Cary before the Civil War. He found that land had been deeded in 1861. So, in 1884, a small frame building was moved onto the lot. A brick veneer church was built in 1925. The church was dedicated in 1935. The church was on the Rolling Fork Charge, but in June 1950 became a station church. An educational annex was added in 1952.

GOODMAN FIRST (*Holmes County: 9750 Main Street, Goodman 39079*). The first church built on the present lot was in 1872, and was jointly owned by Methodist, Presbyterians, and the Masonic Lodge. The two denominations only had church services once a month, but Sunday School was held every Sunday: Presbyterians in the morning and Methodists, Sunday afternoon. In 1924, the Masons and Presbyterians sold their share in the property to the Methodists and the present building was erected. After being on the charge with Pickens for many years, Goodman went to full time status in 1951. A few years later Bill Donald donated a lot, and the parsonage was built. Reverend Jack Williams and his family were the first to live in the parsonage.

GOODWATER (*Clarke County: Hale*). The church was organized in 1876.

GORE SPRINGS (*Grenada County: 300 Graysport Crossing Road, Gore Springs 38929*). The church was organized in 1892.

GOSHEN (*Leake County: Goshen Road, Carthage 39051*). The church was organized in 1848, when a log building was erected. The second and present frame sanctuary was built in 1870.

GOSHEN (*Yalobusha County: Coffeeville 38922*). Goshen United Methodist Church is located about six miles west of Coffeeville on a mail and school route. In 1854, Major William Bobbitt, a land owner in this community, felt the need to have a house of worship; specifically, a Methodist Church. Major Bobbitt and his wife, Elizabeth, gave three and a half acres of land, more or less, where Goshen United Methodist Church now stands. The first people who came to worship at Goshen Methodist Church brought their families in wagons, on horseback, and some families walked to church. The deed states a Worship House must be built on this land. The present building is the third building. This red brick building with three Sunday School rooms now sits on this land. In 1942, the Goshen Methodist Church was destroyed by a tornado.

Grace United Methodist Church, Natchez

GRACE (*Adams County: 2 Fatherland Road, Natchez 39120*). The Grace Methodist Church in Natchez was officially organized on 12 February 1950, as the Quarterly Conference of the Washington Methodist church met with the members of the Grace Church and declared the church officially established. Reverend T. O. Prewitt, superintendent of the Vicksburg District, presided over the Quarterly Conference and gave much encouragement and guidance in bringing the new church into being. The

Washington congregation had given encouragement and help to the project for about a year before the organization emerged. Reverend W. L. Elkin began services of worship in the auditorium of the Adams County Agricultural Building on Liberty Road from the first Sunday of February 1949. By 12 February 1950, there were twenty-eight charter members. When the Mississippi Annual Conference met in Jackson, in June 1950, there were thirty-four members. Brother Elkin was appointed by the Annual Conference to serve as the full time pastor of the Grace Methodist Church and moved into Natchez from Washington.

Grace United Methodist Church, Grenada

GRACE (*Greene County: Highway Ninety-eight, Leakesville 39451*). Grace United Methodist Church was founded in 1967 when the Pine Grove United Methodist Church and the Merrill United Methodist Church united to make a larger and better church for the community. The present Church building was erected during the pastorate of Keith Scott. Since that time the church has been served by the following ministers: Harold Fleming, Harold L. Miller, W. R. Dement, Roy A. Givens, Bob Himbrook, Dennis Harris, Keith Goff, David Huffman, Bert Edwards, John Harper, H. J. Hedgepeth, and Chris Cumbest.

GRACE (*Grenada County: 2315 Carrollton Road, Grenada 38901*). This church was the dream of the Men's Club of the First United Methodist Church. They donated land on Van Dorn Street for a new church in south Grenada. The church in no way was a split from the First Church. Reverend Cecil Williamson was assigned in the summer of 1956 to the charge of Tie Plant, Gore Springs, and to build a new church in south Grenada. The membership met in different places like the National Funeral Home, a Conference tent erected one summer, and City Hall, before the building was started. The name Grace was chosen and the church was officially started on 9 December 1956 with Reverend Cecil Williamson as pastor with fifty-nine charter members. Reverend Wesley Youngblood was the first full-time pastor in 1958. The lot on Van Dorn was sold and three acres on Carrollton Road were purchased on credit. The funds from the sale of the lot helped finance the new building. The first building was started on 17 August 1958 with the addition beginning in October of the following year. The official opening was 17 April 1960.

GRACE (*Issaquena County: Grace Road, Grace 38745*). Grace Methodist Church was organized in 1902, with six charter members; Mrs. Callie Dulaney, Mrs. Sue Harris, Mr. Ernest Jordan, Mr. James C. Means, Mrs. Maggie Jurdan, and Mrs. Mary Birdsong. Mr. and Mrs. L. C. Dulaney gave the church a deed to a lot for five cents on 22 July 1902. Reverend L. W. Felder was the first pastor. The church is located on

Old Highway One between Grace and the New Highway One. On 7 May 1907, the church was destroyed by a storm and destroyed again by a windstorm on 3 October 1919. The old separate Sunday School rooms building was moved in 1955, and the new Sunday School rooms were added to the church in 1962, by Reverend Exo Griffith.

GRACE (*Prentiss County: 800 East Church Street, Booneville 38829*). The church was organized 18 January 1953. The original sanctuary, built in 1954, was a frame building that was later bricked. The family center was built in May 1983.

Grace United Methodist Church, Greenville

GRACE (*Washington County: 1020 South Colorado, Greenville 38701*). The first church started 15 January 1956, and it was decided by the members that it would be called Grace. For thirteen months the church meetings were held at the County Agent's office with Reverend Clinton T. Floyd. The first full-time pastor was Reverend Leon Scott and one of his projects was to get the members to pick cotton and donate their earnings to a fund to build a church. The dream of the congregation was the site where Grace is now located on Colorado Street, but the owners required a larger building than the congregation was able to

build. So they chose as their second choice, a lot on Thomas Street and built a smaller church. The first service was 23 December 1956, at the new home of Grace United Methodist Church. The Church of Christ had bought the property on Colorado. It was nearly destroyed by fire, and they relocated to a new area on South Main. Grace United Methodist Church bought the property from the Church of Christ in 1970, and Grace began remodeling the burned church, which opened 28 November 1971.

Grady's Chapel United Methodist Church

GRADY'S CHAPEL (*Monroe County: Wren*). The church was organized in 1897. This church was once known as Pisgah Methodist Church. The church was once located at the present Pisgah Cemetery. The present frame structure was built in 1897, and a fellowship hall was added in 1987. The deed for the property was recorded 7 September 1897.

GRANDVIEW (*Forrest County: 12 Little Pacific, Hattiesburg 39401*). This church was organized in 1963.

GREAT SPIRIT (*Neshoba County*). This church was organized in 1980.

GREEN GROVE (*Scott County: Forest 39074*).

GREEN HILL (*Neshoba County*).

GREENBRIER (*Monroe County: Becker 38825*). The church was organized in 1850. Records in the Chancery Clerk office in Aberdeen show that on 6 July 1850, William Flynt and his wife Margaret Flynt, in consideration of the sum of ten dollars rendered a deed to the trustees of the newly organized "Green Briar" Methodist Church, South, in the Athens Circuit of the Alabama Conference, for two acres of land. The acres described in a manner so as to include "Green Briar" meeting house and graveyard. The Methodist Church was already in existence at that time. Due to the fact that Greenbrier Cemetery was free burying ground, the citizens of the community saw the necessity to add more to the cemetery, so they purchased one acre for thirty-seven dollars from W. F. Nichols.

GREENDALE (*Franklin County: Roxie 39661*). The church was organized in 1912.

GREENFIELD (*Rankin County: 1060 Greenfield Circle, Brandon 39042*). The church was organized in 1895. That year, a frame building was built to serve the congregation. A second building, the present sanctuary, was erected in 1957.

GREENLEAF (*Tate County: Lewisburg*). This church was organized in 1859.

Greenville First United Methodist Church

GREENVILLE FIRST (*Washington County: 402 Washington Avenue, Greenville 38701*). The first log structure was built in 1836 in "old Greenville." A neat frame building replaced the log cabin in 1846. In 1863, Union soldiers burned the church and all other buildings except two houses. In 1869, the Methodists purchased a pre-cut ready-to-erect building from a Cincinnati firm of architects. This building came down the Mississippi River by boat and was located in present Greenville on Main Street and Walnut Street. This church was later moved to Shelby Street and Washington. In 1903, a new brick church was built which was occupied until 1949, when the present new sanctuary was built. During the construction of the building the congregation accepted the invitation of the Hebrew Union Temple members and held worship services in the Temple. Doctor Harris Hirschberg, Rabbi, composed a special anthem dedicated to Reverend Jeff Cunningham and the First Methodist congregation.

GREENWOOD CHAPEL (*Leake County: Greenwood Chapel Road, Carthage 39051*).

GREENWOOD SPRINGS (*Monroe County: Route One, Greenwood Springs 38848*). On 10 April 1880, Charles M. Jordan and wife, Mary Ann Jordan, deeded to the Methodist Church a parcel of land to be used both as a church and a school. The sanctuary was built the following year. It was known as Quincy Chapel, as Quincy was then the post office for this area. In 1905, the W. B. Todd family gave a plot of ground near the railroad for a charge parsonage. The church services were then moved to a school building near the site of the present church, to be more convenient for the members. In 1928, C. B. Kinard gave the property on which the present church is located. In 1983, many improvements were made. Among them, a large fellowship hall was built, the building was underpinned, and a new piano was purchased. This church is one of four active churches on the Ganman Charge.

Greenwood First United Methodist Church

GREENWOOD FIRST *(Leflore County: 310 West Washington Street, Greenwood 38930).* The earliest record of organized Methodism in Greenwood is from a letter written by W. A. Gillespie. A steward in the Methodist Church, Mr. Gillespie relates that in 1846, a Union church was founded and located on East Market Street. In 1886, the Methodists withdrew and built a small church on the corner of Fulton and Washington Streets. In 1898, a new church building was built on the corner of Washington and Cotton and has stood for a century. In 1924 an education building was added. Membership in 1954, was 2124, and during that year a group left to form the Saint John's Methodist Church. Greenwood First Methodist Church became First in April 1968, and continues to serve the community of Greenwood carrying forth her theme and spirit of "The

Church with a Warm Heart." This church is also listed on the National Register of Historic Places.

GREER CHAPEL *(Rankin County).* This church was organized in 1935.

GRENADA FIRST *(Grenada County: 61 South Line Street, Grenada 38901).* Methodism in Grenada began in 1820. Three ministers from Massachusetts came as missionaries to the Choctaw and Chickasaw Indians, working and preaching until they had enough converts to organize the first church in this area. In the Treaty of Dancing Rabbit, 15 September 1830, the Indians left this area, moving to Indian Territory. Two settlements later sprang up, Pittsburg and Tullahoma. Many years of rivalry and difficulty existed between the two towns until at last they were united on one of the hillsides of Tullahoma on 4 July 1836. The ceremony was performed by Reverend A. B. Lucas, a Methodist minister. The new town was named Grenada. From the time the missionaries arrived in 1820, Methodism grew steadily. The present physical plant is the culmination of many changes and events. The first house of worship was the second story of a store building. The first Methodist

Grenada First United Methodist Church

Conference in Grenada was held there in 1838. Bishop Morris of Ohio rode 800 miles on horseback to attend and preside. Four delegates from the Mexican Mission rode 1,200 miles. The territory embraced six states: Mississippi, Alabama, Florida, Louisiana, Arkansas, and Texas. On 19 July 1839, a deed was secured to property in the town of Pittsburg. The building erected there was only an unpainted structure, but it was considered to be "fairly comfortable." The congregation then had thirty members. On 7 September 1850, James and Harriet Sims deeded to the trustees of the Methodist Episcopal Church the lots where members are still worshipping. The new church, begun in 1850 and completed in 1855, had a membership of 200. The basement was used for Sunday School each Sunday morning and during the afternoons as a place of worship for slaves. By 1916, there were 381 members; by 1928 there were 600, again presenting a need for expansion. On 12 May 1929, 400 people attended Sunday School in a new educational unit. The cornerstone for the present sanctuary was laid on 20 February 1947, and the first service was held on 26 October 1947. In 1971, the west annex, known as the parlor area, was constructed, followed in 1984 by a vast renovation of the sanctuary, basement area, and education building. In 1838, the first Sunday school in Grenada was organized. In the spring of 1895, the Epworth League was begun. On 21 January 1885, the Women's Missionary Society was organized. This church was in ministry to Grenada College and its students from 1884 until 1937.

GRIFFIN CHAPEL (*Oktibbeha County: 212 West Main Street, Starkville 39759*).

Griffin Chapel had her beginning under a brush arbor in an old public graveyard in 1867. Reverend Nelson Drake, a Methodist, and Reverend David Higgins, a Baptist (both ordained), called people together to organize a Union church. This Union church operated two years. Then Reverend A. C. McDonald requested the Missionary Society to send Reverend Mack McLacklin to establish a school and to organize a church in Starkville. Thus in 1869, the Methodist Church was officially born in an old barn near Washington and Gillespie Streets. One year later they moved to the corner of Louisville and Greensborough Street. A plank arbor was used as a place of worship. A two-story plank building was built within two years to be used as a school and as a church. The new structure was named in honor of Reverend Ira B. Griffin and still remains. The church site moved to Main and Cushman where it is in ministry today. This new church site and structure with an educational basement was constructed in 1926, under the pastorate of Reverend G. W. Evans. A new education building was constructed under the pastorate of Reverend W. N. Redmond in 1971, but the dream and groundwork had its beginning under Reverend J. W. Mosley. Griffin was one of the few churches in Starkville that had its doors open during the civil rights movement of the sixties for public community meetings in an effort to help do away with discrimination and segregation. When the Mule Train for Freedom came through Starkville headed to Washington, Griffin was the only church that gave them refuge. They were also a storage place for clothing, food, etc. that came in from areas of the country to the poor. The following ministers had their beginning in Griffin: O. B. Davis; D. W. Williams; Wilson Ashford Jr.; Tyronne Stallings; Ralph King; Marvin King; Maurice King; J. L. King Jr.; D. T. Jackson; Abraham Little; James Henry; and Clarence Allen.

GULDE (*Rankin County: Pelahatchie 39145*). The church was organized in 1876.

Gulfport First United Methodist Church

GULFPORT FIRST (*Harrison County: 2301 Fifteenth Street, Gulfport 39501*). The church was organized in 1896. The church was once known as Twenty-fifth Avenue Methodist Episcopal Church, South. The church was located at Twenty-fifth Avenue and Fourteenth Street from 1900 to 1912. The first building, constructed in 1900, was a frame building. The present building was completed in 1912. The educational unit was built in 1965. Among the prominent persons affiliated with First United Methodist Church were Senator Pat Harrison and Governor Lee Russell. Two former pastors, Nolan Harmon Sr., and C. C. Clark, had sons, Nolan Harmon Jr., and Roy Clark, who became Bishops.

GUNNISON (*Bolivar County: Wrenn Street, Gunnison 38746*). The first land records for Gunnison date back to 1846. It is named for A. N. Gunnison, plantation owner. The village incorporated in 1892. The first church was located at Carson's Landing (Concordia) three miles north of Gunnison in 1832. In the minutes of the Seventh Board of Police (Supervisors) of November 1848, there is mention of a chapel at Concordia. The first log structure was built in 1848, the first church between Memphis and Vicksburg. Doctor Porter from the Louisville, Kentucky, area served as the first pastor. The second church building was built in 1868, and in 1892, moved to Gunnison, being rolled on logs from the Concordia Cemetery to Gunnison for a distance of two miles. This building was torn down in February 1914. The third church building was constructed in 1914, and torn in 1948. The fourth building was built in 1951, and the education building was added in 1961.

GUNTOWN (*Lee County: 1635 Main Highway, Guntown 38849*). Guntown Church may have existed as early as the 1840s, but was part of the Memphis Conference. It first appeared in the North Mississippi Conference in 1870, the year that conference was organized.

HA. BROWN MEMORIAL (*Stone County: Highway Forty-Nine, Wiggins 39577*). Named for the late Reverend Harris A. Brown, a former pastor of the Wiggins Circuit, the church completed a process that began in June 1993, when Bishop Marshall Meadors appointed Reverend Carolyn Abrams to the Wiggins Charge. At that time, the Charge consisted of three United

Methodist churches: Andrew Chapel, Mount Zion, and Saint Paul. The consensus in each church was that it could be more effective by putting its strengths together. The merger proposal was presented during a church conference on 21 October 1993. Each membership was asked to vote its acceptance or rejection. Mount Zion and Saint Paul voted to merge at that time. Andrew Chapel would later vote for the merger on 6 February 1994. The end of the meeting signaled the beginning of the new church, and all church services were held "under one roof" on a rotation basis between sites. The name, H. A. Brown Memorial United Methodist Church, was adopted by ballot during services on the first Sunday in December.

HALES CHAPEL (*Sunflower County: 106 First Street, Inverness 38753*).

HAMILTON (*Monroe County: Hamilton 39746*). In 1871, Mary Whitworth deeded the Methodist Conference a church building known as Sardis Methodist Church and three acres about three miles southeast of Old Hamilton where the Sardis Cemetery and Valley Chapel community now stand. Mrs. Leona Carter was one of the first Stewards; unusual because women rarely served. In 1888 Hamilton Methodists purchased property from L. C. Ross, a Presbyterian, for a sum of ten dollars upon which they built Wesley Methodist Church. In 1905, the membership of Wesley had declined such that they disbanded and joined Methodist friends in North Hamilton in building Friendship Methodist Church, the third location of Methodists in Hamilton.

HAMMITT HILL (*Lafayette County: Oxford 38655*).

HANDSBORO (*Harrison County: 2333 Demeret Drive, Gulfport 39507*). In the early 1850s, a building was constructed in Handsboro to house the newly established Polar Star Masonic Lodge, which today is the oldest Masonic Hall in the state of Mississippi. About the same time, a Methodist church was organized at Handsboro under the Vicksburg District. This church is the first Methodist church established between the Bay of Biloxi and the Bay of Saint Louis. The newly organized Handsboro Methodist Church held their services in the newly constructed Masonic Lodge Hall, until such time as they were able to build their own. James Brown, the owner of Beauvoir, was an ardent and generous member of this first Methodist congregation on the Gulf Coast. He designated one of the cottages, known as the West Cottage, exclusively for the use of the Methodist circuit rider, who usually held services once a month. It is thought that James Brown donated the land and gave generously to the building of the first church several years later. The first Methodist circuit rider to preach at Handsboro was Reverend Gipson, and the first full-time minister, who came to the church once a month, was Reverend McNeal. In 1886 the Handsboro Methodist Church sold their original church which was located on what is now Church Street, to the Black Methodists. This church is now the Riley's Chapel United Methodist Church. It was named in honor of Reverend Riley, who was the pastor at the time the transfer took place. The Handsboro Methodist Church then held their services in the Masonic Hall again for three years. During that time they constructed a new building on Main Street, now Pass Road. This is the building which the congregation is now using for their worship services, and was completed and occupied in 1889. Sometime in the late 1800s, a mission chapel was established in the community of Epico, northwest of Handsboro, just off Courthouse Road.

HARDINS CHAPEL (*Itawamba County: Fulton 38843*).

HARMONY (*Tishomingo County: 149 County Road 229, Iuka 38852*). It is not known exactly how long ago the church was established here, but authentic sources reveal the fact that a small log cabin served the rural congregation during Civil War years. Just afterward, another log building, somewhat larger, was erected, and it also served as a schoolhouse. It stood a few years southeast of the present church site, surrounded by lame oak trees. Around 1885, the growing congregation voted to build a new church of native lumber. Several citizens contributed their choicest pine and poplar trees for the building. Work was donated by local men, and when the building was completed, the women were asked to each give a "fat hen" from her flock to pay for the paint for the building. The building which is now used for worship was erected in 1947, under the leadership of Reverend J. H. Holder, with Mr. Dean Davis as head carpenter. The present building was dedicated in October 1948. Since that time, several Sunday School rooms have been added, as well as a large fellowship hall and other improvements.

HARPERVILLE (*Scott County: 10142 Old Hillsboro Road, Harperville 39080*). In July 1896, Harperville, a pleasant diminu-

tive community, born after the Civil War (1860s) was a quiet village of Scott County north of Forest. The Harperville Collegiate Institution was chartered in 1881. There were some good people numbered among the alumni of this institution. Methodism was introduced into this community just before the turn of the century. They followed the Baptist, Congregationalists and Cumberland Presbyterians. These congregations held worship service monthly in the Assembly Hall of the College. Reverend Irvin Miller, a local preacher, pastor, and merchant from Walnut Grove, introduced "The Methodist 1896 Doctrine" in Harperville and served as the first pastor. Reverend Miller, with another Methodist preacher, Reverend Henry Ballow, the Congregationalists, and Cumberland Presbyterians, held a "Protracted Meeting" for ten days. A number of people expressed an interest in organizing a Methodist church and were ready to join. This was brought about 22 July 1896, with thirteen charter members. Reverend Irvin was appointed as pastor. He came from Walnut Grove and held regular monthly meetings, either in the Assembly Hall of the College or in private homes of the people. The first building was built on land owned by the Harkey family in 1905. The new church was placed first on the Lena Charge 1896 to 1908. In 1909 it was placed with the Forest-Morton Charge. In 1915 it was placed back on the Lena Charge, until it was placed in 1931 on the Hillsboro-Mount Zion-Oak Grove Charge. In 1956, it was to be a station church, and in 1973, it was placed with Forest and Trinity making the Forest

Trinity-Harperville Charge. The members built a parsonage in 1919 under the leadership of Reverend R. H. Clegg. A new meeting house was begun in 1919 on property deeded to the church by Mr. and Mrs. W. D. Harkey for five dollars. This building served well until 1954, and under the leadership of Reverend Nicholas Peace and layman C. S. Sanders, the present building was built.

HARRIS CHAPEL (*Benton County: Highway Seventy-Two and Meridian Road, Ashland 38603*).

HARRIS MEMORIAL (*Hinds County: 4315 California Avenue, Jackson 39213*). The church was organized in 1971.

HARRISVILLE (*Simpson County: 109 Harrisville-Braxton Road, Harrisville 39082*). In 1849, Reverend Godfrey, a Methodist minister, homesteaded a parcel of land where the Methodist Church at Harrisville now stands. He donated a plot of ground for a Methodist church which the members built from hewn logs. The seats were made from large logs split in half, hewn flat with wooden pegs driven in them to serve as legs. The little church grew and prospered and other denominations came to worship with them. The building became too small. A number of Baptists proposed to help build a larger building in which to worship together. The building was completed and on the day of its dedication, Dempsey Touchstone gave it the name Liberty, because the two denominations worshipped there. The Methodists called it Bethel, because this was the name which they had called the first church. Each denomination worshipped there on different Sundays. The first Methodist

pastor was Reverend Godfrey. One of the first charter members was Sally Millsaps Touchstone, the wife of Dempsey Touchstone who was a Baptist. Sally was the aunt of Major Reuben Millsaps, one of the founders of Millsaps College. A cyclone blew the building down. The Methodists preferred to rebuild separately on their own ground. The Baptists acquired a plot across the road and built their own place of worship. This new structure, the second built by the Methodists, was a two-story building in which the Masons occupied the upper floor, and the building faced west on the present site. In 1879 the first quarterly conference of the Rankin Circuit was held at Bethel, presumably Harrisville. Doctor Cain, Conference Historian wrote, "it could have been there forty years before that time." In 1988, a family life center was added, and in 1996, the church built a new parsonage.

HAVEN (*Carroll County: 500 Flowers Street, Vaiden 39176*). The church was organized as a brush arbor in 1870. In 1873, the church built a frame building. This building, which served the congregation for over a century, was destroyed by a tornado on 20 December 1990. Haven constructed a new brick church in 1991.

HAVEN (*Coahoma County: 402 Yazoo Street, Clarksdale 38614*). Haven United Methodist Church was established in 1880. The church was originally named Haven Chapel Methodist Episcopal Church. The name is believed to have been selected to honor Bishop Haven who was serving the Tennessee area at the time of the founding and building of the church. The original church was a frame building located on the

Haven United Methodist Church, Clarksdale

plot where the first parsonage, now the education building, stands. The plot of land on which the church was erected was owned by Milton Carruthers, who deeded it to the church trustees: Ed Pulliam, P. W. Ivy, and Henry Dixon; on 8 July 1905. A year after the deed was received by the trustees, Haven Chapel was partially rebuilt under the leadership of Reverend W. M. Bell. A brick structure was begun which was completed seventeen years later while Reverend F. H. Henry was pastor. During the construction phase, services were held in the basement area of the church. In 1923, the congregation, with the encouragement of Reverend F. H. Henry, completed the present structure. In 1946 the church sanctuary was modernized and the Lillian Rodgers Johnson Day Care Center was established under the leadership

of Reverend W. B. Brump II. In 1976 Reverend T. V. Triplett was assigned as pastor. During his years, the members built a new parsonage, and initiated plans for the centennial celebration. The sanctuary was remodeled and the fellowship hall was renovated. The old parsonage was remodeled and converted into an educational facility. On 10 January 1988, the Reconsecration Service was held. In June 1990, at the Mississippi Annual Conference held in Tupelo, Haven United Methodist Church received the distinction of being named "The Small Membership Church of the Year."

HAVEN (*Montgomery County: 509 Campbell Street, Winona 38967*). The church was organized in 1880.

HAVEN CHAPEL (*Harrison County: 1310 Mills Avenue, Gulfport 39501*).

HAVEN CHAPEL (*Lauderdale County: 1302 Twentieth Street, Meridian 39301*). The Haven Chapel Church was organized in a house on Sixteenth Avenue and Twenty-first Street in Meridian. The church was an outgrowth of the Saint Paul Methodist Church. At the time of the organization in 1885, Reverend W. H. Smith was pastor. The first building of the church was on the corner of Thirteenth Avenue and Twentieth Street, the current site. The contractor completed the building in 1900. In 1906, the church was destroyed by fire. Under the leadership of Reverend N. W. Ross, the building was rebuilt. The present edifice was built under the leadership of Reverend H. C. Clay Sr. During the time of the building of the church, the members worshiped in the Wesley Chapel United Methodist Church, Meridian. The new building was dedicated on Sunday, 27 September 1970. In addition to other ministers of the Mississippi Conference, present at the opening services were Bishop Pendergrass and Reverend Sidney L. Webb, a former District Superintendent, Meridian District.

Hawkins United Methodist Church

HAWKINS *(Warren County: 3736 Halls Ferry Road, Vicksburg 39180).* On 10 June 1951 the Service of Organization of Hawkins Methodist Church was held. This service was directed by Reverend Prewitt and Doctor Tyson. The church was organized with twenty-four members, eight preparatory members, and twenty associate members. The church school was organized on 24 June 1951 under the leadership of Mr. W. B. Baker, superintendent. From September to December of 1951, the church was served by guest pastors from Millsaps faculty, and from elsewhere in the Mississippi Conference. The lack of full-time pastoral leadership did not deter the congregation. The Hawkins' Guild had been organized on 26 September 1951. Strong pastoral leadership for Hawkins Methodist Church was provided by the appointment of Reverend T. L. McCurley Jr. as its first full-time salaried pastor.

Reverend McCurley preached his first sermon on 23 December 1951. A building committee was appointed with Mr. H. A. Walker Sr. as chairman. Active plans for construction of a church building were started. The new church building (the present chapel) was opened for services on 7 June 1953 with Reverend T. O. Prewitt preaching the first sermon to a congregation numbering one hundred thirty. The parsonage, adjacent to the church, was constructed by the Fall of 1963. Ground breaking ceremonies were held for the first floor of the education building in October 1956, and the second floor was completed in 1967. The present sanctuary was formally opened in May 1970.

HAWKINS CHAPEL *(Lincoln County: 1040 Bennie Trail Northwest, Brookhaven 39601).* The church was organized in 1903.

HAWKINS MEMORIAL *(Lauderdale County: 2906 C Street, Meridian 39301).* This church was first known as South Side Methodist Church and was once located at Grand Avenue and Saint Charles Street. The church was organized 28 May 1893. The new sanctuary and classrooms were built in 1906, remodeled in 1947, and an education building was added in 1950. The name of the church was changed to honor a prominent layman, E. B. Hawkins. The church has an archives room which contains a collection of artifacts from the church's history. Deeds were recorded 3 August 1907, and 7 June 1926.

HAZLEHURST FIRST *(Copiah County: 127 Caldwell Street, Hazlehurst 39083).* In 1860, Reverend Andrew J. Wheat, a native of Copiah County and at that time pastor of the Georgetown

Hazlehurst First United Methodist Church

Circuit, led in the movement that resulted in the organization of a Methodist congregation in Hazlehurst. The original church was built on Georgetown Street on the east side of the railroad tracks. In 1869, two lots were deeded to the church at the corner of West Green Street and Highway Fifty-one. In 1870, the original church was moved from one side of town to the other. This process took one month, and Sunday School was held in a different place on three consecutive Sundays as the church moved to the location where the present church stands. In 1893 a new church was built on this site. Five hundred people attended the dedication. The final service was here on 6 September 1927, and the following day workmen began demolition. Two sessions of the Annual Conference and many district meetings of various groups have been held here. Many materials from

this building were used to construct the African Methodist Church in the south part of Hazlehurst. Reverend Doctor C. W. Crisler was in his first appointment when the present church building was completed in September of 1928, with a new parsonage having been completed earlier in that year. The new church building was dedicated in 1937, during his second appointment here.

HEBRON *(Holmes County: 3621 Hebron Road, Lexington 39095)*. The church was organized 11 January 1844. The first building was a log church built in 1844. The log church burned in 1896, and a wooden frame church was completed in 1897. By 1962, the church had completed work on an education annex.

HEBRON *(Jones County: 276 Hebron-Centerville Road, Soso 39480)*. This church was organized in 1889.

HEBRON *(Lee County: 538 County Road 1451, Saltillo 38866)*. Hebron Methodist Church was erected in 1885, and R. B. East was the first pastor. On a hill behind the present church building, George Jim Hester unloaded the first load of lumber for the Hebron Church. The church was built by community workers and was used first for a church and a school. In the 1930s, the original building was torn down and rebuilt. The building was moved to its present location and Sunday School rooms were added. In 1962, the Hebron Methodist Church became a part of the Saltillo Charge, and in 1970, it united with ten other churches in North Lee County to form the North Lee Cooperative Ministry. The United Methodist Men met with the Saltillo United Methodist Men to form a charge-wide United Methodist Men's Club.

HEBRON *(Tate County: Independence 38638).*

HEBRON *(Wayne County: Matherville).* The church was organized in 1840s.

HEIDELBERG *(Jasper County: 210 Magnolia Avenue, Heidelberg 39439).* The church was organized in 1885.

HENRY CHAPEL *(Quitman County).*

HENRY'S CHAPEL *(Neshoba County: Route Three, Philadelphia 39350).*

HERITAGE *(Harrison County: 4322 Popps Ferry Road, D'iberville 39532).* This church was organized in 1921.

HERITAGE *(Lamar County: 3 Barracuda Drive, Hattiesburg 39402).* In 1904, several members of Main Street Church decided to move west and form Red Street Methodist Episcopal Church, South. It was later named Broad Street United Methodist Church and was known throughout the state for its music program. In 1989, the members again felt God's call to move west and became Heritage United Methodist Church.

HERMANVILLE *(Claiborne County: Hermanville 39049).* Reverend Elijah Steele was appointed to the Port Gibson and Hebron Circuit in 1836. Several years later, Reverend Steele was to die a martyr's death at his station, Poydras Street Methodist Church, New Orleans, during a yellow fever epidemic. He refused to leave. Later, it was decided to build a new church and change the name from Hebron to Steele Chapel in honor of Elijah Steele. The railroad reached the Hermanville area in 1879. A depot, named Hermanville, was constructed beside the track. A booming little city sprang up at the point where the

Old Post Road crossed the new railroad. The Old Post Road was modern day Mississippi State Highway Eighteen. In 1884, the decision was made to move the church to the village and change the name from Steele Chapel to Hermanville United Methodist Church. The church used temporary quarters until property was purchased in 1893 and a new church and parsonage was constructed. At that time the Hermanville Circuit was created.

HERNANDO *(DeSoto County: 755 Mount Pleasant Road, Hernando 38632).* The Hernando United Methodist Church was organized in 1836, and at that time was in the Memphis Conference. In 1870, Hernando and Coldwater were made a dual station. Later, Hernando was placed with Hinds Chapel and then with Horn Lake. It became a station church around 1900. In 1839, a lot was deeded to the church by Edward Orne, a land speculator. In 1840, a frame church was built. The next church building was constructed in 1905, on the "town square," directly in front of the county courthouse though that building later burned. Later in 1940, it was voted to build a new church on Depot Street. In 1955, an annex was added. In 1975, a lot was purchased on Mount Pleasant Road, and on 4 October 1981, the first service was held in the present location. During its long history, the church has been part of the Memphis, Holly Springs, Hernando, Sardis, and Senatobia Districts. The number of charter members has been lost, but records show that in 1855, there were 152 white and eighty Black members.

HICKORY *(Newton County: Hickory 39332).* The church was organized in 1860.

HICKORY BLOCK *(Jefferson County: Union Church 39668).*

HICKORY FLAT *(Benton County: 402 Wolf Street, Hickory Flat 38633).* The 1850 report from the Memphis Conference noted that the Hickory Flat Charge on the Ripley Circuit listed a Black and white membership of 320. This church was at old Hickory Flat, about two miles from the present site. The church moved to the "new" Hickory Flat soon after completion of the Frisco Railroad in the 1880s. It is reported that a young minister, Reverend D. M. Gaddis, was accompanied to his new appointment by Reverend H. C. Moorehead. Shortly after his arrival, Reverend Gaddis held a protracted meeting at which there were thirty-seven conversions, a prayer meeting was organized, and two Sunday Schools were started. A new church in the "new" Hickory Flat was built in 1892. Reverend John W. Boswell, presiding elder of the Holly Springs District, built a new home in the young town. Reverend Boswell and his son, John Jr., were responsible for the construction of a new church. This church was part of the Myrtle Circuit which was later transferred to the Potts Camp Circuit. In 1911, the Hickory Flat Charge was established. The present church was built in 1948, during the ministry of Reverend P. B. Grisham, father of Reverend Roy Grisham. The building was dedicated by District Superintendent, L. P. Wasson, on 9 April 1950. An annex was added in the late 1950s. Several ministers have come from the Hickory Flat Charge. Among them are George and Will Baker, Marvin Scott, Henry Clay Moorehead, E. S. Moorehead,

R. C. Moorehead, Grover Moorehead, Richard Fanton Wicker, and Wade Holland.

HICKORY GROVE *(Lamar County).* This church was organized in 1888.

HIGH HILL *(Scott County: Highway 501, Forest 39074).* The church was organized between 1878 and 1882. There have been two buildings. The first frame building was constructed in 1878. In 1961, the church constructed a new brick building.

HIGHLAND *(Lauderdale County: 3411 Twentieth Street, Meridian 30301).* The church was organized in 1946. The first building, a two-story structure, was completed in 1947. A brick sanctuary was built in 1955, and an educational unit was added in 1962.

HINDS CHAPEL *(DeSoto County: Horn Lake 38637).* The church was organized in 1843.

HOLCOMB *(Grenada County: Holcomb 38940).*

HOLDERS *(Jasper County: Lake Como).* The church was organized in 1842.

HOLLANDALE FIRST *(Washington County: 110 East Washington Street, Hollandale 38748).* Methodism in this area had its beginnings in a small community on the east side of Deer Creek across from what is now Hollandale. This community was known as Barefield Colony. In 1864, Mr. Stephen Barefield donated one acre of land as a site for a Methodist meeting house. In 1864 to 1865, under the leadership of Reverend Drake, a circuit riding preacher, a building of worship was erected. In 1885, the Methodists of "Drake's Chapel" acquired a site for a new building. This site is the location of the present church. On 7 June 1888, Reverend J. C. Shumaker, pastor of the Arcola-Indianola Charge reported to the Greenville District, "located some unoccupied territory partially served by local preachers, but the people have very little interest. An old parsonage and church called Drake's Chapel have been ordered sold and money invested in a church building at Hollandale." In 1889, a frame church building was erected on the new site. On 5 November 1896, this building burned. During 1925 to 1926, the frame building of worship being no longer adequate, the present church building was erected on the same site as the frame building. Many people were housed in the church building during the Great Flood of 1927.

Holly Bluff United Methodist Church

HOLLY BLUFF *(Yazoo County: 117 Marshall Avenue, Holly Bluff 39088).* In 1889, a committee went to petition the Methodist Conference that there be a church for the Holly Bluff community. The request was granted. The first preacher, a Brother Ellis, came and brought his parents and two sisters and lived in a cabin on Mrs. Eugenia Lavenia Crippen's place. The first services were held in a puncheon school named Heildberg School. A puncheon building was a building supported by puncheons, which were simply posts supporting the roof. Around 1891, a small church was erected near the same area. Discussion was held over the naming of the church. Sharbrough Chapel was settled on. Most churchgoers attended, though some may have been of other denominations. In those days they held "protracted meetings," which we today call "revivals." The church had no benches, so early each morning Mr. Walton and Mr. Wilbur Sharbrough and the minister built benches until church time. By the close of the meeting all the benches were built and the congregation could sit for the sermon. As most of the people lived on the Yazoo County side of the river, the church was moved to Campbellsville Landing around 1894. There is no record of what type building was used. About 1905, the second Sharbrough Chapel was built near what is now the Will Hegman home. High water was always a Spring problem. Members attended church many times in boats. In 1907 a parsonage was built on the site of what is now the Sam Langley home. It was only used one year and then sold to Mr. J. W. Nabers, who made his family home there. In 1912, another flood year, services were held in the home of F. W. Sharbrough. About 1920 Holly Bluff became a charge with Louise and had church two Sundays a month. The minister lived in Louise. In 1924 a Brother Allsworth came with the idea of a new church, and by 1926, the present church was in use. 1927 brought the big flood. When the levee broke there was only time to see to one's family and possessions, so all the chrch records were lost.

HOLLY BUSH *(Rankin County: Lake Road, Pelahatchie 39145).* The Holly Bush Methodist Episcopal Church, South, was organized by A. D. Miller in 1879, in a one-room log cabin located one and one-half miles south of the present building on land owned by Dick Wilson. Until this time there had been services held by circuit riders. The four acres of land used presently as the Holly Bush Cemetery was given by John McKay in 1880 to be used as a church and schoolhouse. B. P. and J. S. Cawthorn gave the one acre site on which the present church building is located. The church moved from the one-room construction to the church and school building which had been built on the five acres. M. J. Miller was a member of this church when he was licensed to preach. J. E. Williams was licensed to preach in 1894. J. W. Ward, who died while he was district superintendent in the North Mississippi Conference, joined the church at Holly Bush in 1893. In 1913, a new sanctuary was built and the move was completed from the old log cabin to the new sanctuary. In 1944, a new addition was joined to the west of the building using material from the old two-story building of the consolidated school. In 1971 a new fellowship hall was built.

HOLLY SPRINGS FIRST *(Marshall County: Holly Springs 38635).* The Holly Springs United Methodist Church was established in 1837, and the first building was located on the corner of West College and Craft Street. This building later

Holly Springs First United Methodist Church

became a residence. The property was deeded to William Long, who built the new church building in 1849 in partial exchange of materials and labor. The deed which records this transfer also shows that the pews and pulpit from this early church were moved to the new church. The lot for the present building was given to the church by Robert Burrell Alexander, one of the earliest settlers of Holly Springs. The front entrance was added in the 1870s. Access before then was gained by a flight of steps to the second floor from the outside. When the church was built, the board decided to rent pews, a practice which was bitterly opposed by Robert B. Alexander, who felt that every person should have a free seat in church. Consequently, after the members rented their pews, he paid the rent on those remaining, stipulating that anyone who so desired could sit in them. After the court-house was burned during the Civil War, court was held on the lower floor of the church for several years. A Bible, originally the property of the church, was taken back to Deerwood, Minnesota, by Union soldier Daniel Rogers, sometime between 1862 and 1865. It was kept in his family until 1958, when a Rogers' grandson returned it to the church. Federal troops stored gunpowder in the sanctuary and stabled horses downstairs. The pews were pushed together with the seats facing to make feed troughs for the horses. The old parsonage was begun in 1849 and completed in 1862. There are thirteen beautiful memorial windows in the church. The first was placed in honor of a beloved pastor who served from 1888 to 1889, Reverend George S. Inge. The last window was installed in 1954. In 1888 and 1889, the first hand-pumped organ was installed. When Holly Springs United Methodist Church was organized, it was in the Memphis Conference. At a conference meeting in the church in 1868, steps were taken to organize the North Mississippi Conference. This materialized in 1870, so Holly Springs Church claims to be the mother church of the former North Mississippi Conference. Franklin College, later known as Malone College, was opened under the auspices of this church. Three missionaries have gone from the church, Miss Lennie Barcraft, Miss Viola Blackburn, and Doctor Ann Fearn.

HOLMES CHAPEL *(Hancock County: Highway 607, Pearlington 39572).* The church was organized in 1870.

HOMEWOOD *(Jasper County: Highway Eighteen, Rose Hill 39356).*

HOMEWOOD *(Scott County: Homewood).* The church was organized in 1884.

HOPE *(Neshoba County).* Organized in 1873, members met in a church building owned by various denominations, known as Woodland Baptist Church. Elder J. M. Huston was the first pastor. In 1907, services at Woodland were discontinued. The church moved about two miles east and changed its name to Hope Baptist. In 1908, Mr. Ruben Grafton donated a lot where the present Hope Methodist Church now stands, and a building was erected. In 1934, a storm damaged the building, and while repairs were underway, the congregation used the Methodist building. It was destroyed by fire later, and a school building was used for services. The two denominations agreed to build a new building to be shared. In 1956, Hope Baptist voted to sell to the Methodists, and then moved the old Waldo School building to the present site.

HOPEWELL *(Alcorn County: 572 County Road 200, Corinth 38834).* The first Hopewell Methodist Church was started in a one-room log house near the Choate Cemetery in 1890. It was also used as a schoolhouse. There is no date of when it was built. A Mr. Blakney was both minister and teacher. He named the church Hopewell. It was later moved to where it stands today. The first church at this site was a one-room log house built in 1890. In 1915, this building was torn down and the present one was built. There have been a few changes made with the additions of Sunday School rooms and indoor plumbing. The first minister of this church was Reverend Jim Whitehurst. The church was first called Protestant Methodist. The name was later changed to United Methodist. The deed to this land was given to the church by A. L. Wood.

HOPEWELL *(Clarke County: Sykes).*

HOPEWELL *(Jasper County: Hopewell Road, Rose Hill 39356).* The church was organized in 1837.

HOPEWELL *(Kemper County).* The church was organized between 1874 and 1879.

HOPEWELL *(Marion County: 880 Old Highway Thirty-Five, Sandy Hook 39478).* The church was organized between 1846 and 1872.

HOPEWELL *(Neshoba County: Route Two, Philadelphia 39350).* The first frame structure was built in 1883. A second building was completed in 1962.

HOPEWELL *(Wilkinson County: 194 Hopewell Road, Crosby 39633).* The church was organized in 1834.

HOPEWELL *(Winston County: Highway Twenty-Five South, Louisville 39339).*

HORN LAKE *(DeSoto County: Horn Lake 38637).* This church was organized in 1860.

HOULKA *(Chickasaw County: Houlka 38850).* Old Houlka was the oldest settlement in Chickasaw County. It was the seat of Chickasaw Indian culture when Hernando DeSoto came through this area in 1541 or 1542. It was known as Old Agency, because the U.S. Government agent to the Chickasaws was stationed here. The present community dates back to 1836. The Methodist church was organized in 1883.

Houston First United Methodist Church

HOUSTON FIRST *(Chickasaw County: 230 North Jackson Street, Houston 38851).* Houston First Church was organized in 1837. This community emerged as the result of a donation of land by Colonel Joel Pinson in 1836. Pinson also donated land upon which the town's early churches were built. Prior to the construction of a building, the Methodist congregation met at the courthouse. This church was once located at the corner of Highway Eight and Starkville Road. The first wooden frame structure was constructed in 1857. The second brick structure was completed in 1951.

HUB CHAPEL *(Marion County: 343 Old Highway Thirteen South, Columbia 39429).* In 1900, a group of five devoted Christians met in an old dilapidated barn. Their major job was to make plans to build a church. In 1905, Bishop Spellmyer appointed Moses White as pastor. At that time, the church was named Saint Luke Methodist Episcopal Church, South, with a membership of twenty. The original church building was long and straight with only a sanctuary, pulpit, wooden benches, and outdoor facilities. By 1953, under the pastorate of S. L. Webb, the members conceived the idea of building a new church. In 1955, the

Hub Chapel United Methodist Church

trustees purchased land near Highway Thirteen in the Hub community, from the James' family. This is the church's present location. It was decided that the church's name would also be changed to Hub Chapel Methodist Church. In 1957, actual construction of the new building was begun. Reverend S. G. Roberts was pastor and an experienced carpenter who helped to construct the building. On 5 February 1964, under the pastorate of L. W. Smith, the new building was completed. On Sunday, 9 February 1964, a Service of Dedication for Hub Chapel Methodist Church was held. The new church was a wooden white building built with a complete sanctuary, pastor's study, fellowship hall, kitchen area, four rooms upstairs, and a steeple with a church bell. In 1977, plans were begun to brick and remodel the church. In 1979, the church building was remodeled. On 10 February 1980, Hub Chapel held a Dedication Service with Elonzo Harry as pastor.

HULL MEMORIAL *(Newton County: 227 Lawrence-Hazel Road, Lawrence 39336).*

HUNTERS CHAPEL *(Tate County: Route One, Crockett Community, Sarah 38665).* The church was organized 21 May 1878 with five founding members. The first pastor was William Davis. The original Hunter's Chapel sanctuary, built in 1884, burned in 1947, as the result of a grass fire. The present sanctuary was constructed with subsequent additions of classrooms, kitchen and restrooms in 1964, with a further addition of two more classrooms in 1983.

HURLEY *(Jackson County: 21901 Highway 613, Hurley 39550).* The church was organized in 1919.

Independence United Methodist Church, Morton

INDEPENDENCE *(Scott County: 1213 Independence Road, Morton 39117).* Independence Church dates back to the year 1867. In that year, George Washington Holmes was licensed to preach by C. Mack Donnel, secretary; C. F. Gillespil, pastor. Independence was a part of the Strong River Circuit. There are no reports of any other pastors until the years of 1899 and 1900, when a new church was erected. From 1901 to 1904, J. W. Thompson was pastor, and the church reported a Sunday School. In 1951, the congregation built the present church. The new building was dedicated on 3 June 1951, by Bishop Marvin A. Franklin. A parsonage was constructed in the 1960s.

INDEPENDENCE *(Tate County: Independence 38638)*. This church was organized in 1859.

INDIAN SPRINGS *(Alcorn County: 124 County Road 340, Glen 38846)*. Indian Springs community was organized prior to 1859. Indian Springs Church was organized in 1895. There have been three buildings: one each made of log, frame, and brick construction. The present building was erected in 1962. A copy of the church history is in the Archives at Millsaps College.

Indianola First United Methodist Church

INDIANOLA FIRST *(Sunflower County: 205 Second Street, Indianola 38751)*. The First United Methodist Church was organized in 1879 at Indian Bayou with Reverend W. F. Rozell as pastor. Between 1880 and 1900, circuit riders served the church. The structure was completed in 1888 in Indianola with land donated by G. K. Smith. From 1880 through 1900, the new church was served by thirteen circuit riders. In the year 1909, R. O. Brown, the pastor, led the church in trading lots with the city jail, moving to Second Street. The church is now located at 205 Second Street. The period from 1910 to 1930 was known as church development. In 1927, the church began construction of a new brick building. In 1955, a new parsonage was erected on Sunflower Avenue to give space next door for additional church growth. The first addition to the present sanctuary was completed in 1958. In the decade of the sixties the church had the greatest growth. During this time more educational space was added, including a chapel, pastor's office, library, secretary, and business office, all of which were constructed in three stages. Indianola First United Methodist purchased land during this period to start a new Methodist church named Christ United Methodist. First United Methodist has supported this new church since its birth in 1974. The church also supported Rasberry United Methodist Church, an all-Black congregation.

INGOMAR *(Union County: 1110 County Road Ninety, New Albany 38652)*. The church was organized in 1886, and the first pastor was R. A. Ellis. The land for the Ingomar Methodist Church was deeded to the church on 2 November 1888, by T. A. Witt. The building was erected by E. R. (Lige) Hill. The building was only one large room. All the materials used in the first building were made by hand. In the early 1900s, the Baptists and the Methodists used the same building while the Baptists were constructing their building. In 1920, the Methodist Church was damaged by a tornado but the members were able to repair it. The building was used until 1933. Preaching services were held once a month. The building was torn down in 1933, and a new building erected. A few years later four Sunday School rooms and a kitchen and fellowship hall were added. In 1978, four more Sunday School rooms were added. The pulpit Bible which still graces the pulpit was presented to the Ingomar Methodist Church by Mrs. M. J. Buchannan, President, Chickasaw Female College, Pontotoc, which dates back to the 1800s.

INVERNESS *(Sunflower County: 895 Fifth Street, Inverness 38753).* In the 1890s, those of the Methodist faith were meeting with other denominations in a little church in the center of what is now the Hickory Grove Cemetery. The church was a non-denominational church. In 1901, the first Methodist congregation was organized and formed in the Inverness community. Soon after this, a little wooden church building was erected on the present site of the Methodist Church. The first Methodist church building served the people well for a period of nineteen years with Reverend J. T. McCafferty as its first minister. By 1919, the membership had increased to the point that the building was inadequate. During that year and the early months of 1920, plans were made for a new building. On 20 June 1920, the ground was broken for the new building. Nearly two years passed before the new church was completed. A great deal of the interior work, the altar rail, and the choir loft were done by Reverend Sharp. The new church building was completed in May of 1922. The formal dedication service was held on Sunday evening, 22 October 1939, with Bishop W. T. Watkins officiating. On

Sunday, 21 February 1971, the church and parsonage lay in the path of a tornado that completely wrecked the sanctuary, damaged the education building and scattered church records. For the third time in its life the church began making plans to rebuild. The new sanctuary was finished and the first worship service held on Sunday, 7 October 1973. On 31 March 1974, a beautiful Service of Dedication was held with Bishop Mack Stokes bringing the message.

ISOLA *(Humphreys County: 117 West Edna North, Isola 38754).* The church was organized in 1903.

ITTA BENA FIRST *(Leflore County: 201 Main Street, Itta Bena 38941).* Evidently a preaching place for a few years prior, Itta Bena Church was organized 10 January 1894, with first pastor, John W. Price, and seven founding members. The records show, however, that the first members were received 10 August 1897. The only charter member received on Profession of Faith and Baptism was Mrs. Edith Rich (nee Reese) who died in 1983 at the age of 100. A small frame building was erected in 1898, on property secured from C. A. and Lou Haley. This building was moved to another part of town and is used by a Christian Methodist Episcopal Church. In 1911, when an additional portion of a lot was bought from Mrs. S. M. Reese, the present building was erected on the site of the first church. Completed in 1912, the church was dedicated in 1915, by Bishop William Murrah. An education building was added in 1964 under the pastorate of J. C. Williamson and was dedicated in 1980, by Bishop Mack B. Stokes. The church began here as the Itta Bena-Sidon Circuit in the Winona District, was later Itta Bena Station for a time, and again is the Itta Bena-Sidon Charge. Somewhere along the name "First" was given.

Iuka First United Methodist Church

IUKA FIRST *(Tishomingo County: 101 Eastport Street, Iuka 38852).* In 1857, North Mississippi was under the Memphis Conference of the Methodist Episcopal Church, South, and had been served for years by the circuit riders. Two years later, in 1859, there were enough Methodists in Iuka to begin erection of a church, and a foundation was laid. Entrance to the church was by a broad porch on the south side supported by Corinthian columns. There was no center door. The men entered a door on the right and sat on that side while the ladies entered from and sat on the left. There was a gallery provided for slaves. The dark days of the 1860s wrought many changes in the church. The structure served as a hospital, and through its portals were carried the wounded and dying of both armies. The ministers enlisted in the Confederate Army, and Iuka became a mission station. In 1866, a regular station preacher was again in charge. In 1897, the church was remodeled. In the spring of

1898, nearly forty years after establishment, the church was dedicated with Bishop Hoss presiding. In 1906, an apse was added, and in the center was placed an art glass window depicting the Good Shepherd. Bishop Warren A. Candler presided at the District Conference here. In 1900, Bishop Charles B. Galloway delivered the funeral oration of former Governor John Marshall Stone. Bishop Marvin A. Franklin, president of the World Council of Bishops, spoke several times.

JACKSON STREET *(Lincoln County: 1107 North Jackson Street, Brookhaven 39601).* Jackson Street United Methodist Church was organized as a separate church by the First United Methodist Church in Brookhaven on 29 September 1952. While the present church was being constructed, the members met in a house on Rogers Circle, which also served as the parsonage. The church has had only one sanctuary. It was built in 1953, along with two classrooms. In 1956, a kitchen and dining area and three classrooms were added. In 1961, seven more classrooms, a new kitchen, fellowship hall, pastor study, church office, and three utility-storage rooms were constructed.

JACOBS CHAPEL *(Tippah County: 6211 County Road 701, Ripley 38663).* The church was organized in 1887.

JAMES CHAPEL *(Clarke County; Sykes).*

JAMES CHAPEL *(Lamar County).* This church was organized in 1906.

JEFFERSON STREET *(Adams County: 511 Jefferson Street, Natchez, 39120).* Natchez is the center of the section where Methodism had its beginning in Mississippi, but the Natchez Methodist

Jefferson Street United Methodist Church

church was not organized until several years after Tobias Gibson came from South Carolina in the late spring of 1799. At first the membership was very small, and when the first house of worship was built, 25 March 1807, at least half of the trustees had to be chosen from other churches. Until 1825 the Natchez church was part of a large circuit, but with the Annual Conference of that year it was made a station, the first in Mississippi, and has so remained until the present time. The first brick church bore the name Cokesbury Chapel when it was erected in 1807, and became unsafe for use. In 1823, after meeting for some years at some convenient place nearby, a new church was built, which served the congregation until after the Civil War. The first service held in the present building was a funeral on 30 August 1872, though only the basement was then in use. The first service in the auditorium was held by Bishop Wightman on Thanksgiving Day, 30 November 1876. The Natchez church was host to fifteen sessions of the Annual Conference. In addition, the Conference has met on five occasions within six miles of Natchez. The first "Sabbath School" in Mississippi was started in this church in April 1829. The historical marker in front of the church states "The first Sunday School south of Philadelphia, Pennsylvania, was organized here in 1829."

JOHN MEMORIAL *(Leake County).* This church, a part of the Native American ministry, was organized in 1962.

JOHN WESLEY *(Holmes County: Forty-Nine South Lexington Street, Durant 39063).* The church was organized between 1868 and 1870. During the early years, the Methodists and Baptists worshipped together in a frame building due to the difficult economic times following the Civil War. The two denominations agreed that the congregation with the largest membership would get clear title to the property when they parted. In 1870, the two groups were very close in size, but the Methodists won out, and the Baptists built another house of worship. In 1890, John Wesley Church built a second sanctuary. Reverend Donelson Green was pastor. Again in 1930, the church rebuilt, when Benjamin H. Ashford was pastor. The present building was built in 1990. Reverend Alex Turner was pastor. A library was added in 1991.

JOHNS *(Rankin County: Highway Eighteen South, Brandon 39042).* The church was organized in 1890. The church was once known as Salem Methodist Church. Tom Gates obtained a site for the construction of a church. About 1893, the old Burnham (Thames) School was moved to the site located across the road from its present church and used as a house of worship. The current frame building was erected about 1895, when the Salem congregation merged into Johns Church. A request for a post office was made and named Johns. The name resulted from a clerical error, because the named requested for the post office was Johns Place.

JOHNSON CHAPEL *(Leake County: Block Church Road, Walnut Grove 39189).*

JOHNSTON CHAPEL *(Pike County: 2085 Chapel Drive, Summit 39666).* The church was organized in 1909.

JONES CHAPEL *(Leflore County: Carrollton 38917).* The church was organized in 1862.

JONES CHAPEL *(Oktibbeha County: Bradley).*

JONESTOWN *(Coahoma County: Jonestown 38639).* This church was organized in 1890.

JUMPERTOWN *(Prentiss County: Highway Four, Booneville 38829).*

KALEM *(Scott County: Highway Eighty, Morton 39117).* On the fifth day of August 1928, Reverend M. M. Black, first pastor, received into the fellowship several members on profession of faith and organized Kalem Methodist Church. The first meetings of the new church were held in Concord School, which no longer exists, some four miles east of Morton. Continuing to hold services of worship in Concord School, the members rushed to complete their own house of worship on a site some one hundred yards west of Concord School on property situated on the north side of what is now known as Highway Eighty. In 1948, it was determined that the church building needed repairs and remodeling. It was decided that the existing building was inadequate for the needs of the growing community and that a new structure should be erected. Under the leadership of the pastor, Reverend Aubrey B. Smith, volunteers from the membership began construction. The necessary lumber was secured by cutting and hauling logs donated by the federal government, having them sawed into lumber and hauling it to the site of the new church. Other materials were purchased with funds provided by the membership. The work was all done by voluntary labor by members of the church. The first service was held in the new church building in November 1948. On 12 September 1954, Bishop Marvin A. Franklin, formally dedicated the building. Services have been held regularly and continuously since the organization of Kalem Methodist Church, first in Concord School building; second, in the original frame structure; and, lastly, in the brick-veneered, spire-topped church that is a landmark for travelers. Kalem United Methodist Church has been, at various times, a part of the Newton District and of the Jackson District; and has been joined with other Methodist churches in several different pastoral charges, at one time with Forest United Methodist Church; with Morton United Methodist Church; with Trenton and other churches on the Trenton Circuit; and with Independence and Pulaski on the Pulaski Circuit.

KEYS CHAPEL *(Kemper County: Porterville 39352).*

KILMICHAEL *(Montgomery County: Money Avenue at Ridge Road, Kilmichael 39747).* The early 1840s and 1850s saw settlers begin to come into the area. In 1852, the first Methodist church, which was known as Friendship Methodist Church, was built. Approximately twelve families were members. William and Charlotte Flowers were very instrumental in the formation of the church. Reverend L. F. Finch served as pastor for a number of years and during that time, he taught in the local school. From the formation of the first church to date, this church has been in the following districts: Vaiden, Winona, Grenada, Greenwood, Columbus, and Durant. With the advent of the coming of the railroad, it was decided that this church needed a more central location. In 1896, the present church was dedicated. Reverend Amos Kendall preached the dedication sermon. Samuel J. Locke and Arthur Colton built this second church. To the rear of the church an annex consisting of several rooms has been erected. Three persons have entered the ministry from this church: Sanford Brantley, Claude W. Johnson Jr., and Willie Frank Howell.

KINGS *(Monroe County: Route Four, Aberdeen 39730).* The church was organized in 1885.

KINGSLEY CHAPEL *(Hinds County: Mount Moriah Road at Highway 467, Edwards 39066).* Many years ago, a group of settlers moved into Mississippi from Alabama, Georgia, Florida, and other southern states as soon as the period of slavery ended. There was a group of settlers who came to Edwards from Alabama by way of Meridian, and set up to live in homes near Baker's Creek on the old Raymond Road. Back in the fields behind where the Military Road corners with the

Raymond Road, a group of interested Christians decided to come together under a brush arbor and form a Methodist church in 1878. We do not know how the church got its name, but it is believed that it is named for Bishop Calvin Kingsley of New York City, New York, who lived from 1812 to 1870. The church that was rebuilt in 1902 became too weak to stand, so, the members decided to tear it down and build the present edifice in March 1975, under the leadership of Reverend Doctor Oscar Allan Rogers Jr. The cornerstone was built and laid in marble by the architect and builder, Joseph Robinson. After it was finished, pews and other furniture were purchased. A convocation was held in December 1975 and a new cornerstone was laid.

Kingston United Methodist Church, Natchez

KINGSTON *(Adams County: 1090 Hutchins Landing Road, Natchez 39120).* Kingston is the oldest Protestant community in the state. The community was once known as Jersey Town, because many of the early settlers, including Caleb King, settled here from the state of New Jersey. The Congregational Church here, organized in 1798, is said to have been the first

Protestant church in Mississippi. Tobias Gibson organized a Methodist congregation here in 1800, the second Methodist church in the state. In 1803, Lorenzo Dow sold his watch and bought a lot not far from the present church in a community known as Jersey, so called because of the community of settlers from New Jersey. This lot was the first Methodist property in Mississippi. The original membership included seven persons most of whom were related to Jersey settler leader Samuel Swayze: Caleb King; Gabriel Swayze; Lydia Swayze Cory; Prudence Cory; Deborah Luce; Prudence Varnado; and Eliza King. In 1822 Daniel Farrar, son in law of Caleb King, donated a plot on which a second building made of brick was constructed. An 1840 tornado damaged the church. The present lot was given by Alexander King Farrar and his wife, Ann Doughtery, on 13 February 1856. In the present Kingston Church, built in 1856 and dedicated with William Winans' next to last sermon on 3 May 1857, the slave galleries still remain, and the old-fashioned high pulpit still adds a touch of formality and dignity. The ravages of the Civil War impaired Methodists everywhere, and preaching at Kingston was irregularly conducted for a period after the war. A small but faithful congregation has continued throughout each generation since Reconstruction.

KINGSTON *(Jones County: 1419 Second Avenue, Laurel 39440).* The Mississippi Annual Conference of the Methodist Episcopal Church, South, saw the need of a church in this community and sent Reverend A. C. Dickson to Laurel to organize the Kingston Methodist Episcopal

Kingston United Methodist Church, Laurel

Church, South, in 1902 with twenty-three members. They met in the school building until a small frame building could be built. During Reverend Parker's pastorate, 1904, the Epworth League was organized and the Sunday School made into a missionary society. In Brother Alford's first pastorate, 1908, the first parsonage was built on the lot at the rear of the church. In 1913 the Quarterly Conference changed the name of the church from Kingston to Second Avenue. However, the name was changed back to Kingston in 1917. While Brother Greenay, 1925, served the church, Antioch became a part of Kingston and remained a part of the church until about 1939. Kingston sponsored the organization of Justice Heights Methodist Church. In Brother Moore's ministry, 1948, the present building was started. The building was completed by Brother Castle, in 1952. Kingston sponsored the organization of Franklin Methodist Church. The Aycock property next to the church was purchased. The women's work was organized in 1906 as a Women's Home Missionary Society and is now the United Methodist Women. The men were organized later. The following young men have gone from Kingston into the ministry: Morel Wells,

Bufkin Oliver, Eugene Dyess, Willis Cochran, George Whitton, Rex Harris, and Eugene Covington. Two young ladies Wilma Fay Dyess (Crosby) and Betty Dyess (Youngblood) went into full time Christian work.

KOKOMO *(Marion County: 126 Kokomo Road, Kokomo 39483)*. The church was organized in 1911.

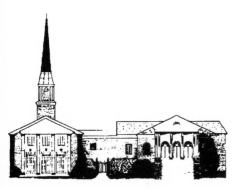

Kosciusko First United Methodist Church

KOSCIUSKO FIRST *(Attala County: Kosciusko 39090)*. With the rush of the immigrants to the central part of the state in 1830, there came many devout Methodists to the town of Kosciusko. The town was named for the Polish hero of the American Revolution, Thadeusz Kosciusko. These early settlers and their friends of other denominations worshiped together in the Academy. The first records show Reverend Elijah Steele organized the Methodists in Kosciusko in 1835. On 9 August 1848, the Methodists bought one-fourth acre of ground and erected a church building. The first church was constructed on the lot which continues to be the location for the present church. It is said that all

denominations continued to worship together, each having a separate Sunday for its preaching date. In this first building, it was the custom for the women and children to sit on one side and the men on the other. The center pews were occupied by the young people and visitors. When the war clouds of the sixties hung heavy over the Southland, the women came to the church and made garments for the boys who wore the gray. During the war, the Annual Conference was held in Kosciusko. During the period of 1835 to 1886, the circuit was known as the Attala Circuit. Later it was changed to the Kosciusko Circuit. The second building was erected in 1871 by a devout member, John C. Lucas. This building was a large frame structure facing south. In 1887, the church was remodeled. A new front and tower were built. Later, memorial windows were added in honor of the founders and active members. In March 1925, the old building was sold. In September 1925, the Methodists moved into the new church, during the pastorate of Reverend A. S. Raper. During the pastorate of Reverend Sam E. Ashmore, 1938 to 1941, the indebtedness on this building was paid in full and the church was dedicated. The present Sanctuary was built during the pastorate of Reverend W. R. Richerson, 1955 to 1961. Since 1872, there has been a Sunday School in the Methodist Churh of Kosciusko. The Epworth League (former name for the Youth Organization) was organized in 1895. Before the days of public schools in Mississippi, the Methodist Church helped to provide education for the people of the community. There were three different Methodist Academies in Kosciusko. One was called "The Kosciusko Male and Female Institute." It was destroyed by fire in 1886. One of the Academies was located on the present site of the City Park. Lucas Avenue was opened up by John C. Lucas so the Methodist preacher could get to the academy from his home on the Natchez Trace, now Natchez Street. Six Annual Conferences have been held here: two Conferences were held in the first building: 20 November 1856, with Bishop George F. Pierce; and 4 November 1863, with Bishop James O. Andrew. Three conferences were held in the second building: 24 November 1875, with Bishop Robert Payne; 2 November 1885, with Bishop Robert K. Hargrove; and 7 December 1904, with Bishop C. B. Galloway. One conference was in the third building and marked the centennial of Methodism in Kosciusko: 4 November 1936, with Bishop Hoyt Dobbs. During the last conference, a marker was unveiled on the parsonage lot, denoting the birthplace of Bishop Charles B. Galloway. In 1967, the property to the northwest of the church, formerly First Baptist Church, was purchased. A new fellowship hall and educational facilities were erected.

KOSSUTH *(Alcorn County: 6 County Road 604, Kossuth 38834).* Originally known as New Hope, the Kossuth community was organized in the 1840s. It was named for Louis Kossuth, an exiled Hungarian who visited the United States in 1851. There were two churches in Kossuth in 1857. The present Methodist church was organized in 1878.

KREOLE *(Jackson County: 4701 Kreole Avenue, Moss Point 39563).* The church was organized 22 March 1924. The church was once a part of the Orange Grove-Pecan Charge. Church construction occurred between 1939 and 1945. The first building was destroyed by fire in 1954. The second building was damaged by lightning.

KYNETT *(Lincoln County: 318 North Second Street, Brookhaven 39601).* The church was organized in June 1873, when Lizzie A. Hoskins donated property to the trustees of Kynett Methodist Episcopal Church. It was once known as Kynett Chapel, and resulted from a merger with Pilgrim Rest Church. The present brick structure was built in the 1950s.

L. L. ROBERTS *(Jefferson Davis County: General Blount Drive, Bassfield 39421).* The church was organized in 1904.

LAGRANGE *(Choctaw County: LaGrange Road, Mathiston 39572).* The date the church was organized is unknown, but it was in the 1800s.

Lake United Methodist Church

LAKE *(Scott County: 24587 Highway Eighty, Lake 39092).* Earliest religious services were held under a brush arbor when a circuit riding preacher came. Later, camp meetings for all faiths were held, usually for a week's duration, with several preachers taking turns delivering the sermons. In 1862, the Lake Circuit was formed and provided a preacher, but things were virtually at a standstill because of the Civil War. Therefore, there was no place for public worship until 1865 when the community's first one-room school was built by a Mr. Chester. Its materials were salvaged from the railroad shops at Lake which General William T. Sherman's troops destroyed on 11 February 1864. All worship services were then held in the small school. Baptist, Methodist Episcopal Church, South, and Presbyterian Christians built the first church building about 1868 and called it the Union Church because it was owned jointly. However, in 1873 the Baptists withdrew from the arrangement and built their own building. The 1868 Union Church building remains as the sanctuary of the Lake United Methodist Church. The bell is from one of the locomotives which was destroyed during General Sherman's invasion of Lake's railroad shops. The first parsonage was built before the turn of the century and still stands today as a private home.

LAKE CENTRAL *(Scott County: Lake 39092).* The church was organized in 1903.

LAKE CORMORANT *(DeSoto County: Lake Cormorant 38641).*

LAMBERT *(Quitman County: Lambert 38643).* The Lambert United Methodist Church, known as the Methodist Episcopal Church, South, began almost as soon as the unbroken wilderness was invaded in early 1900, and a town was begun. Mrs. Fannie B. Allen, later known as "Auntie Allen," inspired in her friends the need for a place to worship. The first church was nothing more than a tent. The pews were heading blocks and the carpet was sawdust. The

Lambert United Methodist Church

earliest church records indicate that Reverend Walter W. Jones came as the first minister in 1903. Soon a frame church building was built. This was called the Union Church where Baptist, Disciples of Christ, and Methodist congregations met for worship. Later it was bought by the Disciples of Christ. In 1903, a group of people met in the home of Mr. and Mrs. Harvey Crossland to make plans for a separate Methodist congregation, and a small frame building was erected where the present church building now stands. Mrs. Fannie B. Allen was the first member of the church. The first Quarterly Conference of 1907 was held in Vance on 6 April. Lambert, Rome, Belleview, Vance, and Marks were on the Vance Charge which was in the Winona District. There were only two church buildings on the charge, Vance and Lambert. Later that year one more preaching station was added, Adam's School. Belleview organized a Sunday School, and a Women's Home Missionary Society was organized during the same year. In 1910, the charge was renamed the Lambert Charge. In 1922, the charge was again renamed the Lambert-Marks Charge reflecting the changes in population. The membership began to rapidly increase in the early 1920s. During the decade of the

1920s, three more preaching stations were added: White's Schoolhouse, Respess School, and Brazil. In the 1930s, Lambert was realigned in the Sardis–Grenada District, a community Men's Bible Class was organized with over 100 members, and a new parsonage was built. In 1940, Center Hill was added. Under the leadership of Reverend R. L. Long and Revered John Millsaps Jr., Lambert became a station church in 1953. During the early 1960s, plans were approved for a new education building. At the Conference level, the North Mississippi and the Upper Mississippi Conferences merged. Within three years, Lambert was realigned twice, in the Delta and the Cleveland Districts.

LAUDERDALE *(Lauderdale County: Lauderdale 39335).* The church was organized in 1874.

Laurel First United Methodist Church

LAUREL FIRST *(Jones County: 420 North Fifth Street, Laurel 39440).* Methodism in the Laurel area began in 1852 in the western part of Jones County in the small community of Union Line. The usual log building was erected, with puncheon floors and benches (broad, heavy timber, roughly dressed with only one side

finished flat). Circuit riding preachers served the church until the Civil War, when it disbanded. The church remained inactive until a Congregational Methodist evangelist held a series of meetings at Union Line and a new log building was erected on the present site in 1891. Church records show that Reverend Lazarus Jackson Jones was appointed to preach at Laurel from December 1882 until December 1883, but Mississippi Conference records show that during the same period Reverend Jones was also pastor at Ellisville Methodist Church.

LEAF *(Greene County).* Leaf River Circuit dates back to 1822. Leaf Church first appeared in the conference appointments in 1926, and was to be supplied, meaning no pastor was appointed.

LEAKESVILLE *(Greene County: Paulding Raod, Leakesville 39451).* Leakesville first appeared in the conference appointments in 1892, with W. J. Dawson as pastor. It was in the Meridian District. In 1896, an article in the *New Orleans Christian Advocate* referred to it as Leakesville Mission, when J. C. Ellis was in his second year as pastor. The article stated the church had a new parsonage and a new church organ.

LEARNED *(Hinds County: Raymond 39154).* Learned was originally a small lumber town named for a Mr. Learned of Natchez who owned the sawmill. The sawmill was built in 1890. A loyal group of Methodists felt the need of a Methodist church in Learned. A site was purchased the latter part of December 1890 from A. J. Lewis. The church was built with contributions and personal labor given by the members. The building was dedicated in the spring of 1892. Reverend N. J. Roberts was pastor of the Utica Charge at this time. Twenty-five new members heard the first sermon preached at Learned Church on 28 November 1891. This new church was first placed with the Utica Charge. The church building originally rested on tall pillars and had high wooden steps. In the year of 1918, there was a tornado in Learned. The wind lifted the church up and set it down on a vacant part of the lot.

Leavell Woods United Methodist Church

LEAVELL WOODS *(Hinds County: 3302 Terry Road, Jackson 39212).* On 4 June 1944, a group of interested residents, under the leadership of Reverend Thomas A. Carruth, pastor of the Terry Charge, met in the home of Mr. and Mrs. K. P. McCluer. The formal organizational meeting took place on 12 August 1944, when some forty-three persons became charter members. Reverend J. H. Hetrick became the first pastor. A small brick chicken house, located on Daniel Lake Drive, was used as the first house of worship. The first permanent building was ready for occupancy on 25 July 1948. Reverend Robert Matheny came to Leavell Woods in 1951. On 14 March 1954, the official opening of the sanctuary took place. In 1956 a

concrete block educational unit was erected behind the Founders Building. It was named after Reverend T. B. Winstead. In 1962 church offices, fellowship hall, kitchen, and church school classrooms were erected. In 1985 under Reverend Henderson Rasberry's leadership, the Bert Jordan Education building was constructed. Over the church's history there have been four parsonages. Out of the membership has come twelve ministers and many outstanding lay leaders, some of whom have served at the national level.

LEBANON *(Prentiss County: Two County Road 7552, Booneville 38829).*

LEBANON *(Webster County: Lebanon, Eupora 39744).* In the summer of 1850, John Wesley Lamb was instrumental in establishing the Lebanon Methodist Church. The first church, built soon after organization, was made of logs. The second one was a boxed building built in 1870. The third building was a high ceiling one-room building with high pitched roof erected in 1901. This building was replaced in 1960, with a brick veneer building with three Sunday School rooms. In the early years there were Black members who worshipped in the afternoon. The church has been on several circuits: First the Walthall Circuit, the Tomnolen Charge in 1908, the Bellefontaine Charge in 1911, continuing until June 1959, and the Eupora Circuit, when it was formed until now. Sam Dodd entered the ministry while at this church.

LEE ACRES *(Lee County: 1601 President Avenue, Tupelo 38801).* On 10 June 1965, the Board of Missions of the North Mississippi Annual Conference of the

Methodist Church purchased four and a half acres of land at the southeast corner of President Avenue and Garfield Street in Tupelo as a site for a future church. In June 1966, Reverend W. R. Lott Jr. appointed Gerald C. Krueger, a lay minister, to survey the Lee Acres area. Gerald and his wife, Nell, began a house to house survey of the area and in just a short while found sixteen persons who were eager to start a new church. Permission to hold services was secured from Reverend Lott, and on 11 September 1966, the first service was held in the William Pechal home on Garfield Street. The budding congregation soon outgrew the home on Garfield Street and moved into a tent on the new property, just east of the location of One D'Ville Place Apartments. On 27 November 1966, Bishop Edward C. Pendergrass, District Superintendent W. R. Lott Jr., and pastor Gerald Krueger led the congregation in the tent in the service formally organizing Lee Acres United Methodist Church. Eighteen persons became charter members that Sunday. With winter coming on, a small one-room structure was built in the fall of 1967, to house the church. In April 1968, the young church looked forward to receiving its first full time minister and voted to purchase a parsonage at 1411 Van Buren Avenue. Reverend Donald Wildmon was appointed as the first full time minister of the church in June 1968. On 20 March 1970, construction was started on the first unit of the new church on the present site.

LEGGETT MEMORIAL *(Harrison County: 1410 Beach Boulevard, Biloxi 39530).* The J. T. Leggett Memorial Methodist Church was organized at Seashore Campground in Biloxi, 23 January 1955. Bishop Marvin A. Franklin made the principal address. Reverend D. T. Ridgeway, superintendent of the Seashore District, presided at the organizing meeting held in the tabernacle. Reverend F. W. Casey, director of the Campground, was acting pastor of the new church. Mrs. J. T. Leggett was enrolled as the first charter member. Seventeen other charter members were enrolled. Over 100 people attended the organizing meeting, and an offering was taken for the new church. The Leggett Memorial church later built a beautiful new sanctuary on the Seashore Assembly grounds, overlooking the Gulf of Mexico.

Leland First United Methodist Church

LELAND FIRST *(Washington County: 202 North Broad Street, Leland 38756).* This church was organized in 1897. An education building was erected in 1963, and a Christian Life Center in 1986. In 1923, a member, Doctor W. B. Lewis, with financial and spiritual support of the Leland Church, left to become a medical missionary in the Belgian Congo. Following the flood of the Mississippi River in 1927, the pastor reported: "Please let it be borne in mind that of the fifteen weeks of this quarter, eight weeks have been embraced by the overflow period that for a while brought almost all church work to a complete standstill." Damage to the outside stucco of the new sanctuary resulted in replacing the lower level of stucco with brick.

LENA *(Leake County: 823 Highway 213, Lena 39094).* This church was organized in 1908.

LEONA *(Jasper County).* This church was founded between 1892 and 1894.

Lewis Memorial United Methodist Church

LEWIS MEMORIAL *(Calhoun County: Calhoun City 38916).* In early Spring of 1906, there were in Calhoun City at least twenty-five Methodists whose membership was in churches throughout Calhoun County. They had a vision of a Methodist Church in the city and set out to establish one. Those twenty-five people became charter members of the Calhoun City Methodist Church and Reverend R. P. Goar was appointed as the first pastor. The church became a part of the Pittsboro Circuit. In 1909 the church became a part of the Vardaman Circuit and remained in that circuit for three years. In 1912 the Calhoun City Charge was established and ministry continued in this fashion for twelve years. In 1925 the Calhoun City Methodist Church became a station church and began to "stand on its own" for the first

time. At the time of the organizing of the church (1906) there was no house of worship in which to hold services, so brush arbors and vacant buildings were used until 1913. In that year, the congregation undertook the challenge of building a permanent structure. Over the years this building was added to and in 1983 it was completely remodeled. Today there is a main sanctuary with all modern features. In 1940 the church was renamed to honor the memory of Reverend T. W. Lewis, who was pastor at the time of his death in 1939. The name was changed from Calhoun City Methodist Church to Lewis Memorial United Methodist Church. In 1985 there were some small churches which closed in the county and again the church became a charge, with Big Creek United Methodist Church.

LEWISBURG *(DeSoto County).* This church was organized in 1879.

Lexington First United Methodist Church

LEXINGTON FIRST *(Holmes County: 108 Tchula Street, Lexington 39095).* At a Quarterly Conference held at Ebenezer on 27 February 1836, a building committee was appointed to build a church at Lexington. This first church, known as the Methodist Episcopal Church, was a one-room frame building on the site of the present parsonage. In 1840, the circuit was changed from Yazoo to Holmes and remained thus for a number of years. In 1844, the name of the denomination was changed to Methodist Episcopal Church, South. The Mississippi Conferences' Fiftieth Annual Conference was held at this church in 1865. The present edifice was completed in 1897, and dedicated debt-free by Bishop Charles Betts Galloway in 1898. In 1930, during the pastorate of Reverend J. E. Stephens, an educational annex was built. Soon after, in 1939, the name of the denomination was changed for the third time to Methodist Church. The present parsonage was constructed in 1941, on the site of the original wood church. The name of the denomination was again changed in 1968, to the present First United Methodist Church. A complete renovation of the sanctuary was undertaken in 1974.

LIBERTY *(Amite County: North Church Street, Liberty 39645).* Liberty is the oldest community in Amite County, having been settled as early as 1790. In 1809, when the county was formed, Liberty was designated the county seat. The church was organized between 1841 and 1851.

LIBERTY *(Benton County: Liberty Road, Ashland 38603).* About 1830 or 1835, Mr. Thomas Elliott gave land to build a church in what was then Tippah, but is now Benton County. A log house was built and was used as a union church for Presbyterians and Methodists until a new frame building was erected in 1897. Then a

deed was secured as Methodist Church, South. The frame building built in 1897, was used until 1921. A larger sanctuary was added for worship, and the old church was made into Sunday School rooms. In 1947, the entire church was reworked, and by 1953, new Sunday School rooms were built. In 1958, it was decided to build a new church in the near future. In December 1961, an annual fund drive was begun in addition to having monthly offerings. The present church was begun on 10 June 1963. It was completed about four months later. The church was paid for on 9 December 1967, and formally dedicated on 5 May 1968, when B. B. Bailey was pastor.

LIBERTY *(Kemper County).*

LIBERTY *(Prentiss County: Highway Thirty East, Booneville 38829).* The history dates back to the Civil War when Arch Street, a Confederate soldier, recruited soldiers here. When the war was over and reconstruction was well advanced, a few Methodists in the community saw the need for a church and organized Liberty United Methodist Church between 1860 and 1874. R. L. George was among those who built the first building. The church was used by several denominations. Preachers were hard to get and in 1918, Brother G. P. Mayo, a Free Will Baptist, was a much loved man of God. After a time, Brother Jim Gullett, a well known and beloved Methodist came to preach on several occasions. In 1925, a Sunday School was started. In 1947, the members voted to build a new church. The new building was erected around the old building, making it necessary for members to attend neighboring churches during the construction.

LIBERTY *(Union County: 1284 County Road 188, Blue Springs 38828).*

LIBERTY *(Webster County: Martin King Drive, Eupora 39744).* The church was organized in 1882.

LIBERTY CHAPEL *(Attala County: Ethel 39067).* The record shows the first worship services were held in brush arbors by Reverend H. Williamson with the assistance of other ministers in 1851. It was first known as Liberty Chapel Campground. In 1853, four and one-half acres of land were donated to the trustees and their successors by Mr. James T. and Martha Mathis. The first church was constructed of wood and built in 1853; the second in 1904. In 1926, Liberty Chapel Church was transferred from the McCool Charge to the Ethel Charge. In 1960, a complete renovation of the exterior and interior was made. New church schoolrooms, new pews, pulpit, and communion table were also added.

LIBERTY HILL *(Attala County: McCool 39108).* This church was organized in 1857.

LINDSEY CHAPEL *(Oktibbeha County).*

LINN *(Sunflower County: Nine Linn Road, Doddsville 38736).* Organized in 1877, the first building was built in 1886 on Sand Ridge, and was called Macedonia. The next building was constructed in 1914, at Linn with Reverend Brooks serving as minister and the congregation claiming the name, New Salem. This building was a one-room frame with annexes added as necessary. The first annex was in 1952. The second annex was built in 1957. An arsonist burned the building on 4 February 1984. With the insurance money and contributions by people from sixteen states, a new modern brick sanctuary, fellowship hall, and Sunday School rooms were built. There being no outstanding debt, the facility was dedicated in November of the same year.

LITTLE CREEK *(Perry County).*

LITTLE ROCK *(Copiah County: Crystal Springs 39059).*

LITTLE ZION *(Clarke County).* This church was organized in 1870.

LITTLE ZION *(Copiah County: 2096 Hawkins Road, Hazlehurst 39083).* The church was organized in 1857.

LITTLE ZION *(Madison County: 400 Church Street, Canton 39046).*

LITTLE ZION *(Rankin County: 816 Second Street, Pelahatchie 39145).* The church was organized in 1927.

LITTON *(Bolivar County: 1868 Litton Road, Shaw 38773).* This community began in 1902, when W. E. Litton moved here from Tennessee. The church was organized in 1914.

LODEBAR *(Rankin County: 675 Highway Forty-Three South, Pelahatchie 39145).* This church got its name from a Biblical town by the same name, which means "without pasture." The first Methodist meetings in this Rankin County community were under a brush arbor near the place where the present church stands. James Brown, and his wife, Nancy, deeded land to this church 13 September 1830. The first church was made of logs and stood where the cemetery now is located. Tradition says this building was destroyed by fire during the Civil War. The second frame building served until 1890, and was located just west of the cemetery. The third building was erected in 1890, and served the church until 1935, when the present building was completed. A fellowship hall was added in 1992.

Lone Pine United Methodist Church

LONE PINE *(Madison County: 708 Lone Pine Road, Canton 39046).* On 18 February 1867, by deed recorded in Book R, Page 176, Britain and Emily Pritchard executed a deed of property in Section 32, Township Nine, Range Four East, containing three acres, together with all of the buildings, and appurtenances thereon, to the trustees of the Lone Pine Seminary and their successors in office as long as said property conveyed shall be used for the purpose of education or the promotion of Christian religion. No definite date of the establishment of the Methodist Church can be ascertained, as so little information is on record. In a reference in the Archives at Millsaps College in Jackson, there is mention of a District Conference held in Jackson on 5 June 1884. On 18 May 1899, an item was recorded in the *Christian Advocate*, published in New Orleans, by Reverend W. Black for the Louisiana, Mississippi and North Mississippi Conferences of the Methodist Episcopal Church, South. "Lone Pine: This is the name of a church on the Sharon Circuit, located in a thickly set grove of oaks. The

pastors of twenty years ago will recall a small two-story California building of fifteen by twenty feet used for grange school and preaching purposes, close by the lone pine. The schoolhouse still stands, but near by the Methodist and Baptists have each erected cozy attractive churches. A more quiet and appropriate place to build a house to the Lord has never appeared to me. Signed: T. B. Holloman, presiding elder of Jackson District." Since the article refers to "twenty years ago," that would be in 1879. A notation found in an old conference report dated October 1912 states that a deed to the Lone Pine Methodist Church property was recorded in the deed records of Madison County on 29 February 1892. On 13 June 1914, an old conference report states: Lone Pine Methodist Church organized a Sunday School about five months before. Lone Pine had no service for three years, 1959 to 1961. On 1 October 1961, pastor C. Y. Higginbotham wote that he had arrived on the Sharon Charge on 22 June, and was kindly received by the good people of the churches on the charge. He wrote "We have reopened the Lone Pine Church, with good prospects for a revival of interest in its activities. A small Sunday School has been organized with an enrollment of twenty or more." The church has remained active since that time.

LONE STAR *(Covington County: Highway Eighty-Four West).* The church was organized in 1940.

LONG BEACH FIRST *(Harrison County: 208 Pine Street, Long Beach 39560).* The first place of worship for the Methodists of Long Beach was in a discarded box car, in 1874. Reverend Joseph Nicholson organized the

Long Beach First United Methodist Church (Old Sanctuary)

church in 1875. Mr. Henry Ware built the first church building and gave it to the congregation in 1879. It was dedicated as a place of worship under the Reverend Joseph McLaurin the third Sunday in October 1880. In the Fall of 1894, a revival was held in the Long Beach church, with fifty-one members added to the church. At the conference that fall, Mr. Sells was returned to the Long Beach Charge and began the new year by urging the need of a new church building. By September of that year the building was ready for use. At the Annual Conference in the Fall of 1903, J. L. Sells was assigned to Long Beach in connection with Twenty-eighth Street Church of Gulfport, with instructions to spend half of his time in Long Beach. There being no parsonage on the charge, plans were made to build one at Long Beach. By April, the parsonage was near enough to completion so that the pastor could move into it.

LONGINO *(Neshoba County: Old Highway Fifteen North, Philadelphia 39350).*

LONGTOWN *(Panola County).*

LONGVIEW *(Carroll County: Highway Thirty-Five North, Carrollton 38917).* The church was organized in 1889.

LONGVIEW *(Oktibbeha County: 1948 Longview Road, Starkville 39759).*

LOST GAP *(Lauderdale County: Meehan).*

LOUIN *(Jasper County: Church Street, Louin 39338).* The church was organized in 1906.

LOUISE *(Humphreys County: Ash Street, Louise 39097).* For many years the Methodist Church of Louise was a part of what was known as the Silver Creek Circuit. Most of the area at that time along Silver Creek was covered with forest and the people lived on the widely scattered plantations that dotted the stream's banks. The circuit, which got its name from the stream, was served by circuit riders. Reverend Green W. Browne is the first minister known to have served the Silver Creek Circuit. He was appointed to the circuit in 1876 finding fourteen members on the entire circuit. By May of that year, however, he had eleven new members, making a total of twenty-five. In Louise, services were held for many years on the corner lot where the old consolidated school, the present firehouse, now stands. In 1909, Mr. William H. Reid gave a lot for the building of a house of worship and a beautiful little wooden church was erected on this lot which was along the highway and in the center of town. All denominations worshipped there so it became known as the Community Church in Louise. The first pastor of this church which became a part of the Louise, Silver City and Holly Bluff Charge, was Reverend R. H. Foreman. Soon after the community church was built, the women of the church organized a Ladies Aid Society and took over the cleaning of the church and furnishing flowers for the altar. The charge was now known as the Louise and Holly Bluff Charge. The church property was sold and a new lot purchased on Ash Street. In 1928, a beautiful brick veneer building was erected during the pastorate of I. H. Sells and a few years later was dedicated.

Louisville First United Methodist Church

LOUISVILLE FIRST *(Winston County: Main at Church Street, Louisville 39339).* The church was organized in 1835. First Methodist Church of Louisville, later known as First United Methodist Church, has been in existence on what is now the block north of Main Street and west of North Church Avenue since it was organized in about 1835 by Reverend Jacob Matthews. Reverend D. Langford was appointed in 1838 to a pastoral charge that included Louisville, then a part of the old Grenada District. At that time the church building, constructed of pine logs, was located on the north corner of the block adjacent to where it now stands. The first parsonage was on West Main Street, where the education building now stands. The first Sunday School was organized in 1876 during the pastorate of J. D. Newson. This was the first denominational Sunday School in Louisville. The old log church

was sold in 1885 and a frame structure was erected on the present site in 1887. A parsonage was built beside it, facing North Church Street. Damaged by a tornado in 1913, this church building was abandoned and a new brick structure was completed in 1918. The church was completely remodeled. The sanctuary took on a new look as the chancel area was reversed. The narthex was also added, making this now the main entrance. A new parsonage, located on White Circle, was built in 1966. In 1994, the adjoining lot on North Church was purchased for future development. Another major renovation was begun in 1995.

LOVE *(DeSoto County: Hernando 38632).* This church was organized in 1872.

Lovely Lane United Methodist Church

LOVELY LANE *(Adams County: Sixty-Five Morgantown Road, Natchez 39120).* The church was organized in 1951.

LOWRY *(Tippah County: 20860B Highway Two East, Ripley 38663).* Lowry Church was organized under a brush arbor in 1926, by Reverend S. T. Ledbetter, an old time circuit rider. The land was purchased from Mr. and Mrs. M. C. Waldon near the Lowry Cemetery. Lowry was the name of a family traveling by wagon train during the

Civil War. The entire family died of "the fever," and were all buried in the same grave. Until 1947, Lowry was a part of the Lowry Charge of the Corinth District. In 1951, the District became New Albany District and Lowry was placed on the Blue Mountain-Ripley Charge. On 16 May 1960, the Lowry Charge was reestablished, but in 1968, the charge was divided and Lowry was placed on the Falkner Charge. On 1 December 1983, Lowry Church once again became the mother church for Lowry Charge. The church began as a small frame building and was renovated several times. In 1962, a brick building was constructed with four classrooms.

LUCEDALE FIRST *(George County: 311 West Main Street, Lucedale 39452).* Lucedale Methodist Church was founded on 26 November 1899 under the pastorate of J. W. Campbell, with a charter membership of twenty-six. The original church was a frame structure built on the corner of Church Street and Mill Street in 1900. The church prospered and a larger more adequate building was needed. A new building that serves as the church sanctuary today was built on Main Street and completed on 10 April 1909. Between 1949 and 1950, under the pastorate of Frank E. Dement, remodeling was done, with the additions of classrooms and a fellowship hall. At this time the entire church was bricked. On 4 October 1964, the name Lucedale Methodist Church was changed to First Methodist Church. With the 1968 merger of the Methodist and the Evangelist United Brethren, it became the First United Methodist Church. Once again due to growth of the church an addition of an office and education wing and family life center was added under the pastorate of H. J. Hedgepeth. This new addition was completed in October 1996.

LULA *(Coahoma County: Lula 38644).* This church was organized in 1925.

LUMBERTON *(Lamar County: Fifth at Eleventh Avenue, Lumberton 39455).* The church was organized in 1882.

LYNCH CHAPEL *(Hinds County: 230 Dawson, Clinton 39056).* This church, dating back to the pre-Civil War period, was founded and organized by Reverend George Washington, a slave who had a dream to one day become a minister. This dream manifested itself as he listened to the available minister on Sunday mornings on the plantations when the slaves were permitted to attend church services. His family obtained their freedom and finally made their way to a small rural town in Clinton. The desire to become a religious leader of his people lingered with him. Upon heeding the call to become a minister, worship services were carried on in a building located on Raymond Road. Since there were no Methodist Churches for Blacks in Clinton, Reverend Washington organized and built one. He secured a loan, purchased land, and built a small frame building on the present site. The church facing the road was given the name Lynch Chapel Methodist Episcopal Church. The present brick church building was erected for worship under the leadership of Reverend Israel Gilchrist. It is important to note that along with the physical changes that have taken place, Lynch Chapel underwent a name change as a result of the merger in 1968 with the Evangelical United Brethren Church. After this union, Lynch Chapel United Methodist Church emerged.

LYNCH CHAPEL *(Scott County)*. The church was organized in 1868.

LYNCH CHAPEL *(Warren County: Redwood 39156)*. The church, dating to just after the Civil War, was organized about 1866 by Dallas Dunn, Robert Brown, Will Smith, Isaac Calvin, Richard Jackson, Shedrick Hicks, Jackson Phillip, and Mrs. Julia Mason. The first church was a brush arbor on the hill near Oak Ridge, and was called China Ridge Methodist Church. In 1869, a small frame structure on a hill near Oak Ridge, was built and was called Lynch Chapel Methodist Episcopal Church. In 1932, the congregation wanted to move the church to the Vicksburg to Yazoo City Highway, and through the generosity of Elijah J. Smith, and his wife Lucy, the plot of ground on which the church now stands was secured. A new building was erected and dedicated under the pastorate of J. H. Jackson.

LYNVILLE *(Kemper County: Route Two, Preston 39354)*. The church was organized between 1920 and 1921.

LYON *(Coahoma County: Webb and Bobo Streets, Lyon 38645)*. The history of this church began with the Delta of Mississippi. Originally, in the 1890s, the parent Methodist church was based on nearby Big Creek, one of the waterways by which early settlers traveled from the hills: the one sure way of traveling in the mud days of the Delta. Many a member came to church in a dugout. Later the church moved to Lyon and met in the Masonic Hall. When the

time came to have a Methodist revival, a brush arbor was built between the Hall and the schoolhouse, and the organ was moved outside for the services. Brother Sanders began to formulate plans for building a church. On 10 December 1895, Mrs. L. E. Bobo gave to the Methodist Church of Lyon its recently released site on what was then the main road through town. The lumber was cut and hauled into town by ox team and wagon, and the congregation spent their own physical labor to erect it. There was a belfry and bell and two doors to enter: one for the men, and one for the women; although they would meet in the vestibule inside. Before even the pews were placed in the new church building, a Christmas tree was set up for the children, and the whole community was invited. The church building survived flood waters of the Mississippi River in 1897, by a six-foot levee thrown in front of it.

M **ABEN** *(Oktibbeha County: Webster Highway, Maben 39750)*. Maben was organized in 1894, with thirteen charter members, as a congregation of the Methodist Episcopal Church, South. On 17 November 1906, a cyclone destroyed the building and worshippers held services in the Maben School building. The second church was built and, in 1959, the second church building was replaced by the present structure. In 1924, Maben-Mathiston Charge was created and this included Double Springs and Providence. Maben, Cedar Bluff, Pheba, Providence, and Double Springs were put together forming the Maben Charge in June 1950. In 1958, the Maben Charge was reduced to Maben,

Providence, and Double Springs. In June 1974, charge lines were officially changed and the Maben Church became full time. Two of the members, the late J. W. Robertson and Stanton M. Butts, became ministers and served throughout North Mississippi.

MACEDONIA *(Chickasaw County: Trebloc)*. This church was organized in 1873.

MACEDONIA *(Lincoln County)*. The church was organized between 1860 and 1900.

MACEDONIA *(Neshoba County: Philadelphia 39350)*. Organized in 1928, the land for Macedonia was donated by W. B. Willis, and was about fourteen miles northwest of Philadelphia in the community originally called Popetown (now Arlington). The church was built under the direction of Reverend Luke Hodges, and named Macedonia by Mrs. Verna Barnes, one of the first members. Sometime in the late 1930s, the church was rebuilt. The Pentecostal Church at Burnside had few members at this time, so it was decided to consolidate the two. In 1958, a new church was built at the intersection of Highway 395 and Nineteen North in the Arlington community. The land was donated by Monroe Tolbert.

MACEDONIA *(Noxubee County: Macedonia Road, Shuqualak 39361)*. This community was settled around 1840, and took its name from the Methodist church that organized in 1854. Captain Charles Thomas was one of the early settlers, and he served in the State Legislature and as Noxubee County sheriff. The first Methodist building was a log structure

completed in 1854. The land for the present church was deeded on 25 November 1872. The second and present frame building was constructed in 1885.

Macedonia United Methodist Church, Shuqualak

MACEDONIA *(Wilkinson County)*. This church was organized in 1860.

MACON FIRST *(Noxubee County: 104 North Jefferson, Macon 39341)*. This is an interesting church built in 1852, while its organization goes back to 4 February 1834. During the Civil War, the state government used this building for a while after Grant's army captured Jackson.

MADDEN *(Leake County: Madden 39019)*. The church was organized in 1925.

MADISON *(Madison County: 2050 Historic Main Street, Madison 39130)*. The arrival of the railroad in 1856 served to promote settlement around Madison. In 1864, the Madison Mission was established by the Annual Conference meeting at Crystal Springs. Harvey Copeland was appointed to serve as pastor of the mission which was to be connected with the Livingston and Pearl River Charges.

Although no longer an active church, the Pearl River Church building, seven miles northeast of Madison, has been preserved and designated an official Methodist Historic Site The Livingston Charge no longer exists. In 1870, the Madison Charge was formed. Following the organization of the church in Madison, the church building on the Magee Plantation was dismantled and moved to Madison. The best of the material was salvaged and used to erect the first religious edifice in Madison Station. This building served the Methodists as a place of worship for approximately sixty-five years. The first report to the Annual Conference from the Madison charge was in 1877. The first multiple year appointment was held in 1872 to 1875 by Warren G. Black, who would later served as editor of the *New Orleans Advocate*. The first Lambuth Day observance was held and the monument erected on the grounds of the Pearl River Church during the pastorate of Henry G. Hawkins. In 1929, Paul H. Grice was appointed to the Madison Charge. Reverend Grice launched a campaign for a new sanctuary. He learned that among the early worshippers at the Madison Church was a widowed mother, Mrs. Susan Montgomery, who had instilled in her eight children her love for the church. Her second child, Robert Montgomery, though settling in Atlanta, never lost interest in the community, and retained membership in the Madison Methodist Church. Upon being contacted by Reverend Grice, he donated funds to underwrite the construction of the new sanctuary as a memorial to his mother. The Susan L. Montgomery Memorial Church was dedicated on 13

July 1930. Full-time service at the Madison Church began on 24 June 1956. In 1968, the educational annex was completed. The church name was changed to Madison United Methodist Church.

MAGEE *(Simpson County: 226 Northwest First Avenue, Magee 39111)*. The church's beginnings predate the town of Magee itself. In 1899, this rural area was sparsely populated. Yet the railroad had just located a new depot here. Methodists on the old Westville Circuit planned to build a house of worship about two miles north of where Magee is today. Mr. J.W. Burnham supervised construction of a building that served well for forty-six years. The twenty-seven member congregation was organized as the Magee Methodist Episcopal Church, South, on 23 September 1900. A final service was held in the old building on 14 January 1946. The first service held in the new sanctuary, the present sanctuary, was on 9 February 1947. The red brick building with white trim and copper-roofed steeple is now a familiar Magee landmark. Then in 1956 an annex was added. In 1985 and 1986, the growing church built a large fellowship hall with a kitchen, an office suite, conference room, choir room, youth lounge, more classroom space and additional rest rooms. The new facility was consecrated by Bishop Robert C. Morgan on 26 October 1986.

MAGNOLIA *(Clarke County: Highway 513 West, Enterprise 39330)*. The church was organized in 1870.

MAGNOLIA FIRST *(Pike County: 110 East Main, Magnolia 39652)*. The family of Peter Felder Sr. came from South Carolina in 1810 and settled on Tangipahoa Creek

Magnolia First United Methodist Church

about a mile and a half from the present location of Magnolia. The next year a Methodist camp meeting was held near Magnolia. Uncertainty exists in regard to the church to which pioneer settlers in this vicinity belonged. In 1856, the railroad station opened at Magnolia. Less than two months after the first train arrived, Ansell H. Prewett and his second wife, Lucinda Barron Prewett, gave a deed on 4 June 1856, to the trustees of the Methodist Church for an acre and a half of land. The first building was constructed either that year or in 1857.

MAIN STREET *(Forrest County: 712 North Main Street, Hattiesburg 39401)*. Main Street United Methodist Church dates its beginnings to one year after the city of Hattiesburg was founded, the year 1883. Over the years the congregation grew to become the largest Methodist church in the Hattiesburg area. Today Main Street is still one of the largest, and is certainly the most richly varied United Methodist congregation in the area.

MAIN STREET *(Hancock County: 162 Main Street, Bay Saint Louis 39520)*. Shieldsboro, now Bay Saint Louis, was know as a preaching place as early as 1842. This church was organized in 1852 and

Main Street United Methodist Church, Bay Saint Louis

services were held in a small building at the corner of Main and Second Streets on property given by John V. Toulme for a church. Records show that the church was known as Saint John's Methodist Church in 1859. The present church building was erected in 1895. The church building was not completed until near the turn of the century. In 1896 the people were worshipping for the second year in an uncompleted building which had no windows or doors. Although the building was dedicated by Bishop Charles B. Galloway in 1897, the year a disastrous fire destroyed about half the town; records also show that in 1900 the new building was wired for electricity. In 1936 a six-classroom annex was constructed at the rear of the present sanctuary; and in 1941 Mr. A. C. Exnicious gave to the church a plot of land adjoining the building lot. Five years later the church purchased from Mr. Exnicious a two-story building which was used for educational purposes. In the 1950s the annex building was renovated and enlarged. Recently, the church constructed a new annex.

MALLALIEU *(Jones County: 1114 North Joe Wheeler Street, Laurel 39440)*. The church was organized in 1905.

MALLALIEU *(Lauderdale County: 2322 Martin Luther King Drive, Meridian 39301)*. This church was organized in 1905.

MALLALIEU *(Lincoln County: 1806 Bassonette Lane SE, Brookhaven 39601)*. This church was organized in 1904.

MALLALIEU *(Sunflower County: 601 North Delmar, Ruleville 38771)*. The church was organized in 1904.

MALLALIEU *(Union County: 410 Apple Street, New Albany 38652)*.

Mamie C. Weaver United Methodist Church

MAMIE C. WEAVER MEMORIAL *(Wayne County: Five Mamie Weaver Avenue, Waynesboro 39367)*. This church was organized in 1920. The church was once known as Chapperall Methodist Church. It was located on Chapperall Pleasant Grove Road until 1979, when the present sanctuary was erected.

MANTACHIE *(Itawamba County: 5905 N. Church Highway, Mantachie 38855)*.

MAPLE SPRING *(Winston County: Highway Fifteen South, Louisville 39339)*.

MAPLES MEMORIAL *(DeSoto County: Olive Branch 38654)*. This church was organized in 1849.

MARIETTA *(Prentiss County: 16 County Road 4060, Marietta 38856)*.

MARION *(Lauderdale County: Marion 39342)*. This church was organized in 1820.

MARKS *(Quitman County: 400 East Main, Marks 38646)*. The first church, a small frame building on Elm Street, was organized in 1879. It had no pews; worshippers sat on planks laid across nail kegs. After this building was destroyed by a storm in 1897, services were held under the trees on River Front until a frame building was constructed in 1904. The church was also used as a school. This building was torn down and plans were made in 1919 to build a new church on Main Street. Financial problems delayed this project until 1923, and Methodists worshipped with the Presbyterians or in the courthouse until a frame church was built. In 1934, the Methodists bought the building formerly used by the Riverside Baptists and converted the old church into a parsonage. In 1950, construction began on the present church building. Services were held in the community house until the present building was completed in 1952. The old frame parsonage was then replaced by a brick building. Two brothers, Jack S. Smith Jr. and Gorton Smith, sons of Mrs. Helen Gorton Smith and the late Jack S. Smith, have entered the ministry from the Marks Church. The Marks Church has been in the Greenwood and Sardis Districts. It has also been a part of the Marks-Lambert and Marks-Belen-Darling Charges.

MARS HILL *(Wilkinson County: 7417 Old Highway Sixty-One, Crosby 39633).* The church was organized in 1859.

MARS HILL *(Neshoba County: Philadelphia 39350).* The church was organized in 1885.

MARS HILL *(Scott County: Forest 39074).*

MARTIN GROVE *(Carroll County: Route One West 39192).* The church was organized in 1883.

MARVIN *(Rankin County: 211 North Church Street, Florence 39073).* The church was organized in 1877. There have been two frame buildings. The first building was constructed in 1887, and the present building was erected in 1904. Additions were completed in 1954 and 1969. The administration building was added in 1982, and the educational unit was completed in 1995.

MARVIN CHAPEL *(Attala County: Old Natchez Trace Road 2247, Kosciusko 39090).* A number of the early settlers were Lutheran, and the community was known as East Union for the old East Union Church, built before the 1860s. As the population shifted, the Methodists, under the leadership of Reverend T. A. S. Adams, organized a church in 1876, called Marvin Chapel. Many of the Lutherans transferred their membership. The chapel was named for Bishop Marvin of the Methodist Episcopal Church. The school maintained the name East Union.

MASHULAVILLE *(Noxubee County: Mashulaville, Macon 39347).* This church was organized in 1857.

MATHISTON *(Webster County: Horton Street, Mathiston 39752).*

MATTHEWS CHAPEL *(Copiah County: 482 Mount Zion Road NW, Wesson 39191).* The church was organized in 1889.

MATTSON *(Coahoma County: Mattson 38758).* On 3 March 1913, Mrs. S. E. Calloway deeded to George P. Hodges and J. L. Ragan, trustees of the Mattson Methodist Church, a plot of land for the purpose of erecting a preaching place and house of worship. Ten years before, Ragan Hodges, and Doctor Glass purchased the town, which had been a lumbering operation. A community had developed around this stop on the railroad. Most of the families, including other denominations, attended the Mattson Church. In 1913, the Dublin Circuit was formed, with the Dublin pastor serving Mattson. In 1924, the appointment became known as "Dublin and Mattson." In 1975, these two churches were placed on a charge with Tutwiler.

MAXIE *(Forrest County: 46 Maxie Church Road, Wiggins 30577).* This church was organized in 1908.

MCADAMS *(Attala County: Road 4167, McAdams 39107).* This community was organized in the 1840s, and named for the son of a Primitive Baptist preacher. On 15 September 1878, a deed was conveyed by Reuben Coleman, which called for two acres of land to be used for a church site and cemetery for Hurricane Methodist Church, about four miles from Kosciusko on old Sand Road. This property was re-deeded in 1904 by Zack Bailey, and in 1911 by E. T. McCrory. In 1892, Hurricane Methodist moved and rebuilt three miles west, and changed its name to Clear Branch Methodist Church. In 1900, Clear Branch moved back to the original site and changed its name back to Hurricane

Methodist Church. In 1912, the members again decided to relocate, because the majority of members then lived at McAdams. The church was placed on the Sallis Circuit. Mr. J. E. Poole deeded one acre near the old McAdams school for the church site. The congregation worshipped in the school during construction of the church. In 1920, the school moved to the site of the Attala County Agricultural High School, so once again the church decided to move. On 28 April 1925, the Quarterly Conference gave authority to build the new church at its present location. A lot was deeded on 30 April 1926, by D. McMillan, to McAdams Methodist Church. The congregation was given permission to remove timber from the Pleasant Hill Church site to raise money for the building. The new church was dedicated in the Fall of 1927. The congregation outgrew this building, and in 1954 tore down the old building. They replaced it with another church building, which was dedicated 20 February 1955.

MCCARLEY *(Carroll County: McCarley Road, McCarley 38943).* This community emerged as the result of the coming of the railroad in 1887. The Methodist church was organized in 1896. There have been two buildings. The first frame building was constructed in 1898. The second and present building was constructed in 1932.

MCCONDY *(Chickasaw County: Highway Forty-Seven North, McCondy 39854).* McCondy is a very old community, dating back to 1836, and named for its first settler, Andrew McCondy. The church was organized on the fourth Sunday of June 1882, when the Methodist preacher from Buena Vista Charge, consisting of five

churches, preached at a schoolhouse near McCondy. The congregation rapidly built an arbor, and after a two week protracted meeting, one hundred people were added to the church. Benjamin Neal deeded property to the Methodist Church on 29 August 1882. The church was first known as Ebenezer. There have been two buildings: the first was made of clapboard in 1882; the second was made of brick in 1941. An annex was erected in 1963.

MCCOOL *(Attala County: McCool 39108).* This community was settled about 1878, and was known as Barksdale until 1883, when the name was changed to McCool in honor of Judge James F. McCool. The Methodist church was founded in 1847, and a new sanctuary and education unit were built in 1924.

MCDONALD *(DeSoto County).* This church was organized in 1889.

MCDONALD *(Leake County: 5379 Utah Road, Lena 39094).* The church was organized in 1942. There has been only one frame building, erected in 1942. The church added a fellowship hall.

MCDONALD *(Pontotoc County: 194 College Street, Pontotoc 38863).* The McDonald Church was organized in 1864, by three missionaries. The church was originally located on what is now Main Street in the downtown section of Pontotoc, but was rebuilt in 1926, on College Street. The church was built on land donated by Judge Bradford who was also one of the founding fathers. Three persons have entered the ministry from McDonald: A. W. Wright, David Lee High, and Cora Givhan Ford.

MCGOWAN CHAPEL *(Clarke County: Hale, Quitman 39355).* The church was organized in 1857.

MCLAIN *(Perry County: McLain).*
MCLAURIN *(Forrest County: Old Forty-Nine East, McLaurin 39401).* This church was organized in 1880.

McLaurin Heights United Methodist Church

MCLAURIN HEIGHTS *(Rankin County: 325 Mary Ann Drive, Pearl 39208).* McLaurin Heights was organized in December 1959. The first building was constructed in 1960. An education building was added in 1970. The present brick building was erected in 1993.

MCNAIR *(Franklin County: Oldenburg McNair Road, Roxie 39661).* The church was organized between 1813 and 1876.

MEADOW CREEK *(Prentiss County: Booneville 38829).* This church was organized in 1943.

MEADVILLE *(Franklin County: 101 South First Street, Meadville 39653).* The church was organized in 1901.

MELLEN *(Kemper County: Lynville).* The church was organized in 1892.

MEMORIAL *(Hinds County: 102 Church Street, Bolton 39041).* Bolton community was settled in 1830 and named for Colonel T. J. Bolton. In 1868, Joel Reynolds, William McNiel, Doctor Robert Dameron, Joe Peebles, and William Kelly pioneered the movement to establish a Methodist church in the village of Bolton.

Four years later, in February 1872, the Dameron family donated a parcel of land for this purpose. The church, apparently located on the deeded property, had been a Union church and was jointly owned by the Episcopal, Baptist, Methodist, and Presbyterian denominations. After the Methodists received the deed to the land, they purchased the old church structure, but continued to let it serve as a Union church. In 1903, the old church structure was remodeled. The new brick church was occupied in 1922. The church has beautiful stained glass windows.

Mendenhall United Methodist Church

MENDENHALL *(Simpson County: 331 Ash Street, Mendenhall 39114).* Prior to the building of the main line of the railroad, about 1900, there was no town or Methodist Episcopal Church at Mendenhall. Methodists of the neighborhood held membership in a church at Jones Branch, near the present site of Meritt, on the Westville Circuit. Reverend H. T. Carley was sent to serve Simpson Circuit for the conference year of 1902 to 1903. Mendenhall was a part of this circuit. The church record contains the names of twelve persons as its original members. In 1902, during the one-year pastorate of Reverend Carley, twelve more people were received into church membership. The first building was constructed in 1909. It was a frame structure, and faced Pine Street. The second and present building was constructed in 1929. The fellowship hall was added in 1959 and 1960.

MERIGOLD *(Bolivar County: South Church Street, Merigold 38759).* This community was founded in 1884 by Frank Merigold. It incorporated in 1902. The Methodist church was organized between 1896 and 1902.

MERRILL CHAPEL *(Pearl River County: South Shivers Street, Poplarville 39470).*

MIDDLETON *(Winston County: Vernon).* This church was founded in 1893.

MIDWAY *(Carroll County: Vaiden 39176).* The church was organized in the 1850s.

MIDWAY *(Jackson County: 10000 Highway Ninety East, Pascagoula 39581).* The church organized 22 May 1994, when the former Orange Grove and Pecan United Methodist Churches merged to form Midway United Methodist Church. Pecan Methodist's building dated back to 1899 when it was used as a schoolhouse. It was deeded to the Methodist Church in 1939. The former Orange Grove Methodist Church was organized in 1894. The new Midway building was erected in 1994, and dedicated in April 1997 by Bishop Marshall Meadors.

MIDWAY *(Lafayette County: 719 Highway Six East, Oxford 38655).* Midway was organized in 1856.

MIDWAY *(Yazoo County: Highway 433, Benton 39039).* In the Fall of 1828, Reverend John G. Jones brought Methodism to Yazoo County. That year a circuit was formed called Yazoo Circuit and for several years the pastors of the circuit on

their way from the neighborhood of Phoenix to the Ebenezer Church and community in Holmes County, stopped at Manchester (Yazoo City) and preached to a small group of interested prospective Methodists. In 1836 a church was formed in Yazoo City with Reverend A. J. S. Harris as the pastor, and that Fall a new circuit was formed called the Benton, Manchester Circuit with Jeptha Hughes as pastor. On 31 August 1857, Adamson Waters deeded property for Midway Church to the trustees of Yazoo Circuit of the Methodist Episcopal Church, South. The first preacher for Midway was probably Reverend Robert W. Lambuth, pastor in charge at the Yazoo City Church, or Reverend Humphrey Williamson, pastor in charge of the Yazoo Circuit. Reverend D. W. Wiggins was the presiding elder. William L. King and Adamson Waters started a movement to build a church. The original building is the chapel, and was built in 1858 and 1859. All building materials in the church were made by hand labor and put in place. In earlier days, the pulpit was in the rear of the church, in reverse order from today, with a slave quarter for the Blacks in the back of the church.

MILITARY *(Lowndes County: Military Road, Steens 39766).* The church was organized in 1872.

MINERAL WELLS *(DeSoto County: Mineral Wells 38648).* This church was organized in 1892.

MINOR MEMORIAL *(DeSoto County: 6930 Poplar Corner Road, Walls 38680).* In 1889, a group of women from the Poplar Corner community, under the leadership of Mrs. C. T. Knight, cleaned out an old

Minor Memorial United Methodist Church

weather-beaten saloon on the northwest corner of Goodman Road and Poplar Corner. They placed some old benches in it and organized a Sunday School. On 27 November 1893, they purchased one acre of land, which is the present site of the church. The first church, a white clapboard frame building consisting of a sanctuary and three classrooms, was completed in 1894, and was known as Poplar Corner Methodist Church. This church was a branch of Stephensons Chapel Methodist Church which belonged to the Memphis Conference of the Methodist Episcopal South, and the first minister who served it was a circuit rider. Several years later, the church became part of Mississippi Methodist Conference and was placed on a charge along with Horn Lake and Hind's Chapel. In 1935, Henry Dent Minor, who was superintendent of the Sunday School and the Bible Class teacher, began making plans to build a new brick church in memory of his wife, Florence Frayser Minor. His nephew, Lucian Minor Dent, who was an architect, designed the plans

for the church making it similar to a colonial chapel on the campus of the University of Virginia. The new Minor Memorial Methodist Episcopal Church, South, was dedicated on 10 May 1936. At the June 1981, session of the North Mississippi Annual Conference, Minor Memorial was named "The Outstanding Church of the Conference for 1980." The Cecil Williamson Ministry gave the church the Evangelistic Award of the Year.

MINTER CITY *(Leflore County: River Road North, Minter City 38944)*. The Minter City United Methodist Church is a white stucco structure located just north of Highway Eight on the banks of the Tallahatchie River cut-off in Minter City. The parsonage for the church is a red brick home just south of Highway Eight, also on the banks of the Tallahatchie. The Minter City Church is a part of a yoked relationship with Schlater Church several miles to the southwest. The pastor also serves the Phillip Presbyterian-United Methodist Union Church seven miles to the east, just off Highway Eight in the town of Phillip. The town of Minter City has been served by Methodist circuit riders since before the Civil War, when the town was named Walnut Grove. The first permanent church structure was erected in either 1866 or 1868, and served as a Union church in which Methodists, Baptists, Presbyterians, Episcopalians, and some others, worshipped together. This early fellowship soon became a Methodist church since the community had been able to arrange for a circuit rider to visit on a regular basis. Since its formation, the Minter City Church has been a part of the Grenada District, the Winona

District, and finally the Greenwood District of The United Methodist Church. The original church structure, after having been damaged by a tornado and fire in 1904, was replaced in that year with the present sanctuary structure. Perhaps the most noteworthy feature of the present church is the beautiful stained glass window at the front. This window, entitled, "Garden of Gethsemane," is flanked by a similar one on the south side entitled, "The Good Shepherd."

MISSISSIPPI CITY *(Harrison County: 219 Courthouse Road, Gulfport Road 39507).* Methodists along the Gulf Coast, including the Mississippi City area, were first served by a circuit rider stationed at Pearlington in the early 1800s. By the early 1840s, Methodists met in the old Mississippi City railroad station, the first wooden school building, and in the old Harrison County Courthouse located on the corner of Courthouse Road and Sixteenth Street near the church, later replaced with the brick building now being restored. In February 1898, an article in the *Mississippi Advocate* appeared begging "every preacher within the bounds of the Mississippi, North Mississippi and Louisiana Conferences to donate ten cents to aid in the building of a Methodist Church in the town of Mississippi City." A lot was donated by W. G. Evans Jr., son of a prominent Methodist minister, in October 1898. This lot is located two blocks east of the present church. The church building, a white frame structure with steeple and bell was completed in 1899, and moved to the Courthouse Road location in 1950. The church was linked with other churches

along the Coast from Ocean Springs to Bay Saint Louis from time to time by the charge system and served by twenty-nine ministers up to the years 1951 to 1952, when the church became a full station. The first service was held in the present building on 2 October 1960.

MIZE *(Smith County: Highway Thirty-Five, Mize 39116).* This church was organized in 1903.

MONTEREY *(Rankin County: 731 Highway 469 North, Richland 39208).* The church was organized in 1900.

MONTICELLO *(Lawrence County: 130 Broad Street, Monticello 39654).* The church was organized in 1810.

MONTROSE *(Jasper County: County Road 20, Montrose 39338).* The church was organized in 1857.

MOODY'S CHAPEL *(Perry County).* This church was organized in 1882.

MOORE MEMORIAL *(Montgomery County: 201 Magnolia Street, Winona 38967).* This church traces its heritage to the Methodist society at Old Middleton, Reverend William Mounger was the first minister. There is no record of the exact date of the move to Winona where the congregation worshipped in the Baptist Church sanctuary, apparently for several years. In 1871 the Methodist Church erected a frame building on the present plot donated by Colonel O. J. Moore, who was called the father of the town. In 1898 a brick building of Gothic style, the present building, was built on the original land. On Christmas Day, 1898, the cornerstone was laid. The official board passed this resolution: "Resolved, that as a token of our high appreciation of the long and devoted service of our departed brother, Colonel O. J. Moore, that the church shall be known as Moore Memorial." Many important conferences were held at Moore Memorial during the early years. It was during one of these conferences that the idea for establishing a Methodist College was conceived. Winona was considered as a setting, but Jackson was selected as a central location, and in 1892, Millsaps College became a reality. In 1948 the church was in need of extensive repair and renovation was made. In March 1959 the congregation voted to purchase the David L. Webster property directly across from the church. It was called the Fellowship House and was to be used as a Sunday School, education building, and future church expansion. A modern brick parsonage was built in 1967.

MOOREVILLE *(Lee County: Highway 371 South, Mooreville 38857).* This church was organized in 1850.

MOOREHEAD *(Sunflower County: 603 Olive Street, Moorehead 38761).* The church was organized in 1904.

MORTON *(Scott County: 29 Second Street, Morton 39117).* Morton does not appear in the list of appointments until 1870, but it is certain that a church was formed here soon after the railroad went through in 1860. Methodism came to Scott County in 1836, when the first church of the denomination was organized by Elizah Steele in the home of Jesse McKay, a few miles west of Hillsboro. In a letter dated 27 August 1966, Doctor Cain wrote, "I am enclosing a list of the District Superintendents as well as pastors of Morton, following the conference of 1877. The Morton Church had been in existence for some fifteen years

before that." Directly after Sherman burned the courthouse at Hillsboro, the town of Morton was surveyed by a man named Whitfield, who compiled a map, showing a plot of property where Morton's water tank is now located, listing it as church grounds. The date of this map is about 1865. The Methodist congregation, described as few in number, but most devout and spiritual, must have used this location, conducting worship in the "old Academy," an impressive old building with stone pillars. Among the old members were Doctor Moore's family, the Cook family, Barnes family, and Flanagan family. Morton was first listed in the appointments of the Brandon District in the year 1870. The first pastor of record was Reverend Claiborne McDonald. He was appointed to the Morton Circuit in 1870, lived about six miles southwest of Morton, and was pastor to the Morton congregation and itinerant preacher to Methodist people in the surrounding territory. Prior to 1870, Morton was part of an even larger itinerant circuit, and was served by a pastor from the Brandon District. From 1915 to 1932, the Morton Church was served by the pastor at Forest. In 1958, the present building on Second Avenue was constructed.

MOSELLE *(Jones County: 1059 Old Highway Eleven, Moselle 39459).* This church was organized in 1912.

MOSES CHAPEL *(Tippah County: 11199 Highway Four East, Ripley 38663).* Moses Chapel was established 26 August 1884, by Mose and Jennie Cox. Mose and his wife journeyed here after the Civil War from South Carolina. They purchased the spot of land and built a church, which was named Moses Chapel Methodist Episcopal Church but later became United Methodist. The name of the first pastor is unknown. The original church was destroyed by fire or storm and another was built. This still stands on the hill. Additions have been made. The Moses Chapel community also had a school to educate their children. This school later merged with other schools. In 1983 to 1984 the church received the "Most Improved Church of the Year" award. Mose and Jennie Cox are the oldest tombstones in the church's cemetery.

MOUNT CARMEL *(Alcorn County: Wenasaga Road, Corinth 38834).* Mount Carmel United Methodist Church is one of the oldest in Alcorn County. In 1973, the one hundredth birthday of this church was celebrated with dinner and singing with several former pastors being present. The church was moved to the present site on Wenasaga Road in 1916, two or three miles southeast of the original building. Since then Sunday School rooms were built, and the church was bricked.

MOUNT CARMEL *(Wayne County: 400 South Spring Street, Waynesboro 39367).* This church was organized in 1888.

MOUNT CARMEL *(Wilkinson County: 1694 Mount Carmel Road, Gloster 39638).* The church was organized in 1855.

MOUNT EVERGREEN *(Tishomingo County: 253 County Road 244, Iuka 38852).*

MOUNT HEBRON *(Kemper County: Tamola).* This church was organized in 1856.

MOUNT HEBRON *(Winston County: Preston 39354).* This church was founded in 1887.

MOUNT HERMON *(Choctaw County: Pine Highway, Ackerman 39735).* Mount Hermon Methodist Church was organized and located in a section of Ackerman known as "K. C. Town" in the 1890s where dense forest hindered its landscaping beauty. Due to the congested and woody area, a growing desire for a permanent location and a better house of worship culminated in the purchase of the present site. With the proper procedure, the site was acquired by warranty deed, and a beautiful frame structure was erected. The pastor, members, and friends of the community felt the need of a building and made personal sacrifices to meet financial obligations. Years later, this structure was destroyed by fire. During the span of time, another house of worship was built under the pastorate of Reverend Jesse Burton. Disaster came again in 1919, when this building was destroyed by a storm that took the lives of several persons. As time passed, this structure was rebuilt and repaired on several occasions. In 1958, under the pastorate of Reverend J. H. Ashford, the church was completely remodeled. The present structure was completed in 1975, under Reverend J. W. Campbell.

MOUNT JORDAN *(Clarke County: Highway Eighteen West, Pachuta 39347).* This church was organized in 1865.

MOUNT LEBANON *(Attala County: Ethel 39067).* The church was organized in 1884. The present brick building was constructed in 1984.

MOUNT LEVY *(Clarke County: Matherville).*

MOUNT MORIAH *(Alcorn County: 1108 Meigg Street, Corinth 38834).* This church was organized in 1866.

MOUNT MORIAH *(Noxubee County: Route Four, Macon 39341).* This church was organized in 1886.

MOUNT MORIAH *(Webster County: County Road 128, Mathiston 39752).* The exact date the church was organized is unknown, but it was in the 1800s.

MOUNT NEBO *(Pontotoc County: Pontotoc 38863).* The first church building for Mount Nebo Methodist Church was built in 1876. All of the first settlers to this community were slaves and their services were held in the homes. Two acres of land were deeded to the trustees of Mount Nebo Methodist Church. During that stormy period, there was much confusion, and the books were lost in a cyclone. Two schoolhouses were also blown away by cyclones. The church was called Mount Nebo Methodist Church in 1876, and later in 1974, it was changed to Mount Nebo United Methodist Church.

MOUNT NEBO *(Prentiss County: 101 County Road 3350, Booneville 38829).* In 1835, an Indian named "Jerry" donated the first land to Mount Nebo Church. It was about one mile north of the present location and known as Bluff Springs. In 1895, Mount Nebo was built at its present location. About one hundred years ago the present church building was constructed. Through the years it has been lovingly cared for and improved. Today, the same handmade benches that have been in the church for over a century are still being used as pews.

MOUNT OLIVE *(Chickasaw County).*

MOUNT OLIVE *(Clarke County: Carmichael).* This church was organized in 1900.

MOUNT OLIVE *(Covington County: 311 South Main Street, Mount Olive 39119).* The church was organized in 1871.

MOUNT OLIVE *(Franklin County: Kirby).* This church was founded in 1850.

MOUNT OLIVE *(Itawamba County: Route One, Tremont 38876).* According to available records, Mount Olive Methodist Episcopal Church, South, bought two acres of land from G. B. Gray on 6 January 1891. According to old church records, Mr. and Mrs. Barnes were among the first members. Elick Patton for whom Patton Flat was named, was baptized on 29 September 1891, by Isaac Raper, the first pastor. In 1897, there were forty-six members, with H. C. Parrot as pastor. There have been two buildings. The first one was torn down and a new one built in 1955.

MOUNT OLIVE *(Jasper County: Hero).* The church was organized in a year unknown, but it was in the 1800s.

MOUNT OLIVE *(Jones County: 8 Arthur Tucker Road, Ovett 39464).* This church was organized in 1902.

MOUNT OLIVET *(Panola County: Sardis 38666).* On 10 May 1873, land was acquired from A. R. Wilson for Mount Olivet Methodist Church. Three church buildings have been erected on this site. The first building, which was a log structure, evidently was erected many years before the land was deeded. The building was replaced by a frame building about the year 1878. It was about the year 1950, that the present building was made possible, and additional classrooms, and a kitchen were added. A foyer was added in 1981. The bricking of the church was started in 1984, and paid for by 1985. Mount Olivet has had the honor of sending out six ministers: J. R. Wilson, R. G. A. Carlisle, W. C. Carlisle, J. A. George, E. B. Wilson, and Ellis Palmertree.

MOUNT OLIVET *(Union County: County Road 151, Mount Olivet Community, New Albany 38652).* Mount Olivet was organized in 1854.

MOUNT OLIVET *(Yazoo County: 3785 Highway 433 West, Bentonia 39040).* The first people to settle in what is known as the Mechanicsburg community were devout Christians. The church may have existed as early as 1829, meeting in homes. On 5 July 1851, Elijah Wasson deeded two and a half acres for a church site. The church was named Mount Olivet. It first appeared in the Conference appointments in 1857. In 1873, forty-five adults were baptized. A new church was dedicated 29 May 1884. This church served the congregation until another was needed in 1947, which was dedicated 5 February 1950 by Bishop Marvin Franklin.

MOUNT PISGAH *(Chickasaw County: 119 Gatlin Street, Okolona 38860).* Mount Pisgah Methodist Church was established in 1867. The Board of Missions made a contribution to the erection of an early church. The first appointment was left to be supplied. Mount Pisgah was the first Black church in Okolona and opened its doors to be used as the first school for Black children to attend. The first teacher was Mrs. Fannie Carter. Services were held three times on Sundays, Sunday morning service, afternoon women's service, and evening service. The present building was constructed and completed by 29 August 1896, under the pastorate of Reverend N. B. Clay. Mount Pisgah, now a charge in the Tupelo District, was once in the Holly Springs, and later in the Aberdeen District. There has been one young man to enter

the ministry from Mount Pisgah, George Legion Kendrick.

MOUNT PISGAH *(Winston County: Mount Pisgah Road, Noxapater 39346).* The church was organized in 1882.

MOUNT PLEASANT *(Copiah County: 3092 Old Highway Twenty-Seven, Crystal Springs 39059).* The church was organized in 1847.

MOUNT PLEASANT *(George County: Route One, Beaumont 39423).*

MOUNT PLEASANT *(Harrison County: Rippy Road, Gulfport 39507).*

MOUNT PLEASANT *(Hinds County: 2590 Maddox Road, Jackson 39209).* This church was organized in 1922.

MOUNT PLEASANT *(Itawamba County: Tremont 38876).* This church was already a close congregation working together in 1844, so it is presumed to be several years older than that. The very first building was a pine log church with seats made out of logs. The next building was built up the hill from that site, where the cemetery is now. The cemetery was started behind this second building, which was also a pine log church that burned down later. The third building, a wooden structure with glass windows, was used as both church and school. This third building also burned. A fourth building was constructed by the people, as the first three had been. This one was also used as a community school. This building also burned. The people of the community built a small wood structure in about a week to get the children back in school and this structure was used until the present church was built. The fifth building is the present one. The best date that can be put together for the construction of this building is about 1930.

MOUNT PLEASANT *(Jackson County: Mount Pleasant Road, Vancleave 39565).* This church was organized in 1850.

MOUNT PLEASANT *(Jefferson County: Highway Twenty-Eight East, Gravel Hill Road, Fayette 39069).* The church was organized in 1876.

MOUNT PLEASANT *(Kemper County: Route One, DeKalb 39320).* On 15 March 1881, Needham Jackson, "for and in consideration of the love and affection I have for the Protestant Methodist as a Christian denomination," gave property to the trustees of Mount Pleasant Church in Kemper County. The deed mentions a church building in existence at that time. Willie A. Jackson, son of Needham Jackson, built a new church about 1896. Another building was built between 1968 and 1969.

MOUNT PLEASANT *(Marshall County: Mount Pleasant 38649).* Prior to 1853, Mount Pleasant Charge consisted of four churches with New Salem, Marshall Institute, and Union. New Salem closed, and Union and Marshall Institute merged with Mount Pleasant Methodist, making Mount Pleasant a station church. The old parsonage of the 1890s was sold and in 1945, a new one was constructed. In the early fifties an addition of education rooms and a kitchen was added. On 1 March 1959, the new pews, organ, and memorial windows were dedicated by Bishop Marvin Franklin The oldest stone in the Mount Pleasant Cemetery is of Mrs. Nancy Person, born 1796, died 1883.

MOUNT PLEASANT *(Rankin County: 1650 Holly Bush Road, Pelahatchie 39145).* This church was organized in 1900.

MOUNT PLEASANT *(Tippah County: Route Three, Walnut 38683).* Mount Pleasant was organized in 1895.

MOUNT PLEASANT *(Yazoo County: Deasonville Road, Vaughan 39179).* This church dates back to the days after the Civil War. The Berry family gave the tenants on their land a plot of land to build a church. This building was destroyed in a storm. The members bought a plot across from the first church. In 1892, they built a second church. The present structure was built in 1917 on the same foundation. The church was renovated in 1976, and a fellowship hall was added in 1995.

MOUNT SALEM *(Hinds County: 11151 Springridge Road, Jackson 39204).* The church was organized in 1880.

MOUNT SALEM *(Lauderdale County: 1010 Forty-Fourth Avenue, Meridian 39301).*

MOUNT SINAI *(Copiah County).* The church was organized in 1870.

MOUNT VERNON *(Attala County: Kosciusko 39090).* This church was organized in 1877. A new sanctuary was constructed in 1921.

MOUNT VERNON *(Amite County: Mount Vernon Road).* This church was organized in 1835.

MOUNT VERNON *(Tate County: Looxahoma).*

MOUNT ZION *(Clarke County: Quitman 39355).*

MOUNT ZION *(Harrison County: 7436 Labouy Road, Pass Christian 39571).* This church, located in the Delisle community, was organized in 1892.

MOUNT ZION *(Holmes County: Lexington 39095).*

MOUNT ZION *(Jasper County: Bay Springs 39422).*

MOUNT ZION *(Jasper County: Sandersville 39477).* The church was organized in the 1850s.

MOUNT ZION *(Jefferson Davis County: Mount Carmel Road, Mount Carmel).* This church was organized in 1817.

MOUNT ZION *(Jones County: 652 Graves Road, Ellisville 39437).* This church was organized in 1903.

MOUNT ZION *(Montgomery County: Kilmichael 39747).*

MOUNT ZION *(Neshoba County: Philadelphia 39350).* Mount Zion is located about eight miles east of Philadelphia. The first community building constructed at Mount Zion was the log church, in the early 1880s. Before that there was a brush arbor church, constructed of pine poles covered with brush and pine straw. A "box" church made of vertically placed, rough-hewn timbers followed the log church, and in 1899 was replaced by a frame clapboard building that stood for sixty-five years. The latter burned in 1964, and the church was rebuilt and dedicated in 1966.

MOUNT ZION *(Newton County: Road 210, Union 39365).* The church group was started in 1861 under a brush arbor with a circuit riding preacher, Reverend W. B. Hines. In 1867, the first building was erected, with J. C. Houston and Mr. and Mrs. J. A. Williams as the first officers. This building moved the church services under a shelter, but the camp meetings continued for years afterward, so long that it was known as the Campground Methodist

Church until the middle of the twentieth century. This community was known as Beech Springs, with two churches, Ebeneezer Baptist and Campground Methodist. It boasted a school, a general store, operated by Mr. Oscar Williams, and, through the years, a Doctor Henderson and a Doctor Reagan. All the records of the early church have been destroyed. In 1918, the church was placed with Union and known as the Union Charge until 1957, when the church was grouped with Hope. In 1972 the church was returned to the Union Charge. The records were destroyed by fire, probably at someone's house. This church has given five young men to be preachers of the gospel: Clay Hillman, Edgar Hillman, Bernard Walton, Byrd Hillman Jr., and Lamar Jackson. Lamar became a Presbyterian minister. The current building is the third church building to be erected. The first was a few hundred feet west of the present location, but the second building was in the current site. The present building is built from material from the second church building.

MOUNT ZION *(Stone County: North Washington Road, McHenry 39561).* The church was organized in 1899. This church was formerly a Methodist Episcopal Church. The first building was a frame structure. The second frame structure was constructed between 1948 and 1949. The third and present building, also a frame structure, was completed in 1982. The second building was damaged by tornadoes spawned by Hurricane Camille in 1969.

MOUNT ZION *(Union County: County Road 227, Baldwyn 38824).* Mount Zion was organized in 1854.

MOUNT ZION *(Wayne County: Buckatunna 39322)*. This church was organized in 1903.

MOUNTAIN RIDGE *(Rankin County: 1773 Shiloh Road, Brandon 39042)*. The church dates back to 1867. Tradition states that it started under a brush arbor. Later a log cabin was built and then a California type building was constructed. The present Mountain Ridge United Methodist Church was founded in 1890. On 5 April 1905, forty acres of land were purchased, and a beautiful frame building was built. This was destroyed by fire by an arsonist in 1909. Undaunted, two months later the church was ready for worship. However, in 1956 the church was burned again by an arsonist. It was rebuilt in 1959. The new building was a frame brick veneer building. The land was deeded to the nine trustees and their successors. From Mountain Ridge United Methodist Church have gone the following ordained ministers: Nelson Collier, Billie Collier, George Taylor, Prince Albert Taylor, Irvin Kersh, and John B. Randolph.

MYRTLE *(Union County: 1035 Church Street, Myrtle 38650)*. Myrtle was first known as Gerizim Methodist Church. Gerizim was located north of the present town of Myrtle. Mr. Johnson gave land for a church and cemetery where the cemetery is now located. The church was moved to the present site, and a new building constructed in 1888 to 1889. There have been three church buildings: one log; one frame; and one brick, erected in 1948. The first service in the new sanctuary was Easter Sunday, 1949. A fellowship hall, dedicated and named for L. H. "Bun" Coffey, was built in 1984, and a Christian Family Life Center was built in 1989. Deeds were recorded 29 December 1892, for the church, and 13 December 1906, for the parsonage.

NEBO *(Choctaw County: Weir 39772)*. This church was organized in 1893.

NEBO *(Greene County)*.

NEBO *(Noxubee County: Route Five, Shuqualak 39361)*.

NEBO *(Webster County: Highway Nine South, Eupora 39744)*. The exact date the church was organized is unknown, but it was in the 1800s.

NETTLETON *(Lee County: 60 Verona Avenue, Nettleton 38858)*. The Nettleton was established in 1890, under the leadership of B. T. Clark, I. E. Roberts, Riley Wiygul, and others. Services were held upstairs in the newly constructed post office building. The property on which the church still stands was deeded to the Nettleton Methodist Church by George Nettleton, President of the Memphis-Birmingham Railroad on 8 September 1891. In a short time, construction of a frame building began. Later Sunday School rooms were added to the front side of the building. In 1947, it became necessary to expand because of the increased membership. A two-story addition was made on the north and east side of the sanctuary At this time, the sanctuary was enlarged, bricked, and completely remodeled. Another education building was added south of the present one in 1955. Two additional rooms were added on the east end of the building in 1966. The sanctuary was beautified by adding stained glass windows during the years 1973 to 1976, in memory or in honor of loved ones.

New Albany First United Methodist Church

NEW ALBANY FIRST *(Union County: 207 East Bankhead, New Albany 38652).* The church was organized in 1874. Prior to that it had been a church on the Pontotoc Circuit before the North Mississippi Conference was created in 1870. Families met for worship in the Grange Hall. There were seven loyal Methodists who were charter members. Reverend Peter Fleming, a young Scotsman, was the pastor. A Sunday School was organized in January 1895. In 1876, the Methodists, Baptists, and Presbyterians, built a Union church where the Methodists worshipped until 1886, when they built their own church across from where the present church stands. Reverend D. W. Babb was pastor when the building program began, and it was completed under the pastorate of Reverend D. L. Cogdell. The present edifice was completed in 1928.

NEW AUGUSTA *(Perry County: New Augusta 39462).* This church was organized in 1904.

NEW BETHEL *(Monroe County).*

NEW BETHEL *(Walthall County).* The church was organized in 1927.

NEW BETHLEHEM *(Kemper County: Route Two, Dekalb 39328).* The church was organized in 1929.

NEW CHAPEL *(Itawamba County: 2965 New Chapel Road, Nettleton 38858).*

NEW CHAPEL *(Lee County).*

NEW CHAPEL *(Scott County: Trenton Road, Pulaski 39152).*

NEW COVENANT *(Hinds County: 5900 Terry Road, Jackson 39212).* The church was organized in 1995. Some years ago, the Terry and Byram Methodist Churches merged. When Byram closed, a new church was formed in 1995, called New Covenant. The first Methodist Church at Byram was originated around 1847 by a circuit riding preacher. This initial site was a log building at Red Hill, with permission granted to use the facility. By 1870 evidence shows the church relocated at Old Byram near the Pearl River. In 1902 the first church building was constructed, but was destroyed by a tornado in 1917. As a small church and part of a circuit pastor system, it was served by student pastors for twenty-five years. In 1973, Byram United Methodist Church became a station church served by one pastor. With the later expansion of the city of Jackson to the south the church merged with the Terry Church, along with plans to build a new and larger facility on Terry Road. On 24 December 1995 the first service was held in the new church on Terry Road under the new name of New Covenant United Methodist Church, under the pastorate of Scott Carter.

NEW COVENANT *(Lauderdale County: 6210 Highway Thirty-nine North, Meridian 39305).* This church was organized in 1991.

NEW FAITH *(Jones County: 978 South Fifteenth Avenue, Laurel 39440).* The church was organized in 1995.

NEW FAYARD CHAPEL *(Harrison County: 14900 Jim Ramsay Raod, Biloxi 38530).* The date of organization is not known. This church was once known as Few Fayard, and was located on Daisy Vestry Road. The wood frame building was destroyed by fire in 1960. The church then met in the home of George Cruthirds, and at the old community center until a new brick sanctuary was built on Jim Ramsay Road in 1964.

NEW FORK *(Franklin County: South Williams Street, Meadville 39653).*

NEW HARMONY *(Tippah County: 1761 County Road 615, Ripley 38663).* New Harmony was organized in 1915, by Reverend S. T. Ledbetter and Reverend Bill James at Smith School in Hatchie. Worship services and revivals were often held under brush arbors to accommodate the crowds who attended. The church was moved from the school to a hill near Hatchie on 1 September 1938, where a church building was erected. The original building was moved to a new location on the Pine Grove Road on 24 April 1961. The two acre lot was deeded to the church by J. B. Coltharp. Clear Creek Methodist merged with New Harmony at this time. New Harmony was on the Lowry Charge until 1964, when it was placed on the Dumas Charge. In June 1985, it was placed on the Lowry Charge again.

NEW HEBRON *(Lawrence County).* The church was organized in 1904

NEW HOPE *(Chickasaw County).* This church was founded in 1885.

NEW HOPE *(Chickasaw County).* This church, attached to the Okolona First United Methodist Church Charge was organized in 1866.

NEW HOPE *(Copiah County: 1114 Montgomery Lane, Wesson 39191).* The church was organized in 1864.

NEW HOPE *(Kemper County).*

NEW HOPE *(Kemper County).* This church was organized in 1869.

NEW HOPE *(Lincoln County: 2320 Highway 550, Brookhaven 39601).* The church was organized about 1860. The first frame building was constructed soon after organization and served the congregation until 1947, when a new brick church was constructed.

NEW HOPE *(Lowndes County: 2503 New Hope Road, Columbus 39702).* The church was organized in 1843.

NEW HOPE *(Monroe County).*

NEW HOPE *(Montgomery County: 393 New Hope Road, Winona 38967).* The church was organized in 1899. The land on which the church and cemetery are located was given on 19 November 1900, to the trustees of the Winona Circuit. The land was a gift from J. C. and Lucy Wright Williams. A tall white wooden church was built about this time. In 1966 a brick building was built to replace it. The first New Hope Church was built of logs and had poles down the middle to support it. This was located on the Bennett Place a couple of hills away from the place the present church now stands. There is an old cemetery near where the first church was located.

NEW HOPE *(Noxubee County).* This church was organized between 1885 and 1900.

NEW HOPE *(Tippah County: 781 County Road 717, Blue Mountain 38610).* This church was organized in 1883.

NEW HOPE (Wayne County: 271 Old River Road, Waynesboro 39367). The church was organized in 1881.

NEW HOPE *(Winston County: Highway Fourteen East, Louisville 39339).* This church was organized in 1870.

NEW HOPE MEMORIAL *(Marion County: 187 Highway Forty-three South, Columbia 39429).* The church was organized in 1866.

NEW LIGHT *(Oktibbeha County: Longview).*

NEW MOUNT ZION *(Clarke County).*

NEW POINT *(Monroe County: Route One, Becker 38825).*

NEW PROSPECT *(Oktibbeha County: 1983 Williams Road, Starkville 39759).*

NEW SALEM *(Monroe County).*

NEW ZION *(Copiah County: 101 West Piazza Street, Crystal Springs 39059).* The church was organized in 1864.

NEW ZION *(Greene County: McLain).* The church was organized in 1946.

NEW ZION *(Marion County: 21 East Marion School Road, Columbia 39429).* In the year of 1890, a group of people in the Lampton Community was organized by Reverend Paul Grumbsy as New Zion Methodist Episcopal Church. The building was a log cabin located at a site known as the Old Mash. Primitive as it was, this was the essential first step. The church was relocated to the present spot in 1892 under the ministry of Reverend Roundtree. One acre of land was given for the New Zion Lampton Church by Mr. and Mrs. Bacus Stepney. The building was a frame structure.

In 1901, the building was completed. In 1923, a brick building was constructed for worship. It was dedicated by Bishop R. E. Jones in 1924. In 1974 members of the New Zion United Methodist Church joined hands following the footsteps of the forefathers and foremothers with Reverend J. C. Killingsworth spreading God's ministry, completing the long task of the construction of a new church.

NEWTON CHAPEL *(Pearl River County: 5 Moore Road, Poplarville 39470).* Newton Chapel was named for Robert Newton, owner of a turpentine company. The church once met in a house owned by Richard Glover. The first building was constructed of logs and framed wood about 1920 or 1921. This building was destroyed by Hurricane Camille in August 1969. The second brick building was constructed in 1971. The cornerstone was laid 25 October 1970 by Reverend Porter Wynn.

Newton First United Methodist Church

NEWTON FIRST *(Newton County: 600 Decatur Street, Newton 39345).* The United Methodist Church in Newton was organized in 1865 and was made a part of the Garlandville Circuit. The preaching was done in an old hospital building and later in an old store building on the site of the present TWL store. A Sunday School for all residents of Newton was held in this building. The first church building was erected in 1867 on the corner of what is now East Church and Decatur Streets and consisted of one-room which was adequate for a small and young town during the hard years of reconstruction. For the next ninety years, Newton Methodists attended worship services at this location. The church was dedicated in 1868. It was repaired in 1893 and a larger steeple added, and it served until it was destroyed by fire in 1899. The membership began to plan at once to build a larger one-room edifice. On 13 July 1899, the cornerstone for this building was laid.

NORTH BEND *(Neshoba County: Owl Creek)*. The church was organized in 1853.

NORTH CARROLLTON *(Carroll County: 402 Williamson Street, North Carrollton 38947)*. In 1889, the railroad came through the area that was then known as Rathbone. When the town incorporated in 1899, it became known as North Carrollton. The church was organized in 1902. The first and only frame church building was constructed that year.

NORTH MAIN *(Yalobusha County: Water Valley 38965)*.

NORTHVIEW *(Warren County: Pemberton and Skyfarm Avenue, Vicksburg 39180)*. The church was organized 2 April 1950. The church was first known as Springfield, and occupied rented space. In 1955, the congregation purchased property, built a brick sanctuary in 1956, and became known as Northview United Methodist Church. An education building was added in 1960.

NOXAPATER *(Winston County: 218 Main Street, Noxapater 39346)*. The church was organized in 1875. The first structure was a wooden frame building, built in 1875. Mrs. J. B. Gunn gave the property for a second church building, constructed between 1911 and 1912. The third and present brick building was started in 1957, and completed in 1961. An annex was added in 1971.

NUGENT *(Harrison County: 13183 John Clark Road, Gulfport 39503)*. The church was organized 23 June 1895. There was a congregation of Methodists meeting prior to that time, but it was on that date that the church building was dedicated. Mr. Henry Beach Carre writing in the 1 August 1895, edition of the *New Orleans Christian Advocate* reported that the Saint Johns Methodist Episcopal Church, South, was dedicated. Doctor J. B. Walker, believed to be a retired pastor from New Orleans, was the driving force in getting the church built. He apparently donated land in the proximity of his residence and made provisions for the materials to be donated. The people of the church and community supplied the labor, and in due course a "plain country church" was completed. The church was furnished with one hundred forty-four chairs with the chancel furniture coming from the Carondelet Street Church in New Orleans. The original Saint Johns was to have a short life. The church burned on Sunday night, 10 February 1901. The whole church was lost, including an "excellent organ." Plans were made to rebuild on the same site. The exact site of the little church remains a mystery. In 1895, Reverend E. T. Breland was pastor of the Whittington Charge and served the Saint Johns Church. The Whittington

Charge was later renamed Coalville. It is generally believed that services were held in the Hudson School building which was adjacent to the church. The replacement for the burned church building is not reported to have been completed until April 1903. The church met in this new building until at least 1912 when the trustees of the Twenty-Ninth Street Charge of the Methodist Episcopal Church, South, purchased the present acre of land. The deeds show that the land was purchased from J. B. Clark for one dollar "as a place of Divine worship for the use of the ministry and membership of the Methodist Episcopal Church, South, at Saint Johns Church at Nugent, Mississippi." From this title record, the church could not have moved to the present site or taken the name Nugent prior to 7 October 1912.

OAK BOWERY *(Jasper County: Route One, Paulding 39439).* This church is located in the Waldrup area of Jasper County.

OAK GROVE *(Franklin County).* This church was organized in 1899.

OAK GROVE *(Franklin County: Route One, Union Church 39668).* This church was founded in 1868.

OAK GROVE *(Itawamba County).*

OAK GROVE *(Lamar County: 4914 Old Highway Eleven, Hattiesburg 39402).* The church was organized in 1936.

OAK GROVE *(Lauderdale County).* The church was organized in 1875.

OAK GROVE *(Tallahatchie County: Charleston 38921).* This church was organized in 1875.

OAK GROVE *(Walthall County: Mesa).* This church was organized in 1896.

OAK HILL *(Lee County: Route Two, Saltillo 38866).* Oak Hill was first a Union Church owned and controlled by the Methodist Episcopal Church, South; the Cumberland Presbyterians; and the Primitive Baptists. The first church deed was signed 11 October 1902. On 23 February 1903, a deed was drawn up that did away with the Union Church and, as the deed states, "It is to be owned and controlled by Oak Hill Church." The first church was a small wood frame building which stood until 1952. A new church was built with a large sanctuary and three small classrooms in the back. Oak Hill was on the Mooreville Charge. In 1955, Oak Hill joined with East Tupelo (now Saint Mark) to form the present charge. The first annex was built in 1961. In 1969, a second annex was added. A complete renovation was made to the sanctuary in 1973, with new pews added. In 1976, a foyer was added at the front entrance. On 14 January 1977, two acres of land were purchased for a possible future parsonage. In 1977, the entire building was bricked, and in 1978, a steeple was erected.

OAKDALE *(Jefferson Davis County: Oakdale Methodist Road, Seminary 39479).* This church was organized in 1936.

OAKLAND *(Yalobusha County: Oakland 38948).* The church was organized in 1838. The sanctuary was first constructed in 1838.

OAKLAND HEIGHTS *(Lauderdale County: Highway Nineteen North, Meridian 39307).* This church was organized in 1959.

OKOLONA FIRST *(Chickasaw County: Main Street at Olive, Okolona 38860).* The church was organized in the 1840s. Named for a Chickasaw chief, the

Okolona First United Methodist Church

community of Okolona had its start in 1845 with the advent of the railroad. The first Methodist church building was on Olive Street until 1908, when the present structure was erected. An addition was added in 1955. The church has a history room containing old rolls, records, and a book on the church's stained glass windows. The Prayer Life Movement worldwide began with the planting of a "Prayer Tree" on the lawn here.

OLD BAY SPRINGS *(Smith County: County Road, Soso 39480)*. This church was organized in 1894.

OLD BETHEL *(Tishomingo County: Red Bud Road, Golden 38847)*. Old Bethel United Methodist Church, located in the south end of Tishomingo County, was built in 1849, on a lot donated by Mr. and Mrs. Joseph Able to the Methodist Episcopal Church. In 1894, the log church was replaced by the present sanctuary. Old Bethel, the name chosen in 1849, was kept for the new building. In 1920, at the suggestion of "Aunt Tula" Montgomery, Reverend W. Bazzle organized the first Sunday School which met in the after-

noons. Bethany functioned as a sister Methodist Church a few years, but in 1940, the trustees deeded the land back, and Bethany's congregation combined with Old Bethel's. From a one-room log church with no windows in 1849, Old Bethel has evolved into a country haven for worship.

OREGON MEMORIAL *(Holmes County: Lexington 39095)*.

OSYKA *(Pike County: First Street, Osyka 39657)* The church was organized in 1894.

OVETT *(Jones County: Main Street, Ovett 39464)*. The church was organized in 1904.

Oxford University United Methodist Church

OXFORD UNIVERSITY *(Lafayette County: 424 South Tenth Highway, Oxford 38655)*. The Oxford University congregation was organized in 1836. The first church building was erected on a lot on Van Buren Avenue. The first building, erected in the fall of 1838, probably was a log structure. When the new church was opened, the pastor was A. J. S. Harris. On 4 July 1851, a new site was purchased on Jackson Avenue near the square, and a brick church building was erected. This church building burned in 1889, and the congregation erected a Gothic brick building on the site in 1890. A location on University Avenue was selected for a new facility, and the lot was bought in December of 1936. The new facility was occupied in 1937. The new sanctuary was built in 1950. The first service was held 21 May 1950. The new education building was completed in 1964, and was dedicated in 1965. In the Oxford Cemetery are the graves of L. Q. C. Lamar and General A. B. Longstreet.

OZARK *(Itawamba County: Kirkville).*

PACE *(Bolivar County: 201 Jenny Washington Avenue, Pace 38764).* This Bolivar County community was established in 1897 by George Arnold. Just five years later, on 18 September 1903, fifteen Methodists gathered in a farm house about five miles south of Pace and organized Pinson's Chapel Methodist Episcopal Church, South, also known to some as Kuhn Church. The first church was located four miles south of Pace in a frame building constructed in 1905. Another congregation in Pace, known as Arnold, joined Pinson's Chapel, which later disbanded and moved to Pace in 1915. The Methodists formed a Union church with the Baptists until 1941. The present building in Pace was constructed between 1941 and 1942. Dedication services were held 26 April 1942, with Bishop W. W. Peele in attendance.

PACHUTA *(Clarke County: Pachuta 39347).* This community was settled in 1882, and named for the Pachuta Creek. The Methodist church here was organized in 1889.

PAINE MEMORIAL *(Monroe County).*

PALESTINE *(Clay County: Route One, Pheba 39755).* Palestine is one of the oldest churches in Clay County. On 9 October

Palestine United Methodist Church, Pheba

1856, two acres of land were deeded to the congregation by A. O. Parker and his wife, Mary F. Foster. The first church was erected on this site, but the original site has become the present cemetery. Palestine is one of the oldest communities in Clay County. In September 1870, Palestine Methodist Episcopal Church was admitted to the North Mississippi Conference. The church was first served by Reverend William Belk, local pastor. In the early 1920s, Archie Murrah, a native of the Palestine community, deeded to the church the property where the present church building is located. A contract was drawn up by B. W. Aldridge, a contractor, in December of 1922 to tear down the old church and rebuild it on the new site, using the material from the old church. In 1967, under the pastorate of R. E. Wasson, the congregation began plans for a new church building. The church met for the first time in their new building on Easter Sunday, 1970. It was constructed next door to the old white frame building. The new building is red brick. On 10 October 1971, the formal dedication was held. Bishop Edward Pendergrass delivered the sermon and District Superintendent Archie Meadows presided.

PALESTINE *(Itawamba County: Ratliff).*
PALESTINE *(Lee County: Nettleton 38858).* This church was organized in 1880.
PALESTINE *(Pontotoc County: 2181 Palestine Road, Pontotoc 38863).* Campground Methodist Church was the mother church of Palestine. The following names were entered in the early "Clap Book of Palestine," as the first to move their membership to Palestine from Campground: Nelson G. Patterson, George A. Montgomery, Mary E. Patterson, Stansil Wood, and Louise Wood. Following is a description of Palestine's early years as a thriving church. "The year is 1904, and the pastor is Reverend R. A. Clark. Services are being held in a frame building large enough to accommodate the huge crowds that gathered there. Members and worshippers used to pack their lunch and go to Palestine for morning services. The biggest day of the year came on 4 July, when everyone would gather at Palestine for an all day singing, dinner on the grounds and worship. The floor of the church was almost blanketed with pallets holding small babies."
PALESTINE *(Tate County: Coldwater 38618).* This church was organized in 1877.
PALMETTO *(Lee County: Palmetto Road, Verona 38879).* Doctor and Mrs. W. H. Calhoun deeded land to the Methodist Conference in 1854. Mason Anderson deeded property for the cemetery in 1869. The first sanctuary was a frame two-story structure that housed the Masonic Lodge. The present brick sanctuary was erected in 1985. The education building was completed in 1958. Among the old artifacts are old lamps, chairs, spitoon, and old electric lights from the old building.

PARADISE *(Tishomingo County: 58 County Road 958, Tishomingo 38852).* The Paradise Church is located in a rural community three miles east of the town of Tishomingo. The first church at this site can be traced back to 1858 and is believed to be even older. On 6 May 1913, the original building burned and the present building was immediately erected. Since then, improvements, such as a Sunday School annex and the purchase of new pews, have been made.
PARIS *(Lafayette County: Paris 38949).*

Parkway Heights United Methodist Church

PARKWAY HEIGHTS *(Forrest County: 2420 Hardy Street, Hattiesburg 39401).* Parkway Heights was founded in 1949 when the city of Hattiesburg began to expand westward. Members held Sunday School in the upstairs classrooms of a school building while a Baptist church had classes downstairs in the auditorium. J. D. Slay and Robert Matheny were the temporary co-pastors who volunteered to serve until the Conference appointed a new pastor. By May 1949, the church had moved into a brick house that would serve as a temporary building. In 1950, the church bought a wooden frame building from Emmanuel Baptist, had it sawed in half, and moved it to their site to use as a fellowship hall. Sunday School classes were meeting in the pastor's kitchen and on the porches. The nursery was kept in the pastor's bedroom. Finally, in 1953, the church bought a lot and built a permanent building where Parkway Heights is today. The education and youth programs expanded into a house which the church bought in 1956, called the Green House. Over the next decade, a full-time choir director and accompanist were hired, a kitchen constructed, and more education buildings built. Because of its proximity to the University of Southern Mississippi, Parkway made a special effort during the 1960s to bring students to campus. The large sanctuary was built to finally complete the original church plans from over twenty years before, and on Thanksgiving Day 1978, the congregation moved into the new sanctuary.

PARKWAY HILLS *(Madison County: 1468 Highland Colony Parkway, Madison 39110)*. The church was organized in 1994.

PASCAGOULA FIRST *(Jackson County: 2710 South Pascagoula Street, Pascagoula 39568)*. Despite the lack of Protestant church houses or congregations, there was no lack of divine services in this area of the Gulf Coast in the 1870s. Reverend Thompson returned to the Moss Point Circuit for 1879, and Scranton-Seashore was assigned the third Sunday for preaching. In the latter part of November, a Methodist church was organized in Scranton (present day Pascagoula). The brief history of 1931 states that "in 1879 Reverend G. H. Thompson held a meeting

at the Academy which lasted for several days at which time a Methodist Church was successfully organized." The initial membership, excluding small children, probably numbered fifteen. Reverend J. W. Williams, probably a local preacher, was active in the Sunday School work even before 1879, and became the first superintendent of the Sunday School when it was organized in 1881. In 1880, Reverend J. M. Weems, served the Scranton appointment each third Sunday with preaching in the morning at Scranton and at Seashore in the afternoon. During his administration the church lot, the lumber, and sufficient money was secured to begin the construction of the church building. First services in the first building were conducted 13 August 1881. It burned 22 October 1884. The second church building was opened 18 April 1886.

Pass Christian First United Methodist Church

PASS CHRISTIAN FIRST *(Harrison County: 526 East Second Street, Pass Christian 39771)*. During the year 1904, Reverend George H. Galloway, pastor of the First Methodist Church of Gulfport, began preaching in Pass Christian on Thursday nights, the first services of record to be held in the town. Mr. Galloway's time was so fully taken up in Gulfport that he could not continue the work in Pass Christian. At the Annual Conference held in the Fall of 1904, Long Beach and Pass Christian were put together as a charge, and Reverend J. L. Sells was sent as pastor. He found one devout Methodist in Pass Christian, Mrs. Sallie McClaugherty, and that the Presbyterians would allow the use of their building for two regular services a month. A Methodist church was organized with a membership of twenty-five, and by August of that year, the membership grew to thirty.

PATRICK *(Tishomingo County: 59 County Road 321, Iuka 38852).* Patrick was originally organized under the name of Mount Pleasant Protestant Church at some time before 8 August 1882. In 1939, it became Patrick Methodist Church, probably due to the fact that it was organized for sometime in the same building with the Patrick Public School of that period. Court records show that on 8 August 1882, Jim Biggs gave, or sold, at one dollar, two acres of land to the trustees of Mount Pleasant Church. The earliest records show J. S. Hanna as pastor in 1899. The oldest tombstone is dated 1878. It is generally accepted that there have been at least four, and possibly five, buildings constructed on the site: two log buildings, and two or possibly three frame buildings. The log buildings stood just east-northeast of where the present building stands. The second from last building stood where the present one is. It was erected about the year of 1919. It was torn down about the year 1941, and the main part of the present building was erected at that time.

PAYNES CHAPEL *(Tippah County: 4521 County Road 611, Ripley 38663).* Payne's Chapel was organized in 1874. The land was deeded to the church by G. W. Mitchell on 14 October 1912. The second

building was started in 1915, under the pastorate of J. D. Boggs. It was sponsored under the leadership of W. L. Adair and wife. It was transferred from the Silver Springs Charge to the Dumas Charge in the late twenties, under the pastorate of Reverend J. N. Humphrey. Sunday School rooms were added in March 1961.

PEARL RIVER AVENUE *(Pike County: 900 Pearl River Avenue, McComb 39648).* While serving the Summit Circuit in 1907, Reverend J. T. Abney saw a need for a Methodist Church in East McComb. In January 1908, Reverend Abney came into the area, found a vacant lot on the southeast corner of Pearl River Avenue and Live Oak Street, stuck his umbrella in the ground, placed his hat on it, and began preaching to a congregation in the open air. After that service, a Methodist church was organized with thirty charter members. In June 1908, the membership erected a wood framed church and began holding services. This church was added to the work of the Summit Charge and became known as the "Summit-McComb Charge." Reverend A. B. Barry was appointed in 1917 and the charge became Southeast McComb Charge. In 1921, Reverend J. A. Wells was appointed to the station charge called Pearl River Avenue. The old frame church was replaced by a two-story building made of brick and dedicated in 1939 when A. S. Oliver was the pastor. A parsonage was purchased in 1921, located on South Live Oak Street. In March 1951, the Gaston D. Strange property on Pearl River Avenue was purchased. On 21 May, the ground was broken for a new brick education building.

Pearl First United Methodist Church

PEARL FIRST *(Rankin County: 226 South Pearson Road, Pearl 39208).* The church was organized in 1909. The church has been known as Pearson Methodist and Pearl Chapel Methodist. The first brick building was erected in 1909, and became the chapel when the second building was completed in 1990. An education wing was added in 1957, and the church parsonage was obtained in 1963.

PEARLINGTON *(Hancock County: 5210 Levee Avenue, Pearlington 39572).* Pearlington is the second oldest continuous community on the Mississippi Gulf Coast. Simon Favre settled here in the 1770s. Pearlington is the oldest Methodist church on the Coast. It was most probably a stop on Pearl River Circuit, organized 1813. Captain Koch, who ran a steamboat up and down the lower Pearl River, recorded in his 1931 log that a Methodist minister regularly visited Pearlington, although there was then no church building. Pearlington Circuit was organized in 1836. An 1851 city plat shows the Methodist Episcopal Church on the same lot as the present structure. A frame building, under construction in the 1880s, was blown down in a storm. A beautiful sanctuary was built in 1894, but burned in 1930. The present frame structure was built in 1931.

Pelahatchie United Methodist Church

PELAHATCHIE *(Rankin County: Pelahatchie 39145).* The first sanctuary was built in 1878, the second was built in 1914, and the third was completed in 1952. The first two were frame structures, and the third was a new brick church built in March 1952 on the northwest corner across the street from the former church at Church and Musterman Streets. The first deed to the church property was recorded 19 November 1886, from Hiram King. The second deed was recorded 25 June 1889 from A. L. D. Rhodes and E. E. Rhodes. A third deed, recorded 4 January 1943, from Mary E. Skulley, is for the property on which the parsonage was built.

PENDERVILLE *(Choctaw County: Weir 39772).* This church was organized in the 1800s.

PETAL *(Forrest County: 418 South Main Street, Petal 39465).* The church was organized in 1908. A building program began

Petal United Methodist Church

in 1915 for a frame building, consisting of a main sanctuary and four small adjourning rooms. The building was completed in 1916. In 1936, church members worked at night to brick the outside of the church. The bricks were a gift of a member, Miss Nancy Stapleton. A Sunday School addition was completed in 1957. The building program was completed in 1988 with the addition of a fellowship hall.

PHEBA *(Clay County)*. The church was organized in 1890.

PHILADELPHIA *(Jasper County: Highway 528 at Highway 503, Heidelberg 39439)*. The church was organized in 1853.

Philadelphia First United Methodist Church

PHILADELPHIA FIRST *(Neshoba County: 563 East Main Street, Philadelphia 39350)*. First United Methodist Church began its ministry in Neshoba County with the establishment of a mission to the Choctaw Indians in the 1820s. In the year 1837, a lot on the corner of Main Street was purchased as a building site. The Methodist Church occupied the first floor and the Masonic Lodge the second floor. At the turn of the century, the old church building was moved across the street into the next block, and a new building erected, but about 1913, the church burned. Rebuilt in 1923, it acquired an annex, brick veneer, and a pipe organ. In the mid-1950s, the church purchased a lot just beyond the downtown area and erected a larger building. Kenneth Jones served as first pastor.

PICAYUNE FIRST *(Pearl River County: 323 North Haugh Street, Picayune 39466)*. In 1907 Reverend P. M. Howse was appointed to be the minister of the Carriere-McNeill Circuit. First services were held in the Masonic Building at the corner of north Haugh Avenue and Second Street and later in the school facilities. The first church building was erected in 1913, during the pastorate of H. P. Lewis. The church became a station church in 1919 with Reverend B. E. Meiggs. Additional facilities were added between 1922 and 1923, during the ministry of Reverend J. H. Moore. Vision led Reverend J. O. Ware to begin another church building in which the first service was held on 23 February 1941, with Bishop Hoyt M. Dobbs bringing the sermon. Bishop J. Lloyd Decell led the congregation in the dedication service on 21 March 1942. During the

Picayune First United Methodist Church

ministry of Reverend C. C. Clark, construction began on an education building. On 20 February 1955, Bishop Marvin A. Franklin led the congregation in the dedication of the education building. Soon the Board began plans toward construction of a new sanctuary and parsonage. Doors to the handsome new sanctuary were opened to worshippers for the first time on 14 October 1956. On this same day the parsonage was dedicated by Bishop Franklin. During the ministry of Doctor Gilbert L. Oliver, the congregation once again responded to the challenge of expanding the church's educational facilities. Housing church school classes, assembly rooms, and a nursery, a new educational annex was placed into service

in the fall of 1967. On 25 October 1974, the education building was destroyed by a tragic fire. Under the leadership of Reverend W. R. Dement, plans were initiated to rebuild the facility, and fifteen months later a spacious new building was dedicated by Bishop Mack B. Stokes.

PICKENS *(Holmes County: 1336 Lexington Street, Vaughan 39179).* The church was organized in 1833. It was known as Cypress and Shiloh Methodist before it became Pickens Methodist Episcopal Church, South. It was located in Yazoo County from 1833 to 1878. A log house was erected in 1833, a wood frame church was erected in 1854, and the present brick structure was erected in 1952. The present building was damaged, but not destroyed, by fire in 1967.

PIERCE CHAPEL *(Attala County: Kosciusko 39090).* This community did not become thickly settled before the 1880s, and was named for the chapel located here. The Methodist church was organized in 1888.

PILGRIM HILL *(Lauderdale County: 4802 Twenty-Fifth Street, Meridian 39307).* About 1870, a few men and women got together and organized a prayer band. They met from house to house and had prayer meetings. From this prayer band, they organized a church. This church was built from brush cut from trees. This was known as the "brush arbor church." In 1870, a small church was built on land given by Mrs. Cissely Watkins. This little church was renovated many times. This church was called Pilgrim Rest Methodist. In 1967 Pilgrim Rest Church was mysteriously burned to the ground. On Easter Sunday, 14 April 1968, Reverend Johnson called a meeting. The purpose of the meeting was the proposed merger of the churches Pilgrim Rest and Rose Hill Methodist Churches. The merger was confirmed in the Annual Conference at Waveland. The church was given the name Pilgrim Hill United Methodist Church.

PILGRIM REST *(Jasper County: Montrose)*. The church was organized in 1900.

PILGRIM REST *(Quitman County: Curtis Station)*. This church was organized in 1913.

PINE FLAT *(Lafayette County: 40 County Road 422, Oxford 38655)*.

PINE GROVE *(Greene County: Leakesville 39451)*. The church was organized in 1837.

PINE GROVE *(Jefferson County: Fayette 39069)*.

PINEY GROVE *(Lowndes County: 102 Fernbank Road, Steens 39766)*. The organizers of Piney Grove knew something of the "rude log meeting houses and uncomfortable churches." The early members were numbered among the first settlers in the county and met in neighbor's homes or log houses. They were organized into little bands, predominately Methodists, by local preachers and old style exhorters. The first organizational meeting of the church was held in 1828 in a log schoolhouse about half a mile southwest of the present building. The second log building was constructed in 1835. An attractive frame building was constructed in 1838. The present building was dedicated in May 1892.

PINEY GROVE *(Winston County)*.

PINEY JORDAN *(Webster County: Eupora 39744)*.

PISGAH *(Panola County: Shuford)*. This church was organized in 1854.

PISGAH *(Pike County: 2048 Highway 570 West, Summit 39666)*. The church was organized in 1893.

PISGAH *(Prentiss County: Pisgah Road, 337 County Road 8301, Rienzi 38865)*. Organized 27 October 1852, Pisgah was originally known as the Pisgah Methodist Episcopal Church, South. It was in Tishomingo County, but county lines were changed, so it is now in Prentiss County. There has been at least three buildings on the land. The original building was there at the start. In addition to the log building and small frame house which was damaged by a storm in 1920, there was a frame building that was added to from time to time. In December 1967, a tornado destroyed that building and the present brick structure was built. Pisgah Church was a part of the Rienzi Charge until June of 1984, when it became a part of the Carolina-Pisgah Charge. The cemetery at Pisgah shows tombstones with the names of Naller, 1862, Allen, 1862, and Cheeves, 1862.

PITTSBORO *(Calhoun County: Pittsboro 38951)*. This county seat community was founded 26 July 1852, along with Calhoun County, and named for Pittsboro, North Carolina. The church was organized in 1853. A new sanctuary and education building were added in 1927.

PLANTERSVILLE *(Lee County: 839 Central Street, Plantersville 38862)*. The Plantersville United Methodist Church had its beginning in a one-room frame school building in the spring of 1907. After a few months, Reverend Jim Cunningham, an evangelist from Dallas, Texas, held a tent

Plantersville United Methodist Church

revival and the church was organized, with nine charter members, and placed on the Verona Charge, Aberdeen District, with D. M. Geddy as pastor. That same year a church site was given by J. W. Towery, and a one-room frame church was built. The deed was recorded in 1908. The original building, built in 1907, was destroyed by a tornado, and the second building was damaged by another tornado in 1910. In 1925, the Doctor Cantrell Sunday School Class became inspired to build a new brick church. Between 1948 and 1978, many events took place in the life of the church. In 1948, John Porter Gunter was licensed to preach. Between 1951 and 1952, a two-story education building was erected. In 1956, the church was placed on the Plantersville-Union Charge, and a new brick parsonage was built near the church. In 1969, the present brick sanctuary was completed, and dedicated on 12 March 1978, by Bishop Mack B. Stokes.

PLEASANT GROVE *(Chickasaw County)*. This church was organized in 1861.

PLEASANT GROVE *(Jasper County: Pleasant Grove Road, Rose Hill 39356)*. Pleasant Grove United Methodist Church had its beginnings as part of the Paulding Charge, which was established in 1837. This charge was one of the largest and most thriving in the state. Pleasant Grove was

established and became a part of this charge in 1850. Prior to 1870, Paulding Charge was part of the Alabama Conference. In 1870 it became part of the Meridian District of the Mississippi Conference. In 1890, Paulding Charge was changed to Rose Hill Charge. Pleasant Grove is the oldest member church on the Rose Hill Charge. When Pleasant Grove Church was established in 1850, the first church building was erected at a location about two miles east-southeast of the present location. This first church had a slave balcony and two cemeteries, one for whites and one for Blacks. The second building to serve as Pleasant Grove Church was constructed in 1870 on the present site. On 20 April 1920, the church was damaged by a tornado and had to be remodeled once again. Then, after surviving three quarters of a century, the original church at the present location was torn down and a new church was built. The church which was built in 1944 stood the shortest time of all the buildings. Only five years after the church was built, it was damaged by winds and had to be remodeled. This building then stood until 1960. In 1960, the third building to house Pleasant Grove Church was torn down and the present church was built. This church was originally built of blocks. Later, bricks were donated by J. W. Moulds and the church was bricked. In 1976, the annex was added.

PLEASANT GROVE *(Kemper County)*. Pleasant Grove Church, located in the southern portion of Kemper County, was established in 1840. The old church building, a white wood frame structure stood north of the present church. The new church building was constructed in the late 1950s and early 1960s. A fellowship hall and Sunday School rooms were added in the mid-1970s. The church is honored to have several members of their congregation devote their lives to the ministry. These men include Lee Crenshaw, Edward McKeithen, Wallace Terry, William Oliver Joyner, James E. McKeithen, Wallace Lucky, Ellis Scott, and Geoffrey Joyner.

PLEASANT GROVE *(Lauderdale County: Lauderdale-Toomsuba Road, Toomsuba 39364).*

PLEASANT GROVE *(Lawrence County: 1100 Pleasant Grove Road, Monticello 39654).* The church was organized in 1886.

PLEASANT GROVE *(Lee County: Pleasant Grove Road, Evergreen Community, Nettleton 38859).* When the Pleasant Grove Church was first organized in 1859, it was located in Pontotoc County. Since then, the county lines have been relocated, and now the church is in Lee County. In the 1940s, three Sunday School rooms were built. Later, around 1960, a fellowship hall was added. The oldest tombstone in the cemetery is 1852.

PLEASANT GROVE *(Monroe County).*

PLEASANT GROVE *(Oktibbeha County: 206 Pleasant Grove Road, Louisville 39339).* The church was organized in 1869.

PLEASANT GROVE *(Panola County: Tocowa).*

PLEASANT GROVE *(Pontotoc County: Pontotoc 38863).* This church was organized in 1863.

PLEASANT GROVE *(Wayne County: 1710 Dyess Bridge Road, Waynesboro 39367).* The church was organized in 1870.

PLEASANT HILL *(Alcorn County: 320 County Road 614, Kossuth 38834).* The Pleasant Hill United Methodist Church was organized in 1881. The first church building was erected in approximately 1883, near the schoolhouse, which was being used for a place of worship at that time. The land on which the church was built, was deeded by G. W. Lawson and wife, for a "House of peace of worship" for the use of the members of the Methodist Episcopal Church, South. The first preacher was either J. W. Honnell or Thomas Taylor. The records are not clear. In 1922, the church was blown from its foundation during a storm. The building was put back on the rock pillars, but the walls could not be completely straightened. They leaned because they were so high. The building was used like this until 1951. In 1951, Doctor J. H. Hughes deeded enough land for a new building and parking area. The land where the old building stood was added to the cemetery grounds. The land for the parsonage was deeded by R. C. Cates in 1882. There were three churches on the charge at that time. They were Pleasant Hill, Wesley Chapel, and Kossuth.

PLEASANT HILL *(DeSoto County: 3987 Pleasant Hill Road, Pleasant Hill 38654).* The church was organized in 1888. The community that is now Pleasant Hill was part of the Chickasaw Territory that was opened for white settlement after the enactment of Andrew Jackson's Indian Removal Bill in 1830. One of the pioneers who migrated to North Mississippi in the newly-organized county of DeSoto was George Robertson. The land he purchased included a natural watering place at the intersection of two paths. First called Robertson's Crossroads, this site was later designated Pleasant Hill. Before the Civil War, the Presbyterians and the Baptists had established permanent houses of worship. Shortly after the war the community became a mission on the Methodist circuit. The small band of believers created for themselves a "society," just as Wesley's early followers had done in England. Led on a regular basis by a local lay pastor, they were visited periodically by an itinerant ordained minister, who conducted revivals, baptized babies, and confirmed new converts to the church. By 1888 this modest beginning had evolved into a permanent position in the Conference. On a parcel of land purchased from W. H. Shinpock, Pleasant Hill Methodists erected their first real church, a small white frame building. By 1895 a new parsonage was ready for occupancy. Later church members added a large cast iron bell to toll the morning service and to commemorate important occasions. The original building burned in 1937 and was replaced by a simple brick structure that featured a small sanctuary flanked by four little Sunday School rooms. The church has added a fellowship hall, classrooms, and extra sanctuary space.

PLEASANT HILL *(George County: Basin).*

PLEASANT HILL *(Lauderdale County: 5019 Zero Road, Meridian 39301).* The church was organized in 1840. Church buildings were erected in 1911, 1948, and 1986.

PLEASANT HILL *(Oktibbeha County: Highway Eighty-Two, Starkville 39759).*

PLEASANT HILL *(Smith County: Highway 581, Raleigh 39153).*

PLEASANT HILL *(Tishomingo County: 201 County Road 193, Iuka 38852).* Pleasant Hill was built about 1875. It was a Methodist Protestant Church, with Reverend Lemuel J. Hubbard as the founder. The church was constructed of rough material. The pulpit and benches were handmade. When the church was completed, it was given the name Pleasant Hill, saying, "The foundation is of rock and will last forever, that's the faith." For more than thirty years, this building was used. In 1905, the original building was replaced with the present structure. In 1920, Pleasant Hill joined the North Mississippi Conference of the Episcopal Church, South. It was put on a circuit with six other churches. In 1921, Mount Evergreen was founded and added to the circuit, making eight churches on the circuit. The Methodist Church became a United Methodist Church when it merged with the Evangelical United Brethren Church on 23 April 1968.

PLEASANT HILL *(Winston County: Griffin Road, Louisville 39339).* This church was founded in 1937.

PLEASANT HILL *(Yazoo County: Firetower Road, Yazoo City 39194).* The church was organized in 1896. The first

Pleasant Hill United Methodist Church, Yazoo City

building was a frame structure built in 1897. The current brick structure was built in 1971. An annex was completed in 1993. The deed for the church property was recorded 31 October 1896.

PLEASANT RIDGE *(Copiah County: Crystal Springs 39059).* This church was founded in 1884.

PLEASANT RIDGE *(Greene County: State Line 39362).*

PLEASANT RIDGE *(Kemper County: John C. Stennis Avenue, Dekalb 39328).* This church was organized in 1837.

PLEASANT RIDGE *(Lauderdale County: Collinsville 39325).*

PLEASANT VALLEY *(Chickasaw County).*

PLEASANT VALLEY *(Copiah County).* The church was organized in 1845. It is the home church of Major Reuben W. Millsaps and Clara Chrisman. It is listed on the National Register of Historical Places.

PLEASANT VALLEY *(Jasper County: Heidelberg 39439).*

PLEASANT VALLEY *(Lee County: Guntown 38849).*

PLEASANT VALLEY *(Marion County: Sandy Hook 39478).* The church was organized in 1845.

PLEASANT VALLEY *(Newton County: 692 Pleasant Valley Road, Decatur 39327).* This church was organized in 1900.

PLIARS *(Oktibbeha County: Starkville 39759).* The date this church was organized has not been determined. There have been two buildings. The present brick structure was completed in 1967. An education building was completed in 1996.

PONTOTOC FIRST *(Pontotoc County: 68 South Main, Pontotoc 38863).* From an article written by Colonel James Gordon in 1895, we quote the following in regard to Pontotoc and its early religious history. "Pontotoc had everything a town needed except churches." The church in Pontotoc must have been organized in about 1836, since at this first meeting mention was made of Campground, Pontotoc, Palestine, and Harmony. Harmony may have been the same church as Glover's Chapel as it is mentioned in some of the minutes and the membership seems to be the same. The first minister listed as pastor was Reverend R. H. Bonner in 1836. He was listed as lay preacher and was one of the founders of the Old Campground Church. The first church building in Pontotoc stood across the street from the present one. The church was a plank building and served the congregation for about seventy years. Pontotoc belonged to the Memphis Conference until 1869. At that time the North Mississippi Conference was organized and Pontotoc was placed within its bounds. In 1910, the present church was erected.

POPE *(Panola County: Pope 38658).* This church was organized in 1845.

POPLAR HEAD *(Harrison County: 13196 Poplar Head Road, Saucier 39574).* The church was organized in 1879. a small church built of logs, located approximately three-fourths of a mile due south of the present building. Large poplar trees were near the church; thus, the name Poplar Head. The first Quarterly Conference held at Coalville on 22 February 1879, indicated there were no Sabbath Schools on the circuit. The pastor's report stated "the spiritual state of the church is not what it ought to be; some of the members are up to Bible standard while some are far from it." In 1882, the pastor's report commented: "We have three Sabbath Schools on circuit, one at Whittington Chapel, one at White Plains, and one at Poplar Head. The one at Whittington Chapel doing tolerably well. The other two are barely living." But things began to improve. In 1886, the building of a new church was authorized for Poplar Head, which was located at the present site, and completed in 1900. Poplar Head went back on Saucier Charge in 1938 and continued until 1957. At that time, having the present building completed, Poplar Head became a station church. They completed a parsonage in 1952.

POPLAR SPRINGS *(Holmes County: 4284 Wash Bailey Road, Durant 39063).* The church was organized in 1920.

POPLAR SPRINGS *(Wayne County: Matherville-Poplar Springs Road, Waynesboro 39367).*

POPLAR SPRINGS DRIVE *(Lauderdale County: 3937 Poplar Springs Drive, Meridian 30305).* Poplar Springs Drive was organized in 1884. A new building was constructed in 1910. The present sanctuary and educational space were constructed in the 1950s.

POPLARVILLE *(Pearl River County: 202 Church Street, Poplarville 39470).* This church was organized in 1883.

PORT GIBSON *(Claiborne County: 901 Church Street, Port Gibson 39150).* Samuel Gibson, the town's founder, arrived here in 1788. The date on which Methodism came to Port Gibson has not yet been clearly established. It is certain that Lorenzo Dow and Tobias Gibson traveled through "Gibsonport" just after it became a town.

Port Gibson United Methodist Church

Although 1826 is recognized as the year in which the Methodist Church in Port Gibson was officially organized, the history of the church dates back to nearly a quarter of a century earlier. As was the custom among the Methodists in their mission work, a Methodist Society preceded the building of the first church in Port Gibson. Some historical sketches indicate that in 1804 an active society existed, with services held in the homes of its members. Records of the Conference indicate that during this time Port Gibson was in the territory of what was called the Claiborne Circuit, embracing all of Claiborne and Jefferson Counties and a part of Warren County. In 1824, Port Gibson was made a station appointment. In that year John C. Burruss (or Burris), one of the most famous preachers in early Methodism, was appointed minister. This was two years before the construction of the first church building, which was accomplished during the ministry of O. T. Hawkins. This church, built in 1826, was not only the first Methodist Church in Port Gibson, but it was the first church of any denomination in the town. It was built on the same spot on which the present church is standing. The cornerstone was laid on 30 September 1826. In 1844 the Mississippi Annual Conference, under Bishop Edmund S. Jones, was held in Port Gibson, the first of four times that the Port Gibson Methodist Church was designated as the site of the Annual Conference. In 1857, it was decided that the church should be torn down and a new church built, using the bricks from the old church. However, the old church burned before these plans were completed. Worship services continued, however, as both the Odd Fellows and the Chistian Chapel offered the use of their buildings.

PORTER'S CHAPEL *(Warren County: 200 Porter's Chapel Road, Vicksburg 39180).* Porter's Chapel congregation has been in existence since 1830; however, it has not always been known as Porter's Chapel United Methodist Church. Originally the land was donated by James and Mary Atkins Porter for the erection of a building to be used by all denominations. The cemetery was available to all as well, and the building was even used for a school at one time. This building was destroyed during the Civil War, as it was being used for a hospital. For many years afterwards the surrounding country was left without a place of worship. Mrs. Ferguson and her family were foremost in the reconstruction of the new building and in 1877, she saw a

second House of God rise on the same site where the first had stood. The date which the Methodist Conference entered the history of Porter's Chapel is unknown, but a clear title was not obtained to the land until 1954, when Mrs. Gertrude Bell, Mrs. W. E. Brister, and Mr. J. L. McCaskill gave the church a quit claim deed. The present sanctuary plans were begun in 1962, when the new parsonage was completed. The first services were held in the new sanctuary in September, 1965. Porter's Chapel has been a part of the charges of Oak Ridge, Bradley's Chapel, Redwood, and Redbone. The old church building was sold and moved on 20 February 1985, and construction began on the same site. The new building was ready for use in May 1986. The old parsonage was also sold and a new parsonage was built on the same site and completed in October 1996.

PORTERVILLE *(Kemper County: Porterville 39352).* This church was organized in 1892.

POTTS CAMP *(Marshall County: Highway 178, Potts Camp 38659).* As Potts Camp became a village and held its first board meeting in 1888, the seventy-five townspeople began to look for a place to

Potts Camp United Methodist Church

worship. The next year, Reverend S. A. Ellis organized Potts Camp Methodist Episcopal Church, South, on 15 October 1889. A small frame building was erected on a parcel of land given by Mary A Reid, daughter of the town's namesake and pioneer settler, Colonel E. F. Potts. It is the site of the present Potts Camp First United Methodist Church. It first became a part of the Cornersville Circuit. In 1893 it joined the Methodist churches at Winborn, Pisgah, Palestine, Ebenezer, and Hickory Flat to form the Potts Camp Circuit, and a parsonage was built. In 1903 the frame church was struck by lightning and burned to the ground, and was rebuilt. In 1926 this frame building was torn down and replaced by a more substantial two-story brick sanctuary. It served as the site of the Corinth District Conference in 1927. On a cold Christmas Eve night in 1929, it burned. It was rebuilt in 1930, as the two-story brick church building of today with an upstairs sanctuary. On 15 October 1989, the presiding bishop of the Mississippi Conference, Robert C. Morgan, preached the centennial sermon.

PRAIRIE CHAPEL *(Monroe County: 10164 Highway 382, Prairie 39756).* Although the exact month of its forming is not known, the Prairie Chapel Methodist Church was born in 1876 when a group of Prairie area residents gathered in the nearby woods to hear a preacher. The first building of the church was a one-room wooden structure located one and a half miles west of Prairie, on land which was deeded to the church by Patrick Hamilton and wife Sarah Paine Hamilton, the daughter of Bishop Robert Paine. The first congregation had a membership of thirty-nine persons, and in

1877, pastor A. T. Ramsey wrote in the minutes of the first Quarterly Conference, "Even though the congregation is small, the spiritual life is good." Methodist churches were served by circuit riding preachers, and Prairie Chapel was on a circuit with Muldon and Paine's Chapel. Prairie Chapel's original building was replaced in 1908 on land which was donated by Mrs. Anna Green Speck. This is the original and present site of the church. This second structure was a wooden building with a sanctuary and four Sunday School rooms. The present brick structure was erected in 1951. A building program was initiated in 1946 during the pastorate of T. A. Filgo, and the ladies of the church began raising the necessary funds. The building was completed and occupied in August 1951. Dedication ceremonies led by Bishop Marvin A. Franklin were held on 31 May 1953. Prairie was on a circuit with Strong, Friendship, and Hamilton Methodist Churches.

PRAIRIE CHAPEL *(Neshoba County: Mount Bethel Road, Madden 39109).* This church is located off Highway Twenty-One on the Mount Bethel Road.

PRAIRIE MOUNT *(Chickasaw County: Troy).* This community dates back to 1836. Littleberg Gilliam was the community's founder, who established an inn on the Old Stage Road. The settlement incorporated in 1852, but later lost most of its residents to nearby Okolona.

PRATT MEMORIAL *(Hinds County: 1059 West Pascagoula Street, Jackson 39203).* Pratt Memorial United Methodist Church was founded as a mission charge on 9 July 1897. It was housed in a small school building and was called the West Jackson

Methodist Episcopal Church. A year or so later a parsonage was built. In 1901, an effort was made to build the first church. Construction was not complete but was successful to the extent that services could be held. Reverend I. L. Pratt became the pastor of the church in 1902 and unfortunately, both the church and the parsonage burned. The pastor and the faithful members built the first sanctuary, naming it Pratt's Chapel in honor of Reverend I. L. Pratt. In 1907, the second parsonage was built and years later the name of the church was changed to Pratt Memorial Methodist Episcopal Church. In March of 1953, the church fell down. The church was rebuilt, and opened on 14 March 1954. In 1956, the parsonage was rebuilt.

PRENTISS *(Jefferson Davis County: 2205 Leaf Avenue, Prentiss 39474)*. This church was organized in 1890.

Prospect United Methodist Church

PROSPECT *(Chickasaw County: Houston 38851)*. In 1863 Grierson's Raiders of the Union Army destroyed all of the land records in Chickasaw County with the exception of two books. For this reason it is impossible to say exactly when Prospect Church was started. In the early 1800s a log meeting house was built on the site now occupied by Prospect United Methodist Church. One of the first preachers at Prospect was Reverend T. J. Lowry. He built a four-room log house near Prospect Church. The first land record for the church shows that on 1 January 1855, Sanford Robertson deeded one acre of land to Prospect Methodist Church. Legible grave markers date back to 1850 in the cemetery, but there are numerous markers that are older and illegible. Slaves were buried in another cemetery directly behind Prospect Cemetery. Slaves attended church at Prospect Church before the Civil War. The present building was constructed in 1962 and dedicated in 1965. It stands next to the old building which is used as a fellowship hall.

PROVIDENCE *(Copiah County: 14012 Highway 474, Hazlehurst 39053)*. The church was organized in 1828. This church is built on the site of one of the earliest campgrounds in the Mississippi Conference. An historic marker was placed here by the Mississippi Department of Archives and History.

PROVIDENCE *(Lafayette County: County Road 108, Abbeville 38601)*. The church was organized in 1882. In the 1920s, the church

Providence United Methodist Church, Abbeville

was located on the west side of Pumping Station Road. The first building was constructed of wood or logs, and the second brick structure was erected in 1972. An education annex was completed in 1984.

PROVIDENCE *(Wayne County: Knobtown).* The church was organized in 1878.

PROVIDENCE *(Webster County: Highway Fifteen North, Mathiston 39752).* Providence Methodist Church is located on a two acre plot. On 22 September 1879, the land was sold to M. R. Rushing and R. K. Hodges. The church was placed here as early as 1880. This two acre plot was donated before 1880, but was not recorded, so it was returned to the State. On 6 April 1880, the church bought it back from the State. Upon this two acre plot of land the first church building was erected. It was a frame building, facing west, where very large, active crowds gathered. There was a one-room schoolhouse. It was a few yards west of the church and faced the east. The first church building was used until about 1919. The year Rex Myrff was pastor, an old church building was purchased and the material from the two buildings were used to construct the building that now stands. It has been remodeled. When the church was rebuilt, it faced north. W. R. McMullin donated an additional one-half acre to the church. In this book, the male and female list was kept separately. In 1963, R. L. Jenkins was pastor. He revised the old membership book.

PUCKETT *(Rankin County: 6412 Highway Eighteen South, Puckett 39151).* This church was founded about 1831. The first pastor was C. J. Carney, who served from 1831 to 1836. The church was known as Clear Creek Methodist Church until 1940, when it became known as Puckett Methodist Church.

PUGH'S MILL *(Oktibbeha County: Highway Twenty-Five, Starkville 39759).* This church was organized in 1890.

PURVIS *(Lamar County: 203 Mitchell, Purvis 39475).* This church was organized in 1884.

PYLAND *(Chickasaw County: Houston 38851).* This church was organized in 1912. There have been two frame buildings. The present building was constructed in the 1930s.

QUINCY *(Monroe County: Greenwood Springs 38848).* This community, named for John Quincy Adams, was settled in 1816.

QUITMAN *(Clarke County: 203 East Franklin Street, Quitman 39355).* This community was settled about 1830, and was named for Brigadier General John A. Quitman, who served in the Mexican War, and later served as Governor of Mississippi between 1850 to 1851. On the 13 March 1844, J. Atkinson of Quitman conveyed to the Alabama Conference of the Methodist Episcopal Church, and to Lafayette Lodge of Free and Accepted Masons, a lot in the town of Quitman. This lot was on Glynn Avenue, and it was here that Methodism had its beginning in Quitman. It was not until the 1853 session of the Alabama Annual Conference that any official record was made of the assignment of a pastor to the Quitman Church, Reverend John C. Stricklin. The local church was then part of the large Clarke Circuit. Seven local preachers were listed as being members of this charge. The Methodist Church building was converted into a Civil War hospital. A band of Union soldiers burned all public buildings in Quitman, including the Methodist Church. The Methodists worshipped with the Baptist congregation. Between 1872 and 1890, local preacher Sterling West came to Quitman and induced the Methodist congregation, though few in number, to reorganize their work and secure their own house of worship. They began using an abandoned building, and, with a membership of approximately twenty-five, began to move under their own banner again. The building next to the Courthouse was used for worship from 1893 to 1927, when a new church building was completed.

RALEIGH FIRST *(Smith County: 163 Main Street, Raleigh 39153).* In 1837, two new circuits were added to the Mississippi Conference: Raleigh and Paulding of the Monticello District. Joel Sanders was appointed the circuit rider for Raleigh Circuit. This was the official beginning of the Methodist Church in Raleigh and the surrounding area. Reverend John G. Jones, in his History of Methodism in Mississippi, published in 1908, described the situation here before 1837: "This new territory had been transiently passed over a few times by the itinerants on their long rounds, but hitherto had been served by a few local preachers who had emigrated into that region with the early settlers, among whom may be honorably mentioned: Ransom J. Jones Sr. and Jacob Carr." The Raleigh Church has had three sanctuaries: the first two were frame, and the present building is brick, constructed in 1951.

RAMSAY MEMORIAL *(Harrison County: 12474 Dedeaux Road, Gulfport 39503).* This church was organized in 1971.

RAPERS CHAPEL *(Calhoun County: Route Four, Water Valley 38965).* Rapers Chapel Methodist Church was organized 15 July 1926, in the Lone Oak School. J. W. Raper was appointed pastor by Reverend E. L. Lewis, presiding elder. Rapers Chapel was in the Grenada District at that time. The first church was constructed in 1927. The present building was built in 1956. In 1976, the fellowship hall was added. The oldest tombstone in the cemetery is R. W. Dulaney, 19 December 1935.

RASBERRY *(Sunflower County: 511 Roosevelt Street, Indianola 38751).* The early history of Rasberry is uncertain since records were destroyed by storms and fire. This church was formerly known as Rasberry Chapel Methodist Church and named in honor of two founding fathers, Henry Rasberry and Lewis Chapel. This one-room frame building was destroyed in a storm in the early 1900s along with the church records. Another building erected in 1923 was also destroyed by a storm. The congregation then erected a brick building with a basement and a parsonage nearby in 1929. This church building lasted from 1929 until 1971, when it was destroyed by fire. In 1973, a five-room church was consecrated, and in 1980, the building was dedicated. The church was without a parsonage until August 1985, when a missionary team from Kokomo, Indiana, built a three bedroom brick parsonage during their two weeks' vacation.

RAYMOND *(Hinds County: 230 West Main Street, Raymond 39154).* The town of Raymond was laid out in 1827. In 1837 Francis Devine deeded to the town of Raymond a lot, and a building was erected.

Raymond United Methodist Church

Two very large rooms were built: one upper story, which was used as a lodge by different clubs of the town; and the lower story as a place of worship by the people of Raymond. The Baptists built their church in 1844, and that same year the Methodists purchased the lower part of the building that they were using, and the first Methodist Church was organized. A balcony was soon erected in the church for the slaves who wished to come and worship. By 1885 the Methodists had erected a new church building. The present structure was completed in 1941. After the church at Raymond became a full time charge in 1953, a parsonage was built and later the educational annex in 1955.

READ'S CHAPEL *(Jasper County: Highway Eighteen, Montrose).* The church was organized in 1904.

RED BANKS *(Marshall County: 405 Yarbrough Loop, Red Banks 38661).* Red Banks was organized in 1886, as a Methodist Episcopal Church, South. Methodists of the community had been members of two neighboring churches, Wesley Chapel and Hebron. Several from those congregations were named as trustees

of the new church in a deed to the one acre lot, donated by Mr. J. P. Norfleet. A sanctuary, still in use, was built in 1887. Through the years a number of additions and repairs have been made. The late Miss Ruby Berkley went from the congregation into full-time Christian service as a commissioned Deaconess, working under the Women's Division until her retirement in 1964.

RED HILL *(Jackson County: 14936 Old River Road, Vancleave 39565).* The Red Hill Methodist Church was organized in 1837 in Jackson County, though this territory was included in the Alabama Conference. Job Foster was pastor of the Chickasawhay Circuit, which extended from the Gulf Coast one hundred miles north, and Elisha Galloway was presiding elder of the Mobile District. Red Hill is not the oldest church in southeast Mississippi, but it is the only church that stands on the original site. Founders of the church were Reverend Henry Fletcher, a local preacher, John Havens, a layman, and members of their families. There have been three church buildings. The first church was made of logs and stood where the present church stands. The second, also of logs, stood about fifty yards further west. The present church was built in 1892. For the first fifty years of its history the church had no deed to the property. When the last church was built a deed was given by Abraham Galloway, a former slave who belonged to a cousin of Bishop Galloway's father.

REDBONE *(Warren County: 43 Burnt House Road, Vicksburg 39180).* The church was organized in 1814. This church has a long and colorful history. It is the successor to Hopewell and Warrenton Methodist Churches, two of the earliest Methodist churches in Mississippi. At one time the church was known as Bethel. One legend has it the church got its unusual name from the Indians who named this area for the red bones they discarded after eating squirrels. The first building, built in 1814, was a log church. The second frame building was constructed in 1832. The present brick building was erected in 1854. A 1917 fire gutted the brick building, but it was restored by 1947. Additions to the building were added in the 1940s and 1970s. The church was used as a hospital for Union soldiers in the Civil War. A historical marker was erected here in 1974. A Revolutionary War veteran is buried in the cemetery. Redbone was selcted Rural Church of the Year for the Vicksburg District in 1956.

REDWOOD *(Warren County: 110 Redbone Road, Redwood 39156).* Soon after World War II ended, it was decided that a church should be organized in Redwood. The church met in the Redwood School auditorium on Sunday afternoons. It was a Union church. Various preachers and laymen from the area shared in the leadership. Three ministers that showed much interest and were very popular were Reverends Oliver Scott, H. L. Daniels, and John Neal from Gibson Memorial Methodist Church. After several years, it was decided to build a church. The decision as to which denomination was reached by vote of the group. The vote indicated that they would build a Methodist Church. Redwood United Methodist Church was organized 4 September 1949. The special meeting was presided over by Reverend

T. O. Prewitt, District Superintendent. In the fall of 1950, the church sponsored an old fashioned tent revival, with a borrowed tent. Reverend Neal brought the message. The church soon raised money, bought a lot, and built a small church. The first service was held in the new building 27 May 1951. Second-hand pews were acquired from the Taylorsville United Methodist Church. The church was dedicated 28 March 1954.

REFUGE *(George County: Agricola).* The people of this community went to Crossroads Methodist prior to the establishment of Refuge Church. This was a long and difficult trip because they had to walk or go by mule and wagon. At first, they built a brush arbor and had services under it. Later, they met in a one-room house. The church was organized in 1921 by Reverend Van Landrum. It was known as Refuge Methodist Episcopal Church, South. The first wood building was constructed in 1924. Lampton Timber Company gave the land for the church. Mr. John Howell gave the lumber for the church. The Mississippi Conference sent Reverend J. C. Jackson as the first pastor. The old church was added onto in 1940, giving the building a "T" shape. On 1 January 1961, a ground breaking service for a new building was held under the leadership of Reverend Fred Buckholtz. The new building was renovated in 1979 after hurricane Fredrick did much damage.

REHOBOTH *(Copiah County: Barlow).* The church was organized in 1839.

REVELS *(Washington County: 711 South Broadway, Greenville 38701).* Revels was established in 1889, by Reverend N. H.

Williams. It was named in honor of Hiram Rhoades Revels, the first Black senator of the United States. The first church was erected on the corner of Muscadine and Gloster Streets, Greenville, in 1901, under the pastorate of Reverend J. M. Walton. The church remained on the corner of Muscadine and Gloster Streets until 1928. Under the leadership of Reverend N. G. Crawford, it was moved to its present site.

REXFORD *(Simpson County).*

RHODES CHAPEL *(Chickasaw County: Route One, Houston 38851).* The church was organized in 1883. The present building was constructed in 1883. Sunday School rooms were added in the 1950s.

RIALS CREEK *(Simpson County: 185 Rials Creek Road, Mendenhall 39114).* Founded in 1860 as Pleasant Hill Methodist Church, the original structure was a log cabin located seven miles south of Mendenhall at what is now the intersection of Airport Road and Rials Creek Road. In 1893 the log cabin was totally destroyed by a tornado. A brush arbor was constructed near what is now the present church site. Services were held in this temporary facility until vandals led the congregation to build a permanent structure. Services were held once a month and usually lasted all day. A frame building was constructed, and in 1909 the congregation approved remodeling and the addition of a steeple and bell. In 1936 the church again underwent remodeling, and the steeple and bell were removed. Pleasant Hill Methodist Church was known locally as Rials Creek Methodist Episcopal Church, South. In 1937, during the tenure of Reverend Raley, the name was officially changed to

Rials Creek Methodist Church. Sunday School was organized in the spring of 1949, with six classes. The Methodist Youth Fellowship was organized in 1950 during the tenure of Reverend Jim Smith.

RICE'S CHAPEL *(Marshall County).*

RICHLAND *(Rankin County: 255 Richland Circle, Richland 39218).* The Richland United Methodist Church began in the 1850s. Church attendance was held in a one room log cabin that was used for the Richland Academy. The logs were brought in on wagons pulled by oxen. A new building was begun in 1859 by Mr. Jaques and was completed in the Spring of 1861. This building served as the Academy and was the Methodist Church until a new church was built in 1908. The Baptists used the church portion of the Academy building on the Sundays that the Methodist didn't use it. In 1881, Mr. Thomas N. Norrell granted a deed for six acres of land and a portion of the Academy building, including the pulpit, pews, and stove to the trustees of the Methodist church. In 1970, the Richland Church purchased the lot where the old Baptist church had been. A family life center was constructed under the supervision of Reverend L. H. Reynolds.

RICHTON *(Perry County: 500 Dogwood Avenue Highway Forty-Two, Richton 39476).* At the beginning of the conference year 1903, Reverend J. M. Massey was sent to organize the New Augusta Charge of the Methodist Episcopal Church, South, Seashore District. The Richton Church was a part of this charge. The first record of the Richton Church paying ministerial support was shown in the First Quarterly

Richton United Methodist Church

building on the same lines of the one destroyed. The first service in the new church was 26 May 1963.

Ridgeland First United Methodist Church

Conference in 1905. In February 1905, C. H. Stevens, C. C. Dearman, and Mrs. Leotis Cantrell were received as the first members of the Richton Church. The Quarterly Conference November 1905, gave authority to the charge stewards to secure a lot and the materials for the construction of the Richton Methodist Church. At this time worship services were held in the Methodist Protestant Church. By 1907 the building was nearly completed. In 1918, the parsonage and lot were purchased. The church annex was built about 1925. The Richton Church became a station church in 1936 during the pastorate of Reverend L. L. Haughton. In 1939, when the Uniting Conference met at Gulfport, the Richton Church became a part of this Conference, therefore, it became known as the Methodist Church of Richton. Between 1948 and 1953, the original church was demolished, and Reverend McKeithen led in the planning and erecting of the colonial style brick edifice. The first service in the church was 5 April 1953, This church was destroyed by fire 12 February 1962. Soon after the fire, committees were named and plans begun for the reconstruction of the

RIDGELAND FIRST *(Madison County: 234 West Jackson, Ridgeland 39157).* This church was organized in 1896. It was once known as Wesley Chapel, and was located on what is now Old Canton Road near the Hinds and Madison county line from 1896 to 1901. The first building was a frame structure, constructed in 1896. The second, and present, building is made of brick, and was finished in 1960. In 1952, a two-story brick education building was built, and in 1991, a multipurpose brick building was added. The church currently has three students preparing for the ministry: Alvin Lingenfelter at Duke, and Sam (Sonny) Burton and Billy Watson at Asbury.

RIENZI *(Alcorn County: 56 Mail Street, Rienzi 38865).* The Rienzi community was settled about 1830. The community was named for a Roman Tribune. Rienzi United Methodist Church was located about a mile west of Roebke Corner and relocated in 1859, near the railroad. A log house was used for worship in 1848 and was approved in 1849 by the Memphis Conference as a charge. A Union Church for Baptists and Methodists was built in 1852. In 1858, a large two-story building was built where the present church now stands. It was in the Iuka District, which was changed to the Corinth District in 1881. In 1886, the two-story building was replaced by a frame building. The two-story building was spared during the Civil War because it contained a Masonic Hall. The building was destroyed by fire on 16 June 1939. It was replaced with a brick building when Reverend Lott was district superintendent and Reverend Goudelock was pastor. In 1950, the brick parsonage was built. The construction of the fellowship hall to the church was completed in the Fall of 1974. Rienzi Charge consisted of four churches from 1907 until 1983. Three ministers were called to preach from this church.

RIGGAN CHAPEL *(Monroe County: Splunge Community, Greenwood Springs 38848).* The Riggan Chapel United Methodist Church was built about two miles north of the present building around the early 1900s, and named for one of the members. The original building has been gone for many years, but the cemetery adjoining the grounds still bears the name Riggan Chapel. The oldest tombstone in the cemetery dates back to 1851. Later, a new church was built across the road from where the church now stands in the Splunge Community. The present church building was finished in 1939, on land donated by B. M. Knight.

RILEY CHAPEL *(Harrison County: 1107 Church Street, Gulfport 39501).* This church was organized in 1880. In 1886 the Handsboro Methodist Church sold their original church which was located on what is now Church Street, one block south of

Pass Road, to the Black Methodists. This church is now the Riley Chapel United Methodist Church. It was named in honor of Reverend Riley, who was the pastor at the time the transfer took place.

Ripley First United Methodist Church

RIPLEY FIRST *(Tippah County: 302 South Main, Ripley 38663).* The first organization of Methodists in Ripley took place on 30 September 1836, under the leadership of Charles P. Miller, a former Tennessean who was a faithful lay leader in the Ripley Church until his death in 1875. It began in a tavern, a block from its present location. The Ripley Church was part of the Emory Circuit which encompassed most of the present Tippah, Benton, Union, and Marshall Counties. Later, with rapid growth of local churches, the Ripley Circuit was established and took in a smaller territory. Ripley was first in the Memphis Conference and became a part of the North Mississippi Conference when it was created in 1870. The first church building in Ripley was a typically crude wooden affair shared with the Presbyterians, and perhaps other Protestants. The Ripley Church moved to its present location in 1850. This building was burned by the Yankees in 1864, because the Confederates reputedly had stored hay for their cavalry there. The next Ripley Church was erected in 1865, and served until destroyed by fire in late 1886. Within a few months another building was completed and put into use. A severe windstorm toppled the steeple from the Ripley Church in early 1925. The congregation decided to replace the small wooden building with a two-story brick building. This structure is still in use, having undergone major interior remodeling in 1964.

ROBBS *(Pontotoc County: Robbs).*

ROBERTS CHAPEL *(Jackson County).* This church was organized in 1855.

ROBINSONVILLE *(Tunica County: Robinsonville).* This church was organized in 1896.

ROCK HILL *(Madison County: Cameron).*

ROCK HILL *(Oktibbeha County: 110 Grand Ridge Road, Starkville 39759).*

ROCKPORT *(Choctaw County).* This church was organized in the 1880s.

ROCKY HILL *(Winston County: 1386 Rocky Hill Road, Louisville 39339).* The church was organized in 1830. The first building was made of logs. It was replaced by a frame building in 1886. In 1906, the sanctuary was remodeled, placing the pulpit on the west end instead of the east. An education unit was completed in 1958. The church received a brick veneer and the inside was paneled in 1962.

ROCKY SPRINGS *(Claiborne County: Old Port Gibson Road, Natchez Trace, Utica 39175).* This community was first settled in 1796 by Nalum Cooper. This church has one of the oldest active Methodist congre-

gations in the state. It dates back to 1805 and its building, erected in 1837, is the fourth oldest in the Conference. Rocky Springs as a small village, was founded about 1796 by settlers moving northeastward from Port Gibson on the old Natchez Trace. Among the early missionaries were Lorenzo Dow, Tobias Gibson, and Moses Floyd. The Rocky Springs Methodist Church was built in 1837 by the wealthy land holders with the assistance of Reverend and Mrs. Thomas Owens. The only change in the appearance of the church in the past hundred years was the removal of the old belfry in 1901. The first pastor, Reverend Thomas Owens, served the congregation until 1859, when age and infirmities forced him to retire from active service and church duties. In May 1863, General U. S. Grant made the Owens' home his headquarters along with his staff for a week while his army of 40,000 troops camped on Little Sand Creek a mile east of Rocky Springs.

ROCKY SPRINGS *(Tishomingo County: 42 County Road 423, Iuka 38852).* The church was organized in 1850.

ROLLING FORK *(Sharkey County: 101 South First Street, Rolling Fork 39159).* It is thought Reverend John Fullerton, a local

Rolling Fork United Methodist Church

Methodist preacher, preached in a log schoolhouse on Rolling Fork Plantation on the bank of Big Deer Creek in 1840 and established the Rolling Fork Methodist Society. This was the first Methodist Society in the area. The church was organized in 1848. In 1869, the church had seventeen members. In 1872, a two-story building was erected on the bank of the creek to be used as a union church and Masonic Lodge. The downstairs part was used as the community school, and for community purposes. This building burned in 1888. The Methodists soon erected a new building. This building served until 1930 when it was destroyed by fire. The church met in the Royal Theater while building a new church. The present church building was dedicated in 1936.

ROLLINS *(Tallahatchie County: 201 Laurel, Webb 38966).*

ROSE HILL *(Jasper County: Highway Eighteen, Rose Hill 39356).* The church was organized in 1896.

ROSEDALE *(Bolivar County: 600 Front Street, Rosedale 38769).* The Rosedale community dates back to 1838, when it was known as Abel's Point. Colonel Lafayette Jones, who owned the landing, renamed the place Rosedale for his plantation home in Virginia. The town was incorporated in 1882. On 19 February 1877, F. A. Montgomery and his wife, Charlotte, signed a deed selling "Lot One in Block Number One in the Town of Rosedale" to the Methodist Episcopal Church, South. In 1889, the present church was built. On 31 May 1893, a cyclone blew the steeple away. An education building was purchased and moved to the present site in the 1960s.

Rosedale United Methodist Church, Lucedale

ROSEDALE *(Jackson County: 25616 Rosedale Church Road, Lucedale 39452).* This church was organized in 1885. Prior to that, a log building, built in 1850, served as a school and church. It was originally known as Rosedale Methodist Episcopal Church, South. There has been but one sanctuary, constructed in 1887. Additions were made to the church facilities in 1952 and 1981. There were numerous renovation projects between 1944 and 1987. The Mississippi Department of Archives and History recognized Rosedale United Methodist Church as an historic site in December 1996.

ROSETTA *(Wilkinson County: 910 South Crosby Street, Centreville 39631).* This church was founded in 1927.

ROXIE *(Franklin County: 214 Third Street, Roxie 39661).* The church was organized in 1876.

RULEVILLE FIRST *(Sunflower County: 100 South Chester Avenue, Ruleville 38771).* Ruleville began in 1868 in the Lehrton area at the home of Berry Stowers Marshall, one of the county's earliest settlers. The church site was in Sunflower County. In the 1870s, a log hut was built. This church was known by several names: Sycamore Grove, Olive Branch, and Lehrton. In 1880, a frame house was

Ruleville First United Methodist Church

constructed which doubled as a school during the week. Reverend J. N. Flowers, who lived at McNutt, was the first pastor and founder of the congregation. In the 1890s, S. T. Jones donated an acre of land on Dougherty Bayou to the Methodists, and under the leadership of Reverend McNabb, a church and parsonage were built. In 1899 or 1900, the Lehrton or Dougherty Bayou Church was moved to Ruleville, being rolled on logs to the lot given by W. F. Wilson. A storm destroyed the church in 1913. A new brick church was completed in 1917. In the early 1900s, the church was part of the Greenville District, later the Winona District, the Greenwood District, and the Cleveland District. In 1953, an educational department and kitchen were added. Reverend J. O. Dowdle's son, Oscar, entered the ministry from this church. The oldest tombstone in the church cemetery bears the date 1856.

RURAL HILL *(Winston County: Highway Fourteen West, Louisville 39339).* This church was organized in 1845.

RUTLEDGE *(Tishomingo County: 170 County Road 159, Tishomingo 38852).* Rutledge was organized in 1904.

SAGEVILLE *(Lauderdale County: Meehan).* The church was organized in 1850.

SAINT ANDREWS *(Lafayette County: North Sixteenth Street, Oxford 38655).* This church was organized in 1962.

SAINT ANDREWS *(Monroe County: 115 Legion Drive, Amory 38821).* Saint Andrews began as a hope for a new church in Amory in the minds of Reverend George Williams and Doctor W. H. Stockton. Reverend K. I. Tucker later worked with Doctor Stockton and others to bring about its beginning. Reverend Tucker suggested the name Saint Andrew. Reverend Bill Jones, Superintendent of the Aberdeen District in 1958 to 1959, was very helpful in the beginning of the church. The church began meeting June 1959, in a tent on the lot where the parsonage was later built in 1961. The church met in the education building, completed in June 1961, until, under the leadership of Reverend J. G. Babb, a sanctuary was built. The sanctuary was completed in February 1981. Persons who have entered full-time ministry from this church are Mack Riley and Billy Funderburk.

SAINT ANDREW'S *(Pike County: 821-A LaBranch Street, McComb 39648).* In 1902 the people of South McComb organized the South McComb Methodist Church with the assistance of Reverend John Chambers. Land for the building was donated by Mr. J. A. Bishop. At the same time the Whitestown Church, organized in 1894, united with the South McComb Methodist Church. Following the appointment of Reverend L. E. Alford in 1904, plans were made to relocate to a more centralized location. The original church building was sold and a lot on LaBranch Street was purchased and a new building erected. The first sermon in the new church was given by Reverend Alford on the third Sunday in July 1904. During the ministry of Reverend A. S. Oliver, Frank Casey, William Morrow, and Alton McKnight accepted the call to the ministry. Also during this time, the parsonage was built on the lot adjoining the church. During World War II the church continued to grow even though most of the young men served their country in the armed forces. In 1950, with Reverend M. K. Miller as pastor, the outside of the church was bricked making it more attractive. The church name was changed in 1957 to Saint Andrew's Methodist Church.

SAINT ELIZABETH *(Lauderdale County: 2804 Saint Luke Street, Meridian 39301).*

SAINT JAMES *(Copiah County: Georgetown 39078).*

SAINT JAMES *(Covington County: Mount Olive 39119).* This church was organized in 1906.

SAINT JAMES *(George County: 3301 Maple Street, Lucedale 39452).*

SAINT JAMES *(Jackson County: 1418 Government Street, Ocean Springs 39564).* The church was organized in 1867. The first structure was a frame building which was remodeled in 1903. The present church building is brick and was built in 1956. It was heavily damaged in Hurricane Elena.

SAINT JAMES *(Lamar County: 316 and 318 Martin Luther King Drive, Lumberton 39475).* This church was organized in 1907.

SAINT JAMES *(Lowndes County: 722 Military Road, Columbus 39701).* The church was organized in 1870.

SAINT JAMES *(Monroe County: 1072 F Avenue, Amory 38821).* Saint James was originated by a group of families living in the Cotton Gin Community in October 1887. The fellowship was conducted under a brush arbor. These families later moved to Amory around the early 1900s. Prior to that date in 1888, a group of Methodist trustees purchased lots eight and nine. It was determined that the original name of the church would be the Methodist Episcopal Church of Amory. Between 1900 and 1924, the name was changed to Saint James Methodist Episcopal Church of Amory. In 1968, a plan of union was adopted that united the Evangelical United Brethren Church and the Methodist Church into the United Methodist Church which is the current name.

SAINT JAMES *(Pike County: Magnolia 39652).* The church was organized in 1863.

SAINT JAMES *(Rankin County).* This church was organized in 1886.

SAINT JAMES *(Walthall County).* This church was organized in 1924.

SAINT JOHN *(Clarke County: Heidelberg 39439).* This church was organized in 1861.

SAINT JOHN *(Forrest County: 121 Sullivan Drive, Hattiesburg 39401).* This church was organized in 1921.

SAINT JOHN'S *(Adams County: 106 Meadowlane Drive, Natchez 39120).* The church was organized in 1871.

SAINT JOHN'S *(Hinds County: 1702 Old Vicksburg Road, Clinton 39056).* In

August 1973, a mission church was started in Clinton. Reverend Keith Tonkel, pastor of Wells Memorial United Methodist Church in Jackson, helped start the church. The congregation met in a trailer belonging to Holy Savior Catholic parish. In January 1974, the congregation adopted the name Saint John United Methodist Church, and six families joined the small church. In February 1974, the church moved into a house on Pinehurst Street, and became popularly known as "the house church" of Clinton. In 1976, the District Board of Missions gave the church $10,000 to purchase a lot at 1702 Old Vicksburg Road. The sanctuary was built, and services began being held there on 20 June. In September 1976, Bishop Mack Stokes dedicated the new building. In 1980, the first full-time pastor, Perry Tanksley, arrived.

SAINT JOHN'S *(Leflore County: 1001 Grand Boulevard, Greenwood 38930).* On Sunday, 13 July 1952, a group of men who were members of First Methodist Church of Greenwood met to discuss the purchase of a lot for a new Methodist Church in North Greenwood. The lot was purchased in August 1952. The new congregation was organized in 1954. The members of this young church selected the name Saint John's on 2 May 1954. The American Legion Hut was chosen for the first meeting place. Two years later, the first building was completed. The service of formal opening in that sanctuary, which is now the fellowship hall, was held on Easter Sunday, 1 April 1956. The sanctuary was consecrated on 12 July 1970, by Bishop Edward J. Pendergrass.

SAINT JOHN'S *(Yazoo County: 321 East Thirteenth Street, Yazoo City 39194).* Bennett Chapel was moved in 1901 from the corner of Eighth Street and Webster Avenue to a lot on Twelfth Street, and the name was then changed to Lintonia Chapel. In April 1920, different denominations held church services there, and a school was started in the church building for children through the fourth grade. In June, a student minister from Millsaps College came to preach once a month until September of that year. Only one or two people came, so shortly after, the college did not send student pastors. In April 1928, several families began to show some interest, and Sunday School was again started. About 1940, many families had begun to move from this area, and the church attendance declined. In November 1948, a special meeting was called by the District Superintendent to see about a Methodist church in the northern part of Yazoo City. A survey was conducted from Canal Street north to determine interested in having another Methodist church. It was determined that there would be interst if the church was moved to a different location. The trustees decided to sell Lintonia Chapel and buy the lot on the corner of Thirteenth Street and Calhoun. In October 1950, a tent was bought and put up for worship service. The people who came together to worship before 1952 became charter members. For a short time, the church was called North Yazoo Methodist Church, and then was changed to Saint John's Methodist Church. The name was drawn from a hat. On 14 April 1952, Easter Sunday, a ground breaking ceremony was held for the first sanctuary. In October 1953, the church moved into the sanctuary. In June 1955, the church bought two lots adjoining the church property. In 1957, an annex to the church was completed.

SAINT JOHN'S *(Madison County: 219 North Hargon Street, Canton 39046).* The church was organized in 1939. This church was once called Northside Methodist. It was located on Yondell Avenue from 1939 to 1963. The first building was a frame structure built in 1939. The second brick building was completed in 1964.

SAINT LUKE *(Bolivar County: 1227 Deering Street, Cleveland 39732).* The church was organized in 1961. Doctor James M. Ewing, a layman of First Methodist, secured commitments from many First Methodist members who contributed sizable sums to sponsor the new church. The first meeting of persons interested in organizing a new Methodist Church was held in the home of Mr. and Mrs. James Pearson on 7 April 1961. Saint Luke opened as a full church with Sunday School and worship services being held in the Pearman Elementary School beginning on 18 June 1961. The church had forty-one members not including children whose parents joined. The charter membership closed on Easter Sunday, 22 April 1962 with 160 members enrolled. Church members met that first summer of 1961 at Pearman Elementary, and plans for building the new church got underway immediately. With the opening of school in September, Saint Luke members began meeting on the second floor of the Bolivar County Courthouse where they continued to meet until they were able to move into their

own sanctuary at Tenth and Deering. Ground breaking service was 3 June 1962; the first service in the present building was 20 January 1963 with the formal opening on 27 January 1963, at which time Bishop Marvin Franklin preached.

Saint Luke United Methodist Church, Tupelo

SAINT LUKE *(Lee County: 1400 Clayton Avenue, Tupelo 38801).* The organizational meeting was held 11 May 1958, in the sanctuary of the First Methodist Church, with Reverend W. M. Jones presiding. At this meeting twenty-seven people presented themselves and were taken in as members. The second meeting was held on 25 May, with twenty-five more people joining. Several names for the new church were presented for consideration and Saint Luke Methodist Church was selected. Rockwell Youth Center was secured as a meeting place, and the first services were conducted 8 June 1958, when eighteen more people joined the church. A Sunrise Service was conducted on Easter Sunday 1961 in the unfinished sanctuary of the church with the congregation sitting on plank benches supported by concrete blocks.

SAINT LUKE *(Wayne County: 6390 County Road 610, Shubuta 39360).*

Saint Luke's United Methodist Church, Jackson

SAINT LUKE'S *(Hinds County: 621 Duling Avenue, Jackson 39216).* Saint Luke's has been known by several names, including Galloway Chapel in 1909, Millsaps Memorial Methodist, and since 1949, Saint Luke's. The church was organized in 1909 under the auspices of First Methodist Episcopal Church, South, now Galloway Memorial United Methodist Church. The first building was begun in 1909, and Reverend J. A. Alford was the first pastor. The church was located on Fondren, and burned to the ground 24 February 1929. The present sanctuary was completed and the first service was conducted 23 February 1930, one day short of the anniversary of the fire. In August 1949, the education building was completed.

SAINT MARK *(Bolivar County: 1312 South Davis, Cleveland 39732).* The church was organized in 1972.

SAINT MARK *(Harrison County: 3350 Twenty-Eighth Street, Gulfport 39501).* The church was organized in 1892. On the corner of Twenty-First Street and Thirty-First Avenue was a brush arbor known as Saint Mark Methodist Episcopal Church. The church was organized under the leadership of Reverend A. C. Lacey, who was the first minister of the congregation. In the infancy of the church Reverend J. A. Patterson was one of the early pastors. According to the first cornerstone, a structure was rebuilt in 1909. However, there is no record of the first building. The records show that Reverend Jossell was the pastor and Reverend S. H. Cannon was the presiding elder at the time that the church was built. A frame and brick building was constructed in 1947. The third metal and brick building was erected in 1993 and 1994.

SAINT MARK *(Jackson County: 1325 Jackson Avenue, Pascagoula 39567).*

SAINT MARK *(Kemper County: DeKalb 39328).*

SAINT MARK *(Lauderdale County: Daleville 39326).*

SAINT MARK *(Lee County: 307 Elvis Presley Drive, Tupelo 38801).* In 1932, this church was organized and became the fifth church on the Mooreville Charge. Reverend J. W. Holliday was the organizing minister. First called East Tupelo Methodist Church, the name was changed to Saint Mark in 1964. The new church was originally in the Corinth District, then in the Aberdeen District before being placed in the Tupelo District. The first property was purchased in 1933, and plans were made for a church home. The basement of the proposed structure, with only a clay floor, was used as a meeting place for a period of time. The sanctuary was dedicated in 1945. In 1954, the church became a part of the East Tupelo-Oak Hill Charge. This arrangement became effective 1 January 1955.

SAINT MARK *(Monroe County: Highway Eight West, Aberdeen 39730).* On 9 April 1962, Saint Mark was organized by a small group of persons who wanted to provide a second United Methodist Church for persons in the Aberdeen community. The original members met in the home of Mr. and Mrs. Frank Barron. Reverend G. R. Meadows was appointed as the first pastor of the new church. The present building was completed 9 June 1963. An educational addition was completed in 1967. A family life center was completed in July 1993.

SAINT MARK *(Neshoba County: Stallo).* The church was organized in 1900.

SAINT MARK'S *(Rankin County: 400 Grant's Ferry Road, Brandon 39042).* The church was organized in 1973 as a chapel in a trailer. The church later built the Wesley Center. The present building was constructed in 1991.

SAINT MARY *(Marshall County: Potts Camp 38659).*

SAINT MARY *(Union County: Saint Mary Road, New Albany 38652).* Saint Mary was organized in 1887.

SAINT MARY'S *(Copiah County: 3009 Harmony Road, Crystal Springs 39059).* The church was organized in 1912.

SAINT MATTHEW *(Lauderdale County: 9238 Cook Road, Bailey 39320).*

SAINT MATTHEWS *(Madison County: 7427 Old Canton Road, Madison 39110).* The church was organized in 1988. This

Saint Matthews United Methodist Church, Madison

church was formed by a group of persons from the now disbanded Wesley United Methodist Church located on Northside Drive in Jackson. The church started in the cafeteria of the State Farm building in Jackson. The present building was constructed by September 1989.

SAINT MATTHEWS *(Monroe County: Amory 38821).*

SAINT MICHAEL *(Noxubee County: Macon 39341).* The church was organized in 1900.

SAINT MORRIS *(Copiah County: Smyrna).*

SAINT PAUL *(Clay County: 330 Fifth Street, West Point 39773).* The church was organized in 1868.

SAINT PAUL *(Forrest County: 215 East Fifth Street, Hattiesburg 39401).* The church was organized in 1882. The first unit was made of wood, and constructed in 1882. This building was destroyed in a windstorm. The present structure replaced the first in 1930, and was made of brick.

SAINT PAUL *(Franklin County: Route Two, Roxie 39661).* The church was organized in 1897.

SAINT PAUL *(Harrison County: 322 Clarke Avenue, Pass Christian 39571).* Sister Corine Sinclair, born in 1879, reported: "The First Methodist Episcopal Colored Church was organized by a group of unknown stalwarts around 1836 in a one-room house between Henderson Avenue and Church Street." Pass Christian was founded in 1839. No records were kept on "colored" churches before a given time. The date of 1852 is used as the official beginning of the Saint Paul Episcopal Colored Church because a cornerstone

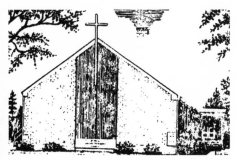

Saint Paul United Methodist Church, Pass Christian

bearing this date was found on the earlier structure. In 1867, land was purchased for the purpose of relocating the Methodist Episcopal Colored Church. The new structure was completed shortly thereafter. This original structure stood, with some renovations, until Hurricane Camille made the old house unlivable in 1969. The city purchased the church property in 1971. Ground breaking service was held on Sunday, 13 August 1972 with Superintendent C. E. Appleberry presiding. Consecration Services were held on 30 December 1973, with Bishop Mack Stokes presiding. Sunday, 20 January 1974, cornerstone laying ceremonies were held. On Sunday, 9 November 1975, dedication services were held with Bishop Mack Stokes, presiding.

SAINT PAUL *(Harrison County: 696 Washington Loop, Biloxi 39530).* This church was organized in 1863.

SAINT PAUL *(Hinds County: 6004 Jimmie Williams Road, Clinton 39056).* Saint Paul United Methodist Church was first founded in 1872, under the name Saint Paul Methodist Episcopal Church of the Tennin community. The founders were just out of slavery and banded themselves

together to establish a church in the Clinton community. Saint Paul's first structure was a brush arbor. The church was first a frame building made from heavy pieces of untreated wood. The building was used for many years as a place of worship and a school. In 1894 the church was rebuilt under the leadership of Reverend R. H. Patton. Twenty-nine years later, the church was remodeled under Reverend J.C. Smoots.

SAINT PAUL *(Jackson County: 3724 Davis Avenue, Moss Point 39563).*

SAINT PAUL *(Jackson County: 800 Porter Avenue, Ocean Springs 39564).* The church was organized in 1853.

SAINT PAUL *(Jones County: 517 Jefferson Street, Laurel 39440).* This church was organized in 1896.

SAINT PAUL *(Lamar County).*

SAINT PAUL *(Lauderdale County: 2705 Thirteenth Street, Meridian 39301).* Saint Paul United Methodist Church was organized in 1868. It is the oldest Black congregation in Meridian. Saint Paul was listed on the National Register of Historic Places, and was officially designated an historic landmark by Meridian. Saint Paul administers the Carnegie Library, built in 1912 as a Black library from the Carnegie Trust. The Library is also on the National Register of Historic Places, and is an historic landmark of Meridian.

SAINT PAUL *(Lee County: 502 North Spring Street, Tupelo 38801).*

SAINT PAUL *(Marion County: 1169 Old Highway Thirty-Five South, Foxworth 39483).* The church was organized in 1875. There have been two buildings. The first was a frame structure. The present block structure was completed in 1956. An addition was made to the building in 1982. Improvements were made in 1991.

SAINT PAUL *(Noxubee County: Macon 39341).* This church was organized in 1867.

SAINT PAUL *(Panola County: Batesville 38606).*

SAINT PAUL *(Pike County: McComb 39648).*

SAINT PAUL *(Tippah County: 510 South Line Street, Ripley 38663).* Organized in 1868, the deed for this church was recorded in February 1870. Among the prominent laity of this church were Ruby Elzy, opera diva, and Ned Barnet, valet to William Faulkner. There have been three buildings in the history of Saint Paul.

Saint Paul's United Methodist Church, Clarksdale

SAINT PAUL'S *(Coahoma County: 1012 West Second Street and Smith Street, Clarksdale 38614).* Saint Paul was organized by members of First United Methodist Church, in order to help Methodism grow in the Clarksdale area. On 6 March 1956, a Quarterly Conference conducted by District Superintendent, Reverend Rufus G. Moore, was held and Saint Paul's was organized as a new church with a number of members from First United Methodist

Church transferring their membership to Saint Paul United Methodist Church. In April permission was given to use the Heidelberg School as the first meeting place for Saint Paul's, and Reverend Gene Russell was its first pastor. Services started the first Sunday in May 1956, at the school and a rented duplex on King Street was used for church school and nursery. During the month of May 1956, the decision to locate the new church on the southwest corner of West Second and Smith was made. Ground breaking for the first unit was held on 23 February 1958, and it was completed in March 1959, with the first service being held on Easter Sunday, 1973. On Sunday, 25 May 1973, Bishop Mack B. Stokes conducted the dedication services. Three young men: J. Torrey Curtis, A. Millsaps Dye Jr., and J. Walt Gaston entered the ministry from this church.

SAINT PETER *(Lafayette County: 40 County Road 104, Oxford 38655).* Saint Peter was established in the mid-1800s. Originally called West Saint Peter Colored Methodist Episcopal, the name was later changed to West Saint Peter Methodist. The church was located on College Hill Switch Road, approximately two and a half miles west of its present location. There were two prior wood structures that were destroyed by fire in the late 1930s. Between rebuilding, services were held under an old fashioned brush arbor. Most of the pews and other furnishings were salvaged from the fires and are now used in the current church. The original building consisted of one-room that was also the local school during weekdays. The present structure was erected in 1953 under the leadership of

Reverend B. J. Cameron, was wood-sided, painted white, and is now bricked.

SAINT PETER *(Lauderdale County: Marion-Lizelia Road, Marion 39342)*. This church was organized in 1990.

SAINT PETER *(Monroe County: Highway Twenty-Five, South, Aberdeen 39730)*. The forebearers of Saint Peter worshipped in the gallery of the white Methodist Church with Reverend Andrew conducting the services. In 1867, the Methodist Church North built a church for the worshippers. They had formerly had services at two other locations in abandoned buildings. Reverend Miles Goodwin was their pastor in 1867. In 1883, the railroad wanted the property for a station and railroad. The city bought a lot, built a church and relocated the congregation. In 1906, the members themselves purchased a ninety-foot lot with a house. The house was used for a parsonage. This church has been in the Aberdeen District and the Aberdeen–Holly Springs District. The original name of this church was Paine Memorial Chapel. Other names have been Saint Paul and Saint Paul Life Boat. Two congregations have merged with this church, and the church has been relocated six times.

SAINT PETER *(Winston County: Route One, Louisville 39339)*. This church was organized in 1896.

SAINT ROCK *(Hancock County: Waveland 39576)*. This church was founded in 1908.

SAINT STEPHEN *(Jackson County: 4517 Old Mobile Highway, Pascagoula 39581)*.

SAINT STEPHEN *(Lowndes County: 800 Tuscaloosa Road, Columbus 39701)*. The church was organized in 1960. There was no church nearer the McBee community than Tabernacle Methodist, Pleasant Hill Baptist, and the churches in the city of Columbus. As the community began to grow, Mr. and Mrs. T. W. Youngblood, Mr. and Mrs. Sam Tidwell, Mr. Weathers, and others in the McBee community erected a large tent on the banks of the McBee Creek at the intersection of Highway Fifty and Lehmberg Road. During the summer preaching was held on Sunday afternoons. A permanent structure was built from contributions of money, labor, and building materials, that is now McBee Baptist Church, but then it was known as McBee Union for the Methodists, Baptists, Presbyterians, and other faiths which met together. All shared in the teaching and preaching services. In 1960 the Methodist Conference found the need of a Methodist church in the community, and plans began for the organization of a Methodist church with the help of Reverend C. L. Rogers of Central Methodist Church. Six acres of land were purchased from Mr. R. W. Bolton for construction of a place of meeting. In December 1960, plans were announced for a full time pastor in March of 1961. On 22 January 1961, Reverend Thad Ferrell, District Superintendent, delivered the sermon and took the fifteen charter members and two others who joined at this time into Saint Stephen Methodist Church from McBee Union Church. On 26 March 1961, McBee Union Church became two separate organizations: Methodist and Baptist, and plans for a building program were underway. Reverend R. K. Hubbard was the first assigned pastor and services were conducted in a building at the Masonic Home until the new church could be built on the purchased property. On 15 October 1961, the ground breaking ceremonies were conducted by Reverend Ferrell for the first building. The first service held in the new church building was on 8 April 1962. On 28 May 1967, Bishop Pendergrass formally opened Saint Stephens new sanctuary.

SAINT STEPHEN *(Webster County: Mabem 39750).*

SAINT STEPHENS *(Yazoo County: 414 East Jefferson, Yazoo City 39194).* After 1865, Blacks of all denominations in Yazoo City worshipped at "the Market Place," an area located on East Jefferson Street just above where Saint Stephens Methodist Church is today. In 1868, one group broke away to form the Bethel African Methodist Episcopal Church, and they erected the present building shortly thereafter. They changed the name to Saint Stephens.

SALEM *(Attala County: Singleton).*

SALEM *(Choctaw County: Highpoint).* The church was organized in 1873.

SALEM *(Choctaw County: Weir Highpoint Road, Weir 39772).* This church was founded in 1873.

SALEM *(Copiah County: 4173 Salem Road, Hazlehurst 39083).* The church was organized in 1877.

SALEM *(George County: Avent).* The church was organized in 1818.

SALEM *(Lafayette County: 208 North Fifth Street, Oxford 38655).* Salem was organized in 1865.

SALEM *(Noxubee County: Macon 39341).* This church was organized in 1881.

SALEM *(Noxubee County).* This church was organized in 1850.

SALEM *(Tishomingo County: 170 County Road 159, Tishomingo 38852).* This church

Salem United Methodist Church, Tishomingo

was organized in 1850, and is also known as Rutledge Salem United Methodist Church. The history of this rural church goes back to the early days of Tishomingo County. At least three buildings have stood at one time or another on the present site of the church. They served from time to time as both school and church for the small community. It is thought the first church was built there in the 1860s. This structure, a log building, was replaced around 1880 by the building used until 1961. This in turn was replaced by a new church building, a native stone and concrete structure. The pews presently in the church were made about 1906. The Salem Church began having services every Sunday morning in June 1982. A fellowship hall was added in 1991.

SALEM *(Union County: 1521 Highway 355, Etta 38627).* The church was organized in 1840.

SALEM *(Wayne County).* This church was organized in 1893.

SALTILLO *(Lee County: 134 Walnut Highway, Saltillo 38866).* This church was organized in 1896.

SAMUEL CHAPEL *(Leflore County: 208 Lincoln Street, Itta Bena 38941).* The Samuel Chapel United Methodist Church has been God's house of worship in the small town of Itta Bena, for over one hundred years. In 1880, a one-room frame building was erected in the Southeastern section of Itta Bena. The building was then named Samuel Chapel Methodist Episcopal Church. In 1911, the frame building was replaced by a brick structure under the leadership of Reverend Troupe. The old church was demolished in 1968, and a new church was rebuilt through membership financing and carefully planned loans. Under the leadership of Reverend M. J. Stalling, dedication of the new Samuel Chapel was held 20 February 1977. Reverend L. T. Brazial entered the ministry from this church.

Sand Hill United Methodist Church

SAND HILL *(Greene County: Highway Forty-Two East, Richton 39476)*. The church was organized between 1952 and 1953. This church merged with a congregation known as Community People. The present building was a frame structure completed in 1953, and later bricked. A fellowship hall was added in 1988. The deed for the property was recorded 9 March 1988.

SAND SPRINGS *(Pontotoc County: Route Two, Pontotoc 38863)*. The Sand Springs congregation was meeting with the Hurricane Baptists and other denominations in 1921, with thirty members. The congregation built their church one and one-half miles west of Hurricane, near the Sand Springs Cemetery, in 1928. Reverend R. M. Pappasan, the first pastor, had previously worked with the congregation while at the Hurricane Baptist Church. The church was remodeled in 1964, when Reverend Royce Linton was pastor. The church, built primarily for the benefit of the cemetery, was non-denominational; however, anyone was allowed to preach who used "sound" doctrine.

SANDERSVILLE *(Jones County: Sandersville 39477)*. The church was organized in 1884.

SANDTOWN *(Neshoba County: Philadelphia 39350)*. Sandtown Church, known in its earlier years as Pine Grove, is eight miles east of Philadelphia. Sandtown is one of the oldest churches in the county. Around 1834, a few pioneer families from Alabama settled around the site where the present church now stands. Their church was called Pine Grove. The first church was south of the cemetery. The second church was built around 1857. The third church was built during the period of 1890 to 1891, west of the present church. In 1916, the fourth church was built, but later was torn down to make way for the fifth and larger building.

SANDY HOOK *(Marion County: 493 John Ford Home Road, Sandy Hook 39478).* In the early 1800s, the wagon train stopped at the area of the present Hopewell United Methodist Church. While the early settlers camped in their tents and wagons, the first building that was erected was a church building made of logs, where the people could worship. Lorenzo Dow was among the first Methodists to preach at least one sermon in this area. Around 1806, Reverend John Ford and his brothers settled at Sandy Hook, near the Louisiana state line on the west side of Pearl River, and Methodism took root in this area. John Ford was already an ordained Methodist minister. Four of his sons later became Methodist ministers, and one of them, Thomas, organized the first Methodist church in Jackson, now known as the Galloway Memorial Church. The first Methodist congregation in this area probably was organized at Fordsville, the present Sandy Hook. After the Civil War, there was a schoolhouse directly behind the present Sandy Hook Methodist Cemetery. Services were held there from time to time. In the early 1900s, the railroad came through Sandy Hook. A large school building was built and the Methodists and Baptists worshipped in this building. Around 1907, the Methodists formally organized as a church and asked the conference to appoint a minister. In 1909 the conference sent Reverend Jasper L. Smith to the Buford Charge. Sandy Hook became a member of this charge, which had five churches. This was Reverend Smith's first appointment and he formally organized the

Methodist Church at Sandy Hook. The present building was completed in late 1928, and opened for worship in January 1929. Reverend J. L. Decell delivered the sermon. The church was dedicated 25 October 1940.

SANFORD *(Covington County: Old Highway Forty-Nine, Sanford).* This church was organized in 1906.

SANTEE *(Jefferson Davis County: Santee Church Road, Santee).* The church was organized in 1852.

SARDIS *(Panola County: Sardis 38666).* The church was organized in 1850.

SARTINVILLE *(Walthall County: 6 East Sartinville, Jayess 39641).* The church was organized in 1813.

SATARTIA *(Yazoo County: 110 Richards Avenue, Satartia 39162).* The church was organized in 1872. Mrs. Amelia Richards deeded to G. W. Ward, J. R. Bell, James Keene, George Martin, and John Slation, as trustees for the Satartia Methodist Episcopal Church, South, two lots for one dollar consideration. The deed is dated 27 November 1896. For many years prior to the erection of the church building, services were held regularly (prayer meeting, Sunday School, and preaching) in the first floor of the Masonic Building. This two-story building stood south of the street, across from the drug store, formerly Leo Martin's Store. Various other denominations held services in this building also. A new building was underway in 1898. During the latter part of Reverend F. M. Williams' ministry, a move was started to build the present building. It was completed and dedicated during the time that C. C. Evans was pastor.

SAUCIER *(Harrison County: 24135 Church Avenue, Saucier 39574).* The church was organized in 1907.

SCHLATER *(Leflore County: 201 West Gleason Street, Schlater 38952).* This church was begun 23 December 1885, in the home of Mr. and Mrs. Daniel Bluett at McNutt. Two traveling ministers stopped at the home of the Bluetts and discussed Christianity and a future place for worship. After prayer, Mr. Bluett, Mrs. James, and a slave, Sandy, were converted. The ministers had religious tracts, and Mrs. James brought some for distribution. This church was organized in 1885, with J. L. Futral as pastor. Services were held in homes, then in the courthouse at McNutt. In 1887, the charge consisted of two churches, McNutt and Sunnyside of the Grenada District, and W. S. Shipman was pastor. The Shellmound Church united with Schlater in 1890. In 1915, Campbells Chapel from Quiver River community united with this church. The first building was replaced by a brick structure in 1949. A cornerstone was dedicated 10 June 1985, on Church Centennial Day with Ed Temple, pastor, and Doctor W. J. Cunningham, presiding. Milton Peden is the only member of this church to become a minister.

SCOOBA *(Kemper County: Scooba 39358).*

SEBASTOPOL *(Scott County: 71 Highway 492, Sebastopol 39359).*

SEE'S CHAPEL *(Panola County: Crenshaw 38621).* The first building was made out of hewn logs around 1855. This little structure was erected near the Jasper Jaco home in a pasture. It was used for a schoolhouse. Some of the church members not only worshipped but attended school there. In 1860, Sam Henry Nelson donated land to the trustees of the Methodist Episcopal Church to build a new house of worship which stood amid oak and cedar trees beside a rural road. The first pastor of this church was Reverend A. J. See for whom the church was named in 1866. The building was a plain one-room structure. There were three large windows on each side. It had two doors in front and one in the back. The church was lighted with candles. The charge was changed in 1870 to Longtown Circuit. Reverend Ben P. Jaco, son of Jasper Jaco, joined the North Mississippi Conference in 1890 and preached at See's Chapel until 1895. With a growing membership, the people began to think of a new building. A group of men met in the home of Mr. Sam Nelson and decided to build a block church. Immediately, the building was begun. All the men in the community helped Mr. F. M. Vanderburg, who was in charge of the project. The church was completed in 1928.

SEMINARY *(Covington County: 208 Pine Street, Seminary 39479).* This church was organized in 1890.

SENATOBIA FIRST *(Tate County: West Gilmore Street, Senatobia 38668).* The Senatobia Methodist Episcopal Church, South, was organized in 1880. The church was built on a lot across the street from the present building on Gilmore Street. In 1925, Sunday School rooms and a ladies' parlor were added. The church burned on Sunday, 13 March 1932. At the end of six months, a new church had been built.

Senatobia First United Methodist Church

During the time of construction, Methodists continued their services in the Christian Church, and in the upper story of the Tate County Courthouse. In the fall of 1955, the ground breaking took place. The last service in the old church was held 7 October 1956, followed by a communion service in the new education building. Completion of the sanctuary was observed with a consecration service 19 November 1961. Following the unification of First Methodist Church and Evangelical United Brethren in 1968, the church officially became the Senatobia First United Methodist Church.

SENEASHA *(Attala County: Highway Fourteen East, Goodman 39079).* The church was organized in 1828, and is named for the creek that flows nearby. After

the death of Tobias Gibson, Doctor Talley was commissioned a missionary to the Choctaw Indians in December 1827. With the approval and support of Colonel Greenwood Leflore, camp meetings were born, and Seneasha was the site of one of the campground missions to the Choctaws. In 1828, Seneasha School was established. White people had begun to settle here by this time. In 1835, Elijah Steele was assigned to the Seneasha Mission, and the boundaries were set "from the forks of the Pearl River to include Rankin, Leake, Neshoba, and Attala Counties." In 1836, the Seneasha Mission became the Attala Circuit. The need for spiritual revivals was great. This began the famous Seneasha Campground Revivals, held in late summers. The first annual conference of the Methodist Protestant Church in Mississippi was held at Seneasha Campground, beginning on Friday, 23 September 1841. Elisha Lott was one of the leaders. At this time the Methodist Protestant conference territory consisted of the states of Mississippi, Louisiana, and Texas; Texas being considered a foreign territory since it had not been admitted to the Union. Many more annual conferences would be held at Seneasha Campground: 1842, 1858, 1872, 1875, and 1879, to name a few. An attempt to unite the Methodist Protestant and the Methodist Episcopal Churches in 1870 was unsuccessful. Four churches chose to remain Methodist Protestant: Seneasha and Pisgah in Attala County and Mount Pleasant and Pleasant Grove in Kemper County. Significantly, the first Annual Conference was held at historic Seneasha. The union of the two branches of the church did not come about until November 1939. The original church-school building was demolished by a tornado in the late 1800s. A new two-story building was built to serve as a church, a school, and a Masonic Lodge. The one-room church continued to serve the congregation for many years. The need for Sunday School rooms and a bigger sanctuary culminated in the building of the present edifice. After three years of hard work and much prayer, Bishop Marvin A. Franklin dedicated this facility on 13 October 1957.

SEVEN SPRINGS *(Hinds County: 4668 Seven Springs Road, Clinton 39056).* A group of local community members met to worship God in a tent under a hollow bush in the community of Raymond in 1881. The families in the community decided that they were tired of getting wet in the tent every time it rained. They made plans to build a church building. In the process of clearing the area for the building they discovered that springs surrounded the area. There were seven of them, so they decided to name the church Seven Springs, because of the beautiful, clear, fresh water from the springs. Three years later a fire destroyed the original building and the growing congregation and community rebuilt the church, which is the existing building today, with a few additions.

SHADY GROVE *(Alcorn County: County Road 402, Corinth 38834).* The exact date that Palestine was built is not known, but it was in existence in 1845, as part of the Memphis Conference on the Jacinto Circuit according to minutes from the old conference. A leather-bound record book

from Palestine Church was found in an old trunk in February 1950. The first date recorded in this book was 7 April 1846, and it contained all the records of the church. Palestine was destroyed by fire during the Civil War. Soon after the Civil War was over, a new church was built about a half mile west of where Palestine was. The new church was named Shady Grove. The first church building was small, but was later enlarged. It served as a schoolroom. Shady Grove produced several preachers, William Ira Smith and W. G. Burks. The Shady Grove building was abandoned in 1902, when it became dilapidated due to a storm that tore up the church building. In 1912 the people built and painted the church themselves. The present church building was constructed in 1965, with the first service being held in December of 1965.

SHADY GROVE *(Attala County).* This community was settled after the Civil War. The first school was built in 1874, and was also used as a church until Reverend N. C. Wasson moved here and organized a church in 1880. The Methodist church dates back to 1873. A new sanctuary and education unit were built in 1956.

SHADY GROVE *(Calhoun County: Banner 38864).* This church was organized in 1881. In 1906, a sanctuary was completed. The education building was added in 1953.

SHADY GROVE *(Montgomery County: 590 Minerva Road, Kilmichael 39747).* The church was organized in 1957.

SHADY GROVE *(Tippah County: 11 County Road 431, Ripley 38663).* Shady Grove was organized in 1905.

SHAEFFER'S CHAPEL *(Lowndes County: 1007 Shaeffer's Chapel Road,*

Columbus 39701). When worshippers gather for services at historic Shaeffer's Chapel eight miles southwest of Columbus, they are continuing a tradition begun there well over a century ago. Shaeffer's Chapel was organized between 1820 and 1860, and began as a woven brush arbor. The congregation was meager with a few white settlers and their children sitting stoically on the front rows, and Blacks and Indians filling in behind. The pastor was an energetic circuit rider known as Reverend George Shaeffer. There are no definite records to this effect remaining, fire having destroyed them, but the vision which began sometime in the 1870s or early 1860s was the erection of the present Shaeffer's Chapel. A newspaper clipping states that the present building was built in 1860.

SHANNON *(Lee County: North Street, Shannon 38868).* The Shannon Methodist Church was organized in 1869 with seventeen members. Reverend E. B. Plummer was the first pastor. In 1871, John Simonton deeded a one-half acre lot on which the church was built in 1872. Originally in the Aberdeen District, it became a part of the Tupelo District in 1965. The building was remodeled in 1906. In 1926, it was bricked and Sunday School rooms added. The education building was built in 1958, and the sanctuary remodeled in 1964. A parsonage was built in 1883, and replaced with a new parsonage in 1952. Several persons from Shannon have entered the ministry. They are: William Edwin Vaughan, Richard Robbins, and Gary Phillips.

SHARON *(Madison County: 111 Old Highway Sixteen East, Canton 39046).* The

Sharon Methodist church in Madison county was organized in 1836, while Orsamus L. Nash was presiding elder of the Choctaw District, and John Ira Ellis Byrd was pastor of the Madison Circuit. The following year, the youthful William Hamilton Watkins served his first year in the pastorate on this circuit. The deed to the property bears the date of 7 June 1836, and included land for a district parsonage, the first in Mississippi; a parsonage for the circuit, the second in this Conference; and for the church. About 1837 there was established in the town of Sharon two schools, which under varying names continued until after the Civil War. The original school was reorganized in 1842 as Sharon Female College, and Madison College for boys was established in 1861 by the removal of Brandon College from the latter place.

SHAW *(Bolivar County: 117 Bayou Street, Shaw 38773).* In the late 1800s, the area now known as Shaw, named for N. A. Shaw, was cleared from a cane break swamp. Early settlers braved malaria, yellow fever, and floods, and the town grew. By 1889, the need was seen for an organized Methodist church. The members first met in the Little Red Schoolhouse and then built a frame church to fit the growing membership. The church burned and a brick church was built by Adonis Simpson, a member, with help from other members. A new education building was added in 1965 under Doctor C. P. Parker with Bishop Franklin at the dedication. The church was in the Greenville District until 1953, when it was placed in the Cleveland District.

SHELBY *(Bolivar County: 1201 South Broadway, Shelby 38774).* Colonel M. D. Shelby of Claiborne County bought thousands of acres here in 1853. In the early days, itinerant preachers, including Reverends O'Bryant and Hume, visited Shelby two or three times a year, and conducted worship in the homes of the residents. In 1856, Colonel Shelby had his slaves construct a small log building that was used as both a school and church, known as Holmes Lake Methodist Episcopal Church, South. The present Shelby United Methodist Church was organized in 1888.

SHERMAN *(Lee County).* This church was organized in 1910.

SHERMAN HILL *(Scott County: Forest 39074).*

SHILOH *(Attala County: Vaiden 39176).* The church was organized in 1854.

SHILOH *(Itawamba County: 1704 Shiloh Road, Mantachie 38855).*

SHILOH *(Lee County: Shiloh Road, Nettleton 38858).* Originally, there were two churches in the vicinity of the present Shiloh United Methodist Church, Palestine and Mount Zion. These churches soon consolidated to form the present church. In 1903, the original structure was built by Frank Monaghan who suggested it be named for the Biblical city of Shiloh. This was done, and one acre of land was deeded to the Methodist Conference by William T. Coggin. At this time a pastor, W. G. Mosier was appointed and the church was born. In 1934, the structure was destroyed by a storm, and again the members saw the need to relocate the church site to its present location on Shiloh Road. As the framework

for the present structure came together, (much of the lumber was salvaged from the original church), the church members rejoiced. The present church site was given by Mr. and Mrs. Gilbert Conlee during the pastorate of Reverend J. E. Lawhon in 1934. Persons who have entered the ministry from Shiloh include: Ewell Payne; T. Herbert Minga; James Noel Hinson; and Danny Dabbs.

SHILOH *(Panola County).* This church was organized in 1874.

SHILOH *(Rankin County: 2394 Shiloh Road, Pelahatchie 39145).* The church was organized in 1826. The community was settled by immigrants from South Carolina. The campground, founded in 1832, is still in use, with a camp meeting each August. Shiloh built a new sanctuary in 1997. An historic marker was placed here by the Mississippi Department of Archives and History.

SHIPMAN *(George County: Lucedale 39452).*

SHIPMAN'S CHAPEL *(Bolivar County: 1595 North Bayou Road, Cleveland 38732).* Shipman's Chapel United Methodist Church had its beginning during the pastorate of Reverend William Sharp Shipman. At the time Brother Shipman was pastor of the Methodist Episcopal Church, South, in Cleveland. It was through his dedicated leadership that a small congregation of Methodist people was formed some three miles north of Cleveland on Jones Bayou Road. It was this group of people that lovingly named their church building, Shipman's Chapel Methodist Episcopal Church, South, in honor of Brother Shipman, in March of 1893. In September of 1892 a revival was held in the community. Ten people affiliated with the church due to the evangelistic fervor of the guest preacher, Reverend Thomas B. Clifford. While Brother Clifford led the church in the revival services, Mrs. Clifford organized the women into a prayer group. On Easter Sunday, 1893, a Charter Service was held with fifteen becoming members of the church. The first church building was erected on a piece of ground given by Mr. J. M. Switzer, Mr. B. F. Beevers, and Mr. Thomas Howell. The property deed was dated 24 November 1892. By the time of the Charter Service in 1893 a small church had been built directly across the road from where the present church is situated. The present building was dedicated 21 May 1944. Additions to the building were made in 1958 and 1960.

Shrock United Methodist Church

SHROCK *(Attala County: Shrock Community, Goodman 39079).* In the year 1858, Joseph K. Shrock purchased a large tract of land in the southern end of Attala County. He was a progressive farmer and merchant, and soon established a sawmill, cotton gin, and grist mill. There were

neither schools nor churches in the area, and a dire need was felt for both of these institutions. In the year 1862, Mr. Shrock built a small building that served as a private school for his children and the children of the other farmers in the community. The little building also served as a Methodist church and stands much the same today with the exception of a few external changes. Joseph K. Shrock saw the need in the community and was responsible for providing the people with both spiritual and educational opportunity.

SHUBUTA *(Clarke County: Highway Forty-Five, Shubuta 39360).* This old community appeared on Benard Roman's map of 1772. The present community was established about 1833. The Methodist church here was organized in 1843.

SHUQUALAK *(Noxubee County: Highways Twenty-One and Twenty-Nine, Shuqualak 39361).* People began moving into this area shortly after the Treaty of Dancing Rabbit Creek in 1830. About 1850 a survey was made through Noxubee County for the purpose of building a railroad. This led to the birth of the town of Shuqualak. The coming of the railroad in 1856 started a rapid expansion in Shuqualak and the immediate area. The town of Shuqualak was first incorporated 16 July 1859. The Shuqualak Baptist Church was organized about 1855. On 18 November, at a meeting in Shuqualak, several persons were organized into a Presbyterian Church of Shuqualak. Mr. D. F. Constantine of Jefferson County, Alabama, deeded to trustees on behalf of the Presbyterian Church and the Methodist Episcopal Church, South, property in the town of Shuqualak to erect a house of worship of God. On 16 June 1867, the Presbyterian elders resolved themselves with a committee to confer with leading members of other churches for the purpose of establishing a Union Sabbath School in the town of Shuqualak. 16 February 1878, *The Macon Beacon* stated "Union Church nearly complete." On 27 October the trustees of Shuqualak Methodist Church were instructed to execute a quit claim in favor of the Presbyterians. There have been three sanctuaries. The first one, built about 1905, was frame. It burned in 1914. The second frame building, built in 1915, suffered a similar fate, and burned in 1934. The present brick building was constructed between 1934 and 1939.

SIDON *(Leflore County: East Railroad Street, Sidon 38954)*. The first mention of Sidon in the conference minutes was between 28 November and 5 December 1855. The conference was held in Vicksburg, and Bishop Cavanaugh presided. Levi Pearce was presiding elder of the Yazoo District. Calvin McGuffey was listed as being assigned to Sidon. Sidon was listed on a circuit with Greenwood and Carrollton and was called Marion. The church in Greenwood was a union church of Methodists and Presbyterians. Other churches included on the circuit were Leflore, Leflore Quarter, Vicks Quarter, Smith, Pickety, Holly Grove, McNutt, Hazel Dell (Shepardtown), McLemore, Doctor Ball's, and Evans Plantation. The name Sidon was first used in Quarterly Conference of 5 February 1855. At the Quarterly Conference of 10 November

1855, held at Roebuck, Edwin Mortimer, pastor in charge, petitioned the Bishop to divide the Greenwood Circuit into two missions to be called Roebuck and Tallahatchie. No record of a church building is found until the present property was acquired in 1904 from Russell and Callie F. Jones of Sunflower County. The original building was a white clapboard building with a steeple and bell. The building burned in 1930. The church was rebuilt the same year. Sidon has always been on a circuit: first with Greenwood and then in 1897, with Itta Bena. In 1905, it was placed with Tchula and in 1916, Tchula was separated, and Sidon remained with Cruger until sometime in the 1960s. In 1966, Sidon was placed with Itta Bena.

SILOAM *(Clay County: West Point 39773)*. The church was organized in 1869. The church was once at a location just across the road from the present building. The present brick structure was built in 1956. Other additions were constructed in 1962 and 1970.

SILOAM *(Prentiss County: 90 County Road 4101, Marietta 38856)*. Siloam was organized in 1870.

SILVER CITY *(Humphreys County: Carter Road, Silver City 39166)*. For many years the Methodist Church of Silver City was a part of what was known as the Silver Creek Circuit. Most of the area at that time was covered with forest and the people on the widely scattered plantations, that dotted the banks of the stream from which the circuit got its name, were served by the Methodist circuit riders. Reverend Green W. Browne was appointed to the Silver Creek Circuit in 1876. Reverend Martin Anding Bell served in the years between 1881 and 1885. During these years church services were held in the homes in the area, in school buildings, and on adjoining plantations. The exact date for the organization of the Silver City Methodist Church is not known. It first appeared in the appointments in 1872. It went by the name Silver Creek until 1903, when the name was changed to Palmetto Home. That name was used only one year. It was changed to Silver City in 1904. The property or the date of the first building is not known, however records show a new church building was constructed in 1906. The present church was built in 1964. The church was in the Jackson District until 1906, in the Vicksburg District 1906 to 1910, in the Port Gibson District 1911 to 1920, and in the Vicksburg-West Jackson District, now the West Jackson District.

SILVER SPREE *(Clarke County: Eucutta).* This church was organized in 1865.

SINGLETON *(Leake County: Singleton Road, Carthage 39051).* The Singleton Methodist Episcopal Church was founded in 1896. The land for the church was donated in 1896 by W. A. Turnage. The name Singleton comes from the first minister, Reverend O. R. Singleton. The church was often referred to as "the church with the steeple and bell," as the first school was in the church building. Reverend Singleton and his daughter were the first teachers. In 1934 the church building was destroyed by a storm but rebuilt that same year. In 1974 the church now standing was built during the pastorate of Clark Howell. In 1975, the old church building was remodeled to include Sunday School

rooms and a fellowship hall. Ground breaking ceremonies for the new fellowship hall were conducted in November of 1994 and construction was completed in November 1995.

Sledge United Methodist Church

SLEDGE *(Quitman County: Sledge 38670).* The church was organized in 1901. The original frame building, built in 1918, was bricked in the 1940s, and more work was done in the 1960s.

SMITH CHAPEL *(Jones County: Laurel).*

SMITHVILLE *(Monroe County: Smithville 38870).* As early as the 1830s, there was a Methodist Church in the Smithville vicinity. This church was known as Siloam and was located about two and a half miles east of Smithville near the Burdine Cemetery. This church had the charge name, Bull Mountain Mission, and belonged to the Alabama Conference. Reverend John Gilmore served as pastor in 1838 to 1839. In 1840, the charge name was changed to Athens and was still in the Alabama Conference. In the 1850s, a small group of Methodist believers assembled and planned to establish the Smithville Methodist Church. The lot on which the church building was to be erected was purchased from C. N. and Mary Ballard on 19 July 1858. The first church was a one-story wooden structure. The church remained on the Athens Charge and Alabama Conference until 1869. Most of the pastors, or circuit riders as they were called, served for only one year. In 1870 the Smithville Church became part of the Athens Charge and North Mississippi Conference. From 1838 until 1874, while Smithville was part of the Athens Charge, the District was Columbus except for 1865 when the District was changed to Athens. This change lasted for only one year. In 1875 another change was made when the Athens Charge became part of the Aberdeen District. Five years later in 1880, still another change occurred when Smithville Church became the Smithville Charge. The church building that was first built in Smithville was used as a place of worship until 24 December 1884, when it was destroyed by fire. It burned immediately following a Christmas celebration held at the church, and it is said that the fire started from candles on the tree. All the church records were destroyed. The Smithville people went about planning another building. Within a few months they had built another house in which to

worship. This was a wooden structure painted white with green shutters at the windows. The pillars were made of native rock and the sills were made of hewed logs. The church had two entrances on the front. For the first time in its history, the Smithville Church was made the Fulton and Smithville Charge in 1884. Smithville became the parent church of Amory in 1889. The charge was changed to Amory and Smithville while remaining in the Aberdeen Conference. In 1899 it became the Fulton and Smithville Charge. From 1901 to 1903 it was part of the Amory-Nettleton Charge. Finally, in 1904, Smithville Church acquired the name, Smithville Charge. In 1960 the Smithville Charge was placed in the Tupelo District.

SNOWDOWN *(Tishomingo County: 274 County Road 246, Iuka 38852).* Snowdown was organized in 1845 as a Methodist Episcopal Church, South. It derived its name from the fact that it was snowing at the time leaders met to build a log structure on a two acre plot donated by Stephen Standifer Hogue for the church and cemetery. This structure burned. The second building doubled as a place of worship and a public school from the early 1900s until 1925. It had a front and back door, three rows of pews and shutter-covered windows. In 1903, an additional eight acres were purchased from Mrs. Belle Pledge. In 1927, a brick church was built. An education annex was dedicated in 1966. The Women's Missionary Society was organized in 1927 and the Circuit Men's Club in 1958. Snowdown formerly was a part of an eight church circuit, but is now one of three churches on the Iuka, South Charge.

SNOWTOWN *(Chickasaw County: Troy).*
SOUL CHAPEL *(Jones County: Rainey Community, Moselle 39459).*
SOUTH UNION *(Choctaw County: South Union Road, Ackerman 39735).* The church was organized in 1865. Following the Civil War in l865, the older churches were organized and were served by pastors. One of these churches was South Union, nestling in the dense pine forest near a spring. The original church at South Union was built of huge logs near the spring. It was built with an apartment back of the pulpit for the accommodation of the slaves, where they worshipped. In this crude structure the congregation worshipped for a few years following the Civil War. The preaching day was on Thursday and only once each month. The original log structure at South Union was eventually replaced by a better and more commodious church, better suited to the needs of the people. In 1872, the campground was laid off in a square. The land was given to South Union for this purpose by Mr. Parham Pollard. The encampment was in the shape of a square. The large shingle-covered tabernacle was built by Mr. Arthur Tenhet. The first tents that were erected around this tabernacle for the encampment of the worshippers were somewhat crude in style and structure. These camp meetings were first held the third Sunday in August but in 1892 they were changed to the fourth Sunday in July, at which time they continue to be held, beginning on Friday before the fourth Sunday and closing the following Wednesday night. The campground suffered destruction by a tornado in 1883, and fire in 1914, but always rebounded with faith to hold the annual camp meetings.

Southaven First United Methodist Church

SOUTHAVEN FIRST *(DeSoto County: 8613 Bunker Hill Drive, Southaven 38671).* The First United Methodist Church began with a congregation of sixteen members in 1962. In 1961, land was bought on Bunker Hill Drive, by a church organization in the Southaven subdivision. In 1962, a tent was erected on the lot to be used until a sanctuary could be built. First services were held on 13 May with sixteen members being placed on the church roll. In September, a metal building was erected to be used as a sanctuary and education building. In 1964, a wing was added with nine classrooms and a pastor's study. In 1974, the present sanctuary was erected along with six additional classrooms.
SOUTHSIDE *(Neshoba County: 910 Range, Philadelphia 39350).* This church was organized in 1947.
SPARTA *(Grenada County: 1329 Scott Road, Holcomb 38940).* The church began as a log cabin in 1835. The present structure was built in 1898. The pews, pulpit, altar rails, and table were hand carved by the early carpenters. There is an Indian grave in

Sparta United Methodist Church

the cemetery. Sparta was in the Grenada District before becoming a part of the Greenwood District. Jack Smith, former Superintendent of the Greenwood District, began his ministry for the Lord on the Holcomb Charge, of which Sparta Church is a part.

SPRING GROVE *(Attala County: Goodman 39079).* Spring Grove Methodist Episcopal Church South was organized and built in 1880. Some of the names of the preachers that served during these early years were Dollar, Worsham, Smith, Oaks, McWhorter, and Giddy. Little else is known about this church in the beginning days of Methodism in Mississippi. The old church was dismantled and the present building was erected in 1913 under the pastorate of Reverend W. F. Rodgers. The deed from E. L. Mabry Sr. and Hattie Mabry for the church and one acre of land was recorded on 26 July 1913. An interesting part of the deed states that the "church shall own one-half interest in the spring on or near said Church lot."

SPRING HILL *(Clarke County: DeSoto).* The church was organized in 1880.

SPRING HILL *(Holmes County: 230 Truly Road, Lexington 39095).* The church was organized between 1840 and 1886.

SPRING HILL *(Jasper County).* This church was organized in 1900.

SPRING HILL *(Jasper County).* This church was organized in 1863.

SPRING HILL *(Kemper County).*

Spring Hill United Methodist Church, Meridian

SPRING HILL *(Lauderdale County: 6614 Zero Road, Meridian 39301).* This church was once known as Spring Hill Methodist Protestant Church. The Meridian and Bigbee Railroad gave land for this church in the early 1900s. The church was organized in 1900. The original building was destroyed by a tornado in 1934. The existing sanctuary was built shortly thereafter, and remodeled in 1980. Two Sunday School rooms were built in 1954, and more educational space was added in the 1980s.

SPRING HILL *(Tishomingo County: 479 Highway 364, Tishomingo 38873).* The church was organized in 1909, with fourteen charter members. The church worshipped in a schoolhouse from 1909 to 1911. In 1911, a church building was built. The present church was erected in 1956.

SPRING RIDGE *(Hinds County: 9534 Spring Ridge Road, Terry 39170).* In the late 1820s, groups of settlers from Kentucky and the Carolinas traveled south down the Natchez Trace into Mississippi. Gradually, as they settled eastward on the Trace, they established a community there, naming it Redwine Branch, after one of the settlers. It was in 1830 that the little community formed a Methodist congregation, Redwine Branch Methodist Church. They had no building, so worship was held in various homes in the community by preachers known as "circuit riders" traveling the Natchez Trace between Nashville and Natchez. Records show that in 1852 the trustees purchased the land where the church is now located. A sanctuary was erected using slave labor and hand-cut lumber and building materials donated by members of the community. By this time the community had become known as Spring Ridge, due to the many natural springs found at the base of the long ridge in the area, so the congregation changed its name to Spring Ridge Methodist Church. This building stood for more than one hundred years. In 1954 plans were made to build an education building. In the Spring of 1956, work was completed on the new structure. On the morning of Friday, 13 April 1956, as workmen were completing the exterior of the new building, fire broke out in the adjacent sanctuary. In just minutes the grand, 104-year-old house of worship was nothing but a smoking ruin. Only a few of the old handmade wooden pews and a few other items were saved. On 13 July 1956, just three months after the disastrous fire, the new sanctuary was completed. The church had always been on a circuit, sharing its pastor with one or more other area Methodist churches. In 1973, it was a charge of its own, with its own pastor. The church now owns about

ten acres, which includes the historic old Spring Ridge Cemetery, with graves as old as the 1840s.

SPRUELL *(Monroe County: Route One, Smithville 38870).* The church was organized in the Summer of 1900. Spruell Chapel Church was moved from Standford or Blue Creek to its present location in the Fall of 1905. Reverend Money Young and Reverend Agnue were the leaders in the movement. The new church was named for Anthony Spruell. Under the leadership of Reverend James Washington, a block building was erected in June of 1977.

STALLO *(Neshoba County: Highway Fifteen North, Philadelphia 39350).*

Starkville First United Methodist Church

STARKVILLE FIRST *(Oktibbeha County: Lampkin Street at Meigs, Starkville 39760).* First United Methodist Church at Starkville was organized in 1835, on the same spot where the present church is located. There were seven charter members and Jacob Matthews, a visiting circuit rider, present. The first church, built in 1839, was a two-story brick building with a slave gallery on three sides. For some reason the walls soon had to be propped up so a second larger church was built in 1850, with slave galleries on three sides. A third, much larger wooden church, was built in 1885. When the present fourth church was built in 1925, the stained glass windows were given to the Guntown Methodist Church. In 1962, a three-story annex of Sunday School rooms was added.

State Line United Methodist Church

STATE LINE *(Greene County: Highway Fifty-Seven, State Line 39362).* Sometime during the year 1876, the pastor at Waynesboro, Reverend Hiram R. Singleton, sent an article to the *Advocate* in which he stated that a new Methodist congregation had been organized at State Line. He stated further that this made the third church he was serving as pastor: Waynesboro, State Line, and "another little church in a community beside the railroad between Waynesboro and State Line," which probably was Winchester. No record has been found as to how many charter members there were. For the first years the Methodists in State Line worshipped in a building used by both the Baptists and Methodists. It was in this building that the first revival services were held the following summer, in 1877. State Line

Methodists had their own campground, known by two names: Smith Mill and Moungers Creek Campground. It was located in the Battle Community. The first camp meeting there began on the first Sunday in August in 1879, with the State Line pastor, Reverend W. B. Hines, in charge. An estimated 600 people attended on that first Sunday, and eighteen conversions were reported. These camp meetings were held annually for about five years and then the project was abandoned. The first sanctuary was constructed in 1883, and dedicated 6 January 1884. The first addition was constructed in the 1930s. In the 1950s, a fellowship hall was added to the building.

STEVENS CHAPEL *(Neshoba County: West Gunn Street, Philadelphia).* The church was organized in 1911. Stevens Chapel was organized by Edd Stevens and his wife, Julia, in 1911, in the parsonage of the Philadelphia Circuit. In 1913, a church building was built on West Gunn Street, and a modern brick facility was built in 1950 at the same location.

STEWART *(Montgomery County: Stewart 39767).* The date of organization of the Stewart church is unknown. There have been two buildings, one frame, and the present brick one.

STONEWALL *(Clarke County: Stonewall 39363).* The Stonewall community was established in 1868 with the creation of the Stonewall Manufacturing Company, a cotton mill, named for General Stonewall Jackson. The church was organized in 1872. The town did not incorporate until 1965.

STRICKLAND *(Marshall County: Wyatte).* This church was organized in 1871.

STRINGER *(Jasper County: Old Highway Fifteen, Stringer 39481).* The church was organized in 1910.

STRONG *(Monroe County: Aberdeen 39730).* The church was organized in 1856. Strong was originally known as Paine Memorial. The first building was on Aberdeen-West Point Road. Late in 1900, the church moved two miles east of Strong, and the name was changed to Strong in 1930. The present structure was built in 1925, and an activity hall was added in 1995. A half-acre was deeded and recorded 12 November 1921 by Asa Watson and his wife.

STURGIS *(Oktibbeha County: Sturgis 39769).* The church was organized in the 1880s.

SUMMERVILLE *(Jackson County: 4100 Dutch Bayou Street, Escatawpa 39552).* Early historical written records for Summerville United Methodist Church were not available. Oral reports from a few senior citizens reveal the first Black Methodist church in Escatawpa was located on a plot of land known as The Bottom, now known as Lilly Lane. The members built a second church on Highway Sixty-three. The second church was destroyed by a storm. The third church was built on the same site and dedicated in 1910. Reverend Lee was its first pastor. The Highway Department purchased the church property to construct Interstate 10 in 1970. Using the money received for the property, the present structure was completed.

SUMMIT *(Pike County: 1107 Baldwin Street, Summit 39666).* The church was organized in 1859.

SUMRALL *(Lamar County: 145 Center Street, Sumrall 39482).* This church was organized in 1903.

SUNFLOWER *(Sunflower County: Sunflower Avenue, Sunflower 38778).* The church was organized in 1899. The records available about the beginning are scant, but the first church home was built on this same spot, a small frame building that served as a schoolhouse during the week and a house of worship on Sunday. Sunflower Methodist Church was then a part of the Moorhead Charge, and the first pastor, Reverend Walter G. Harbin lived at Moorhead. The charge then was in the Winona District. The first frame building was erected in 1902. The Sunflower Charge was organized at the Annual Conference in New Albany in the Fall of 1915. Churches in the Sunflower Charge have changed from time to time, with Fairview and Doddsville having been in the charge at one time.

SUQUALENA *(Lauderdale County: Highway 494, Meridian 39305).*

SWEET PILGRIM *(Clarke County: Eucutta).* The church was organized in 1932.

SWEETWATER *(Copiah County: Midway).* The church was organized in 1824. This church has two distinctions. It is the oldest Methodist organization in Copiah County, and it originally had a charter from the legislature, granted by the fourteenth session of that body in November 1830. Only one other Methodist church, the church at Port Gibson, still exists from a number chartered by the state. Sweetwater Church was organized in 1824, when John Ira Ellis Byrd and Lewellen Leggett were pastors of the Claiborne Circuit. William Winans was then presiding elder of the Mississippi District. The first church building was constructed of logs on the site of what is still known as Sweetwater Cemetery, on the road from Barlow to Caseyville, a few miles from Highway Twenty. For twenty-five years Sweetwater Church stood on this spot and served as the mother church of Methodism in southwest Copiah and adjoining counties. In the early 1850s, the log church was abandoned and a new frame church was erected just across the Homochitto River, three and a half miles from the present community of Caseyville. For a little more than thirty years, Sweetwater stood on this spot. It was then resolved to build a new church near Midway, on a spot four miles south of Pleasant Valley.

SWIFTOWN *(Leflore County: Highway Seven, Swiftown 38959)* This church was organized in 1920. The church has been at its present location since 1920. There have been two sanctuaries, one frame, and one brick. Both buildings are still in use. The church was damaged by a tornado in 1971. The present building was constructed in late 1971 and early 1972.

SYLVARENA *(Smith County: Highway Eighteen, Sylvarena 39422).* The church was organized in 1924.

SYLVESTER *(Newton County).*

SYLVESTER *(Scott County: Harperville 39080).* This church was organized in 1949.

TABERNACLE *(Attala County: Highway 5053, Ethel 39067).* In the 1870s, the Tabernacle Methodist Church was established and became the center of the community that adopted its name. The name was suggested by J. S. Rone, businessman. The church was once located across the road from its present site, where the cemetery is located.

Tabernacle Church was established in 1875. The church was used as a school, and in the Spring of 1905, one of the pupils put a broom in the stove and started the fire which burned down the church. In the Fall of 1905, work began rebuilding the church. Lumber was brought to the site by ox wagon. The church was finished by the Spring of 1906. According to old records, there were no full-time pastors, but the church was served by a pastor probably once a month. There was a District Conference at Tabernacle in April 1906, the pastor was J.A. Goad. In 1945, the present church was built, moving across the road to land donated by Mr. and Mrs. Doss Ray. The old church was torn down, but some of the lumber was used in the new church. The first services were held in the new church March 1946. The pastor was J. L. McElroy. In 1972 work was begun toward the new addition on the back of the church.

TABERNACLE *(Lauderdale County: Highway Nineteen South, Meridian 39301).* The church was organized in 1885.

TALOWAH *(Lamar County: 226 Yawn School Road, Lumberton 39455).* This church was organized in 1917.

TAMOLA BETHEL *(Kemper County: Tamola).*

TANNERS CHAPEL *(Jackson County: 2907 Yellow Bluff Road, Lucedale 39422).* The church was organized in 1882. There have been two buildings. The first frame building was constructed in 1882. A block building was erected in 1964, and the first building was made into a fellowship hall.

TAYLOR *(Lafayette County: 06 County Road 3065, Taylor 38673).*

TAYLORS *(Marshall County).* This church was organized in 1896.

TAYLORSVILLE *(Rankin County: Jackson SE).*

TAYLORSVILLE FIRST *(Smith County: 311 Highway Thirty-Seven North, Taylorsville 39168).* When the town of Taylorsville came into existence, there was no church. Religious services were held in the school building. On 5 June 1902, a small group of men and women, under the leadership of the first pastor, Reverend R. A. Gale of Raleigh, organized a Methodist church. After organization and while the membership was enthusiastic, plans were made to build a church. With the woods full of long-leaf yellow pine trees, materials were easily accessible; thus a huge, square church was begun about 1902. In July, a tropical storm blew the framework down. The charge was called the Okahay Charge, with some seven or eight churches to be

Taylorsville First United Methodist Church

supplied and cared for. While Brother Walton lived there, a new parsonage was built and furnished. Brother Price held a lay-rally and, as a result, a men's prayer group was organized. When Brother Martin came, he helped build a new education building on the north side of the church. It was finished in 1968.

TCHULA *(Holmes County: 123 Main Street, Tchula 39169).* The church was organized in November 1883. Reverend N. G. Augustus was the first pastor. He preached in the lower story of the Masonic Lodge. In 1886, money was raised and a church building was constructed. This was the first church building in the town of Tchula. A new sanctuary and education building were completed in 1925.

TERZA *(Panola County: Terza).* In 1857, the land for the church building site was deeded to the trustees. No written record was kept until the year 1892. At that time there were twenty-three men and forty-five women on the roll. Terza was then a part of the Eureka Circuit. Sometime within the year, or the Winter of 1894 to 1895, the original church building burned. The church was rebuilt and services resumed in the present building in the spring of 1896. Late in 1960, the membership decided to remodel the old church structure. Terza is the oldest church in South Panola County.

THAXTON *(Pontotoc County: Highway 336 West, Thaxton 38871).*

THIRKIELD *(Franklin County).*

THIRKIELD *(Newton County: 114 Bolden Street, Union 39365).* The church was organized in 1920.

THORN *(Chickasaw County: Houston 38851).* On 25 May 1892, William Thorn became postmaster of the post office, thus creating the Thorn community. The Methodist church was organized in 1908.

Thornton United Methodist Church

THORNTON *(Holmes County: Highway Forty-Nine East, Bee Lake Road, Thornton 39172).* Thornton United Methodist Church was organized in 1887. The present frame building was erected in 1887 or earlier. There have been no additions to that structure, but the church was renovated in 1950. The deed was recorded 8 February 1887.

THORNTON CHAPEL *(Madison County: Way at Davis Roads, Canton 39046).* The church was organized about 1855, and

Thornton Chapel United Methodist Church

has a mourner's bench. The church was once known as Persimmon Grove. According to records, the original site was very close to the present site. Doctor Thomas C. Thornton, a native Virginian, was president of Madison College in Sharon from 1851 to 1860, and was the first pastor. The first frame building was constructed in the mid-1850s. This building was still in use when the new sanctuary was built in 1963, and was converted into fellowship and education space.

THRASHER *(Prentiss County: Thrasher Community).*

TILLATOBA *(Yalobusha County: Tillatoba 38961).* This church was organized in 1892.

TILLMAN *(Carroll County: Highway Thirty-Five, North Carrollton 38947).* This church was once located at another unidentified site, and known as Tillman Chapel.

TILTON *(Lawrence County: Hulon Brister Road, Jayess 39641).* The church was organized in 1881.

TIPPO *(Tallahatchie County: Tippo 38962).* In the late 1800s a school and Methodist church were built in a clearing on Tippo Creek, known as Needmore Cemetery today. The first sermons at Needmore were by circuit riders. The present church record book dates back only to 1922. The name of the Needmore Post Office was changed to Tippo when it was moved in 1908 to a spur of a railroad built from Philipp to Charleston. About 1925, a tree fell on the Needmore Church. Some lumber was salvaged from the damaged church, sold, and funds placed in an account to be used for a new building. The members started having services in a new consolidated school building at Tippo. For about twenty-two years worship services were held in the school building by Methodist, Baptist, and occasionally Church of Christ ministers. In 1947, the consolidated school building at Tippo burned and worship services were held in a home. School was held in the Church of God. Reconstruction of the school was begun in 1948. Under the direction of the church stewards the church was constructed at the time of the rebuilding of the school. During the construction a thunderstorm caused the collapse of the framework of the building. The frame was raised again, but to this day the outside walls of the sanctuary visibly bulge outward. The building was completed in 1949, but was not dedicated until it was debt free in 1954. Services were still alternating between Methodist and Baptist ministers. The altar railings were obtained from the Webb Methodist Church which had joined Sumner in building a new church on Highway Forty-nine. The bell tower was added to the church yard in 1973.

TISHOMINGO FIRST *(Tishomingo County: 15 Natchez Street, Tishomingo 38873).* In 1907 there was no house of worship in Tishomingo, a town only in its infancy. A group of Methodists, led by Reverend W. L. Broom, began worshipping in and about Tishomingo until the building of a church in 1915. Having completed a parsonage just a few years earlier, lumber was brought in by train from Corinth and hauled by wagon from the Tishomingo depot to the building site. The church was completed in 1916. In 1954 an educational

annex was added during the pastorate of Bill Appleby, almost doubling the size of the building. In 1979 and 1980, the church and parsonage were bricked, an effort dedicated to the memory of T. E. Finch. By 1995, the church had outgrown the space capacity for Sunday School and, led by pastor Steve Kennedy, a renovated structure was added for use as classroom and meeting space.

TOPEKA *(Lawrence County: China Grove Road, Jayess 39641).* The church was organized in 1941.

TRANQUIL *(Monroe County: Wren).* On 6 February 1847, land was deeded to the Methodist Episcopal Church, South, by Milton Crawford, Aaron Redus, Middleton Westbrook, and their wives. The deed was recorded on 19 May 1847. The first building was built the same year and was "a frame, dropped sides, with studdings and braces morticed in the sills." A cemetery was begun by the church and later Tranquil School was begun near the church. The oldest marker in the cemetery bears the date 1856. Before Tranquil was organized, the people worshipped at "Campground." The church was named by Lemon Shell for Tranquil Church near Greenwood, South Carolina. Tranquil was in the Alabama Conference until 1866, when it was transferred to the Memphis Conference and made part of the Okolona Circuit. In 1871, Tranquil was transferred from the Memphis Conference to the North Mississippi Conference. In 1915, the original building was torn down and a new one erected. In 1920 a tornado destroyed the 1915 building. The third building is still in use today. It was dedicated July 1922. Tranquil became a full-time church in 1962. In 1973, the Wren Charge was formed with Grady's Chapel. The importance of Tranquil in Monroe County history is emphasized by the historical marker placed by the Monroe County American Revolution Bicentennial Committee in January 1977.

TREMONT *(Itawamba County: 291 Bankhead Highway, Tremont 38876).* The Tremont Church was organized in 1892. That summer during the week that the Baptist Church was having a revival in their log cabin, the Methodist people used a brush arbor just behind the log cabin to hold a protracted meeting at the same morning and evening hours. The Tremont Methodist Church was organized from this beginning. The present building was constructed in 1937, and was bricked in 1971. Lumber from the old church was used in the present one.

TRINITY *(Harrison County: 5007 Lawson Avenue, Gulfport 39507).* The church was organized in 1958. The church was first

Trinity United Methodist Church, Gulfport

known as Bayou View Methodist. The first building was a quonset hut. The second building, the present fellowship hall, was opened 29 March 1959. The present sanctuary was dedicated 15 April 1961. Numerous education building programs reflect the rapid growth of Trinity's membership, one of the largest in the Conference. The latest education annex was completed in 1995.

TRINITY *(Washington County: 850 McAllister Street, Greenville 38701).* The church was organized 8 April 1949. Two sanctuaries have been constructed. The first was in 1956. The second was in 1966, and is a brick structure. The 1950 building serves as education and fellowship hall space.

TROY *(Pontotoc County: Troy).* The church records for Troy go back to 1882 showing the appointment of John E. Thomas as pastor. Records also show continuous appointment of pastors since that date.

TRUSLOW *(Tate County: Truslow Road, Sarah 38665).* The church was organized 12 January 1903. The original building was rebuilt in 1955. This is a block and frame building. Sunday School rooms were added later.

TULA *(Lafayette County: 267 Highway 331, Oxford 38655).*

TUNICA *(Tunica County: 1043 School Street, Tunica 38676).* The church was organized in 1890. The first building was a frame structure built in 1892. This building served the congregation until 1908, when it burned. That building was replaced in 1908 by another frame structure. In February 1909, Mr. Leo Lesser delivered the deed to the Methodist Episcopal Church, South. The building was dedicated

Tunica United Methodist Church

9 April 1916. A new brick house of worship was built in 1942. That same year, the education building and parsonage were built. The present building was dedicated 22 March 1942.

TUPELO FIRST *(Lee County: 412 Main Street, Tupelo 38801).* The First United Methodist Church of Tupelo was organized in 1867 by nine devout persons. The wounds of the Civil War were still very deep, and Tupelo was a sparsely settled community in the prairie section of northeast Mississippi. Lee County was carved out of portions of Itawamba, Pontotoc, and Chickasaw counties a year before, and

Tupelo First United Methodist Church

Tupelo was named county seat. The junction of two railroads in the little community held promise of new growth upon the ruins of war. For the first three years, Methodists met at the Baptist Church. In 1870, the same year the North Mississippi Conference was organized, the Methodists of Tupelo built a small but sturdy frame structure as a house of worship. For two decades, Tupelo was served once or twice a month by the Methodist minister living at Verona. In 1890, Tupelo became a station church when Reverend N. G. Augustus was appointed full-time pastor. The new sanctuary was completed in 1899. Bishop W. A. Candler dedicated the new sanctuary on 4 October 1903. In 1904, a splendid new pipe organ was installed.

TUTWILER *(Tallahatchie County: Tutwiler 38963).* In the 1890s, Reverend E. S. Lewis established a preaching place in the railroad depot freight room in Tutwiler. In 1898, the first church building was constructed on the bank of the Hopson Bayou. On 14 March 1899, Tutwiler was incorporated. A deed was given to the church in March 1902, by A. J. Rylee. After a storm demolished this building a few years later, the members worshipped at Cherry Hill Methodist Church in Dublin, about five miles distant. In 1913, the second church was built on the present site which was donated by the Clay family. In 1953, the third church was completed during the stay of Reverend W. L. Wallace Jr., and the members moved in during March of 1953. The church was dedicated during the stay of Reverend C. P. Parker with Bishop Marvin A. Franklin presiding on 20 January 1957.

TYLERTOWN *(Walthall County: 902 Beulah Avenue, Tylertown 39667)*. The church was organized in 1895.

TYRO *(Tate County: Tyro)*.

ULMER CHAPEL *(Leake County: 1474 Ravvit College Road, Lena 39094)*.

UNION *(Amite County: 6126 Perrytown Road, Crosby 39333)*. The church was organized in 1826.

UNION *(Choctaw County: Weir 39772)*. This church was organized in 1960.

UNION *(Kemper County: Firetower Road, DeKalb 39328)*. The church was organized 14 May 1860. The first building was a frame structure that served the congregation until 1905. The second frame building was built in 1905. A fellowship hall was added in 1983. The deed was recorded 14 May 1860.

UNION *(Lee County: Highway Six, Plantersville 38862)*. This church was organized in 1858.

UNION *(Newton County: Union 39365)*. The church was organized in 1864.

UNION CHAPEL *(Newton County)*.

UNION GROVE *(Chickasaw County)*.

UNION GROVE *(Scott County: Harperville 39080)*. This church was organized in 1880.

UNION GROVE *(Tippah County: 500 County Road 549, Ripley 38663)*. In 1873, on a bluff overlooking the bottoms of White Oak, stood the center for both religion and education for the community, the Union Grove Methodist Episcopal Church. The original structure was destroyed by fire. In the days that followed, the men of the community got together and decided to move to a new location.

Boards were used as seats, the sky served as the roof, and sage grass, red oak, and hickory trees surrounded the location. The two acre site was used by both Baptists and Methodists, each denomination having two Sundays a month. By 1906, Union Grove Church had approximately fifty members, and the new building was completed. The pastor was Reverend J. J. Johnson. With strong determination and faith, a new church was built in 1972.

UNION HILL *(Kemper County: Gholson)*.

UNION HILL *(Union County: 1154 County Road 51, Myrtle 38650)*. Union Hill was organized in 1860.

UNION MEMORIAL *(Holmes County: Pickens 39146)*. The church was organized in 1886 as a Colored Methodist Episcopal Church. It had but one wooden sanctuary, built in 1885 or 1886, until the present structure was built in 1991.

UNITY *(Smith County: Highway Thirty-seven North, Taylorsville 39168)*. This church was organized in 1905. An education building was added in 1996.

USHER VALLEY *(Pontotoc County: Algoma 38820)*. This church had its beginning in approximately 1896. The first church was erected in Algoma, near the Macedonia Road. At this time, a church cemetery was started on land sold to the church by Mr. Joe Calhoun. After several years, this building was destroyed by fire after which services were held in an arbor built from posts and branches. Although members were few, a new church building was soon started in 1921. One acre of land was donated by Mr. and Mrs. Walter Williams for a permanent church building. In 1967, under the leadership of Reverend

J. H. Marshall, definite plans began for a larger brick building. In 1976, the new church was finished. Cornerstone laying ceremonies were held on 8 February 1981, and also a dedication service. Donnell Cherry was called into the ministry from this church in 1984.

Utica United Methodist Church

UTICA *(Hinds County: 315 East Main Street, Utica 39175).* The first church in the village of Cane Ridge-Utica was a union church about 1823. The preachers would have been the Methodist circuit riders, and perhaps Reverend Van Brock, a Baptist minister who lived in the village. In 1829, the Baptists organized a church and built their first building before 1840. About 1830, the members of the Christian Church (Disciples of Christ) began to meet at preaching places outside the village. In the 1840s, the Christian Church consolidated several preaching places and built a building in the village of Utica. As soon as the first settlers arrived, the Methodist Episcopal Church began to send Methodist preachers. Reverend Thomas Nixon served Bayou Pierre Circuit from December 1833 to December 1835. He then located and lived in the Bear Creek community, located

a few miles southeast of the of Utica. It is thought that Reverend Thomas Nixon organized the Methodist Society at Cane Ridge-Utica while he traveled the Bayou Pierre Circuit during the years 1834 and 1835. The name of the village was changed from Cane Ridge to Utica on the counsel of Ozias Osborn, a homesick New Yorker, who had settled in the area, and recommended the name Utica, for his home town in his home state. The post office was established at Utica, Mississippi, 30 June 1837. On 19 August 1847, James C. and Winnifred Lee transferred title of the Utica United Methodist Church, a lot to Thomas Nixon, and the trustees of Utica United Methodist Church. The church was built before the end of the year. Later that year, Utica Masonic Lodge, and Utica Sons of Temperance purchased and built a Lodge Hall upstairs in the Utica United Methodist Church building. All three organizations shared the space until 1900. In 1878, the Woman's Missionary Society was organized in the Mississippi Conference. Utica United Methodist Church soon organized a Woman's Missionary Society chapter. Utica United Methodist Church was on the Crystal Springs Circuit between the years 1847 to 1857. It was changed to the Cayuga Circuit from 1858 to 1885. In 1885, the parsonage was built at Utica and the name changed to the Utica Charge. Soon, both Masons and the Methodists needed more room. The Methodists bought the Masons Lodge Room, remodeled it and made it into Sunday School rooms during the pastorate of W. H. Lewis in 1900. Also in 1900, Miss Molly Cessna became a missionary. The church building burned in 1932. Everything was lost. After the fire, the present brick chapel was constructed. In 1941, the Sunday School annex was constructed.

VAIDEN *(Carroll County: 102 Court Street, Vaiden 39176).* Vaiden was once an Indian settlement known as Shongola in the early 1820s. It was named for Doctor C. M. Vaiden, through whose property the railroad ran. The church was organized in 1871.

VALENA C. JONES *(Hancock County: 248 Sycamore Street, Bay Saint Louis 39520).*

VALLEY CHAPEL *(Monroe County: Route Two, Hamilton 39746).* Valley Chapel was once known as Piney Grove Methodist Church. The name was later changed to Valley Chapel after the church acquired its present location. This is the second building to be located at this site. Under the leadership of Reverend Benjamin Wax, plans were made to erect a new building. The building was completed and consecrated in June 1980.

VALLEY HILL *(Carroll County: Highway Eighty-Two, Greenwood 38930).* The church was organized in 1902. An extinct community of Donley was replaced by Valley Hill in 1857 with the settlement of Major James Simpson Hemphill.

VAN VLEET *(Chickasaw County: Houston 38851).* The settlement was named for the Van Vleet Drug Company, and was settled prior to 1860. A post office was established here in 1891. The Methodist church was organized 1840.

VAN WINKLE *(Hinds County: 3810 Robinson Road, Jackson 39209).* The church was organized 3 February 1946. The first service in the first building was on 13 April 1947. The first service in the present building was held on 20 November 1955. An activity building was added in 1972. Van Winkle United Methodist Church and Trinity United Methodist Church merged in 1990 under the name Van Winkle United Methodist Church. Reverend Gerald Lord, who was Dean at Candler School of Theology, and now serves as Associate Director of Colleges, grew up in this church.

VANCLEAVE *(Jackson County: 13613 Highway Fifty-Seven, Vancleave 39565).* This church was organized in 1870.

VARDAMAN *(Calhoun County: Vardaman 38878).* This community, settled about 1872, was known at various times as Ticky Bin and Timberville, but settled on the name Vardaman, in honor of James K. Vardaman. The Methodist church was organized in 1909. A new sanctuary and education building were completed in 1966.

VERNON *(Winston County: Vernon).* This church was organized in 1921.

VERONA *(Lee County: 212 East Main Street, Verona 38879).* This church was once known as Suderman, and faced east on the corner of Cobb and Main Streets. This first building, built in 1860, was a frame structure. The second structure, built in 1901, was also frame, and faced south at the corner of College and Main. The 1966 building, at the same location, is brick. An educational unit was added in 1958. The property deed was recorded 24 February 1899. The Winnie Wharton Library in the church contains artifacts and records of the church's history.

VICTORIA *(Marshall County: Victoria 38679).* The church was organized in 1848. The first frame building was built that same year. That building was destroyed in a tornado or wind storm. The present building opened 27 January 1951.

VINCENT *(Grenada County: 610 Plum Street, Grenada 38901).* The church was organized in 1866. It was once known as Vincent Chapel Methodist Episcopal Church. A frame building was erected in 1866. The sanctuary was fire bombed twice. The present building was constructed in 1980.

VINCENT CHAPEL *(Carroll County).* The church was organized in 1866.

VOSSBURG *(Jasper County: Vossburg 39366).* The church was organized in 1867.

WALDEN CHAPEL *(Holmes County: 308 Franklin Road, Goodman 39079).* The church was organized in 1867. The church was first called Sand Flat. There has been only one frame sanctuary, constructed in 1867, renovated in 1941, and bricked in 1979. An education annex was completed in 1979. The deed was recorded 22 January 1868.

WALLACE CHAPEL *(Sunflower County: 148A O. W. Savell Road, Drew 38737).* This church was organized in 1945.

WALNUT *(Tippah County: 241 Highway 354, Walnut 38683).* This church was organized in 1907.

WALNUT GROVE *(Leake County: 211 Spruce Street, Walnut Grove 39189).* In 1860, land was granted by the McNair family for a church to be built in old Walnut Grove, today known as Old Town. The first appointment of pastor was mentioned in

the 1867 minutes of the Mississippi Methodist Conference held at Natchez. In 1895, a new second church building was built and dedicated by Bishop Charles B. Galloway. In 1925, a new parsonage and church building were built under pastor Van Landrum in new Walnut Grove after the town moved a few miles south due to the building of the railroad. In 1958, a tornado devastated Walnut Grove, damaged the church, and destroyed the parsonage.

WARREN HILL *(Smith County: Louin 39338).* This church was organized in 1900.

Washington United Methodist Church

WASHINGTON *(Adams County: Highway Sixty-One, Washington 39190).* Washington United Methodist Church, in Adams County near Natchez, is the oldest church of the Methodists in Mississippi. It was organized by Reverend Tobias Gibson of South Carolina soon after coming to Natchez in the spring of 1799. Washington became the only Methodist congregation in the old southwest, the nearest congregation being hundreds of miles away. So annual conferences in Louisiana, Texas, Alabama, and Florida, may also point to Washington Church in their conference histories. The place of organization was a small schoolhouse on the opposite side of the highway from the present church, but further down the road toward Natchez. Here candidates for membership were received, eight in all: Randall Gibson, a cousin of Tobias Gibson; his wife, formerly Harriet McKinley (an ancestral relative of President William McKinley); his sister, Mrs. Edna Bullen; Celeb Worley, a young man from Pennsylvania; William Foster and his wife, Mrs. Rachel Foster; and a slave man and his wife, Prince and Mary by name, who were slaves of William Foster. From the flyleaf of an old Bible published in 1825, we learn that additional names were added to the roll by the time the organization was completed at a later date in the home of Randall Gibson as follows: Mary Harris, Ann Downing, Robert Foster, Reuben Gibson, and Fanny Gibson. For about ten years the young and growing congregation held its services in two places, first in the schoolhouse where it was organized, then in a small frame church, built, it is thought, near the Jefferson College gate. Here the trial of Aaron Burr was held, in part at least. In 1810 this church was burned and the congregation, which had grown, found itself without a place of worship. Lorenzo Dow, the noted evangelist, bought a lot, one-half acre, just inside and to the right of the college gate, from John Foster and Mary, his wife, on 22 May 1809. This lot he deeded, on 20 November 1811, to the trustees. It was exprssed in the deed that these trustees

should erect and build a house or place of worship for the use of the members of the Methodist Episcopal Church. The erection of a brick church followed. It was in this church the Constitutional Convention of 1817 met and on its site the monument now stands. Other notables who visited the area include: Andrew Jackson, whose soldiers camped here in April 1815 and were served a banquet upon their return from the New Orleans campaign; Lafayette, who visited the area; and Jefferson Davis, who was a student here. The Presbyterian church had been moved to Pine Ridge, leaving the town of Washington with two churches, Methodist and Baptist. The Annual Conferences of 1819 and of 1821 met in this church, presided over by Bishop George, and attended by large congregations. A new church building began not earlier than 1827 was probably completed in 1829. This was the present church building, which has, however, been remodeled and repaired since that time, the galleries having been removed in 1902. Less than ten years after the building of the church the charge, which included Washington, had lost more than half its former strength and was referred to as a "broken-down circuit." The Civil War almost completely wrecked Methodism in the community of its birth. For ten years after the war very little preaching was done in the Washington Church and in 1877 only eleven persons were found who claimed membership in the church there. A considerable revival took place in 1879 and by 1883 there were thirty-eight members in the church. Of course the Black members, of whom there were more than four hundred before the Civil War, were gone into the various churches for Black people. The church building at Washington still stands in a good state of preservation after over 150 years. With the exception of the church at Woodville, it is the oldest Methodist building in Mississippi. The lot on which it stands was bought from Maria Spencer on 13 August 1825.

WASHINGTON *(Chickasaw County).* This church was organized in 1900.

Water Valley First United Methodist Church

WATER VALLEY FIRST *(Yalobusha County).* Water Valley, the "cradle of North Mississippi Methodism," is the site of numerous activities in Mississippi Methodist heritage. In addition to its selection as the location of the first North Mississippi Conference, formed of portions of the Memphis, Alabama, and Mississippi Conferences, Water Valley was the site of the other annual conferences. A Methodist church was first organized in Water Valley in 1845, in a log schoolhouse. The original church, with a charter membership of eighteen persons, was part of the

Coffeeville Circuit until after the Civil War, 1866, when it was made a station. The first church was built in 1855. In 1871, a new church structure called the Wood Street Methodist Church and a new parsonage were built. The first Mississippi Orphans Home, Methodist Episcopal Church, South, was built in Water Valley. The home, which could accommodate 125 children, was located one mile south of Water Valley. Completed in March 1898, it was used until destroyed by fire on 11 July 1904. The home was rebuilt in Jackson, near Millsaps College. The first Minister's Relief Association was established here on 4 December 1879. The present First United Methodist Church building was erected in 1950, during the pastorate of R. G. Meaders. The first services in the new church were held 2 April 1950, with Bishop Marvin A. Franklin delivering the Palm Sunday message. Dedication services were held 28 March 1954.

WATERFORD *(Marshall County).* This church was organized in 1949.

WAVELAND *(Hancock County: Vacation Lane at Central Avenue, Waveland 39576).* The church was organized in 1950.

Wayne Haven United Methodist Church

WAYNE HAVEN *(Wayne County: 5197 Highway Forty-Five North, Waynesboro 39367)*. The church was organized in 1965. Wayne Haven United Methodist Church is a Native American congregation. The new congregation was created with the merger of Hiwannee and Highway Churches. The present church building was constructed in 1965. The deed for the church was recorded 26 September 1972.

Waynesboro First United Methodist Church

WAYNESBORO FIRST *(Wayne County: 702 Turner Street, Waynesboro 39367)*. The first church built in Waynesboro was in 1858. Colonel John C. Patton, a layman of some means, recognizing the need of a place for religious worship, was instrumental in having this building erected. It was a two-story frame building, the upper story being used for a Masonic Hall, and the lower as a place of religious worship. The Protestant Methodists were the first to use the church, and among their preachers were Claiborne McDonald and Phillip Napier, both of whom afterward united with the Methodist Episcopal Church, South. The Methodist Episcopal Church, South, was organized in Waynesboro in 1860. Waynesboro was then on the Clark Circuit with Joshua T. Heard as pastor. In 1871 Waynesboro was placed in the Wayne Circuit with James Shanks as pastor. In 1874 Waynesboro and State Line formed a charge. During J. V. Penn's pastorate, a new church was built, and dedicated in 1893, by Reverend T. L. Mellen, presiding elder. In 1903, Waynesboro was made a station church. On 12 April 1936, the First Methodist Episcopal Church, South, was dedicated to the service of God by Bishop DuBose. The pastor was A. M. Broadfoot. The present church was erected in 1960.

WEBB SUMNER *(Tallahatchie County: Webb 38966)*. As early as 1834, there are records of traveling preachers setting up brush arbor meetings along the Tallahatchie River. The first churches for Methodist people were built along the rivers and bayous and many people still remember the old church being there before the Methodist churches of Webb and Sumner. In 1962, the people of the Webb Methodist Church invited the people of the Sumner Methodist Church to join them in building a common place of worship. The Sumner Methodist Church accepted the invitation and the birth of the present structure was conceived. The Webb Sumner United Methodist Church was organized on 8 November 1964. The first pastor was James S. Price. The people worked hard to pay for the building and on 22 August 1971, the Service of Dedication and Note Burning was held, less than a dozen years after the birth of the idea for the new facility. In 1982, the church celebrated the ordination of Hugh Clark to the ministry. Hugh was the first member of this church to enter full-time service in the ministry.

WEEMS CHAPEL *(Pearl River County: 810 Third Street, Picayune 39466).* The church was organized in 1914. The church was named after Black store owner, George Weems, who donated the land and unpainted building that he used as a tool house for a place of worship. A new frame building was constructed in 1928. It was equipped with the latest conveniences of that time. The church was renovated in 1952. The exterior of the church was covered with bricks. In 1983 a brick structure was built. The building programs started as a result of an increase in membership and the deterioration of the building. The first shepherd of Weems Chapel was Reverend E. P. Chapman. Under the leadership of Reverend W. M. Emerson, a new building with electric lights was constructed. Reverend C. F. Jackson is credited with adding the social hall to the wooden structure. Under the leadership of Reverend L. W. Smith, the church was completely renovated in 1952. Reverend Phillip Heidelberg was appointed pastor of Weems Chapel in 1979. During his administration, the debt on the parsonage was paid off and the new church was erected in 1983. The consecration service for the new church was held 23 October 1983. Reverend T. D. Gilbert, the Hattiesburg District Superintendent was present.

WEIR *(Choctaw County: Marion Kelly Drive, Weir 39772).* This community was founded by Colonel John Weir, a Civil War veteran, about 1867. The church was organized in 1880.

WELLS MEMORIAL *(Hinds County: 2019 Bailey Avenue, Jackson 39213).* The expansion and growth of the Northwest Jackson area sparked the need for the organization of a Methodist Church in this area. Mr. and Mrs. C. S. Weir had recently come to Jackson to make this city their permanent home. They were residents of this area and they became concerned that there was no Methodist church. Mrs. Weir called Reverend C. E. Downer and made plans for the organization of a Methodist church. An organizational meeting was held on 21 November 1926, with seventy-six charter members. Reverend Downer became the first pastor, and during his period as pastor, the church was built. The church membership grew and an appeal was made to the City of Jackson and they received permission to use Galloway School as a meeting place, and the congregation worshipped there for a full year. Through the work of the members, a ground breaking was held in the Fall of 1927 and work on the brick veneer building was begun. Doctor F. W. Featherstun presided at these ceremonies. Mr. Weir suggested the name as Glendale for the church and the membership accepted this as the proper name. Reverend Wells came to the church in the depths of the depression and the darkest hours that the congregation has ever known. Reverend Wells was killed in an automobile accident in 1947 after fifteen years of service. The church name was changed to Wells Memorial as a memorial to Reverend J. A. Wells.

WESLEY *(Attala County: 207 South Natchez Street, Kosciusko 39090).* From

1879 to 1880, the Mississippi Mission Conference showed a decline in membership. This was probably a result of the Black exodus to the North. In the midst of the decline a new congregation, Wesley Methodist Church in Kosciusko, was started. The first pastor was Marcus Nevils from 1880 until 1882. The congregation held together until a church was built in 1881. The site chosen was perhaps the highest hill in Kosciusko near the downtown area facing South Jackson Street. This was known as the Starkville District. In 1956, the old structure was torn down, the hill leveled to the street, and a new church was built in the space of the old church and the parsonage. This church was built during the administration of Reverend B. F. Harper in the year 1957. He was a minister to the entire city. He started the first ministerial alliance. The oldest tombstone in the cemetery is that of Ike Presley, dated November 1926.

WESLEY *(Bolivar County: Green Street, Mound Bayou 38762).* The church was organized in 1887.

WESLEY *(Jackson County: 8900 Old Spanish Trail, Ocean Springs 39564).* This church was organized in 1985.

WESLEY *(Lauderdale County: 1500 Eighth Street, Meridian 39301).* This church was organized in 1950.

WESLEY *(Lee County: 111 Roosevelt Street, Tupelo 38801).* The Wesley Church was organized 6 January 1946, with thirty-three members in the Rankin Schoolhouse until a church was built and opened on 28 March 1948. The first pastor was Dorsey Allen. The First Methodist Church of Tupelo, parent church, paid one-half of the building costs and made liberal contributions to Wesley each year until it could carry on alone. The latest improvements have been the acquisition of the Sample property adjacent to the church and the parsonage renovation in June 1981.

WESLEY *(Leflore County: 800 Howard Street, Greenwood 38930).* Prior to its existence, there were no worship facilities for Black Christians in the Greenwood area. However, a place was reserved for Black worshippers in the Union church where all of the white denominations of Greenwood worshipped. John Wesley Dunn, who was presiding elder of the Greenwood District from 1877 to 1879, organized worshippers in Greenwood, in 1870 with twenty-five to thirty members. In 1878, Wesley Chapel, later renamed Wesley Methodist Episcopal Church, was erected on Washington Street. This was the second church built in Greenwood. The site of Wesley Chapel remained at the Washington Street location from 1870 until 1890. The frame building was moved to a new location and remained there until it was destroyed by fire on 4 January 1920. Work on the present brick structure was begun in 1921. Reverend H. B. Hart was pastor at the time. Formal dedication for the present structure was January 1922.

WESLEY *(Lowndes County: 511 Airline Road, Columbus 39702).* In April 1956, Doctor Golding preached at First Methodist and Central Methodist, acquainting the congregations with plans for establishing a new church in East Columbus. He invited all interested parties to meet with him in his residence on 13 May 1956. Twenty-three men and women responded, even though these twenty-three people were already established in one of the other two Methodist churches. Doctor Golding authorized Reverend Dorsey Allen, pastor of Central Methodist Church, to organize the new church, the first in the district for many years. Forty-five members were admitted by letter. Several men in the group suggested that with a little work, the three-stable barn could be made into a picturesque and romantic temporary meeting place. On 14 June 1956, the first pastor, Prentiss M. Gordon Sr. and his family were welcomed as they moved into the parsonage. The church was now ready for that first service on the following Sunday, 16 June, and Wesley Church was off to a running start.

WESLEY *(Monroe County)*.

WESLEY *(Noxubee County)*. This church was organized in 1851.

WESLEY *(Quitman County: Route One, Sledge 38670)*. The church was organized between 1950 and 1973. It was known as Alexander African Methodist Episcopal Church in 1950. In 1973, it was dedicated and renamed Wesley United Methodist Church. The church was renovated in 1981 and in 1996.

WESLEY *(Rankin County: 105 Pearl Street, Brandon 39042)*.

WESLEY *(Warren County: 1318 First East, Vicksburg 39180)*. This church, dating back to the pre-Civil War period, was organized by slaves whose masters were Methodists. For a number of years, the slaves attended the same worship services as their masters until 1858, when the white Methodists decided to build a new structure. The old

building at the corner of Grove and Cherry Streets was given to the slaves, and was called Wesley Chapel Methodist Episcopal Church. Although the Black Methodists had their own building, they were still served by a white minister. The Black congregation remained at that site for a number of years, but by the 1860s their growing numbers made a new structure necessary. Through the generosity of a white couple, Jefferson and Julia Hedrick, they were able to secure the site on which the church now stands. The new edifice was completed in 1865, the same year that the Mississippi Annual Conference adopted the general procedure of assigning the white ministers to a definite station and "Colored Charge." Desiring a more modern structure, a new church was built under the pastorate of S. A. Cowan and dedicated in 1886. For several years thereafter Wesley was the host church for meetings of the Mississippi Conference. By the 1920s the church became one of the largest and most influential in the city and attracted a number of nationally and internationally known Black orators and musicians.

WESLEY *(Winston County: 507 Jones Avenue, Louisville 39452)*. Wesley United Methodist Church had its beginning when a community of Christians agreed to band themselves together and worship God in a place of their own, because there were no Black churches for them to attend. Prior to this banding, the Blacks attended church with their masters or employers. They met in homes, under shade trees, and brush arbors to worship God and plan for the future. The church was organized in 1874 and established in 1876, on a site not far from the church structure now in use, south of Cox Street, now known as John C. Stennis Drive. It was then called Louisville Methodist Church. Reverend Daniel Yarbrough was the first pastor. Its humble beginning was a brush arbor that Reverend Yarbrough and a few loyal followers built. The first land was purchased from Judge W. D. Conwell. They bought one-half acre of land on 25 September 1883. Their church grew and was blessed. Additional land was purchased. It is believed that the first small church structure was built under Reverend Orange Grant in 1884. Brother Lias Gage hauled the first stones and lumber for the building and the growing congregation moved from the brush arbor near the present site on Jones Avenue. This small church was used for worshipping God on Sunday and became the first schoolhouse for Black children in Louisville.

WESLEY CHAPEL *(Carroll County: Vaiden 39176).* The church was organized in 1880.

WESLEY CHAPEL *(Chickasaw County: Houston 38851).* This church was organized in 1851.

WESLEY CHAPEL *(Clarke County: 800 Beech Street, Enterprise 39330).* This church was organized in 1912.

WESLEY CHAPEL *(George County).*

WESLEY CHAPEL *(Jasper County).* The church was organized in 1900.

WESLEY CHAPEL *(Jones County: Ellisville 39437).* This church was organized 14 February 1917.

WESLEY CHAPEL *(Lauderdale County: Highway 145, Meridian 39301).* This church was organized in 1956. Rex Alman was the first pastor.

WESLEY CHAPEL *(Lauderdale County: Meridian 39301).* This church was organized in 1912.

WESLEY CHAPEL *(Leake County: Hayes Street, Carthage 39051).*

WESLEY CHAPEL *(Newton County: Hickory 39332).*

WESLEY CHAPEL *(Panola County: Highway 315, Sardis 38619).* The two acres of land on which the Wesley Chapel is located were given by James F. Buchanan and wife, Mary E. Buchanan, to E. E. Arnold, L. D. Foster, J. M. Hudspeth, N. A. Roberts, and R. M. Arnold, trustees of Wesley Chapel Methodist Episcopal Church, by deed dated 30 August 1911. The church was organized in 1912, and a sanctuary was constructed that same year. The first pastor was James Bernard Conner. For many years, Wesley Chapel was one of five churches which comprised the Sardis Circuit and was in the Sardis District. This circuit's parsonage was located west of Sardis. A number of years ago, Wesley Chapel was placed on the Tyro Circuit, and later was attached to the Como United Methodist Church. The church was originally a one-room structure. The oldest tombstone in the church cemetery is dated 1915.

WESLEY CHAPEL *(Pearl River County: Highway Forty-Three North, Poplarville 39470).* The church was organized in the 1890s in an old school building. Professor White taught at this time. This first building was located one-half mile south, across Route Forty-three, the Gainsville-Columbia Road. It was an early lumber structure, covered with hand-hewn boards. Inside was a small rostrum with a hand-made pulpit on each side. In front, behind the pulpits, and on each side of the rostrum were choir benches. In front were two sections of narrow benches, and five or six wide ones to the rear. This building was torn down about 1926, and the present one built. Burt Seal supervised the construction, and some of the windows from the old Stewart School were used. Lumber was also donated by Hugh L White. The land was given by the H. H. Stewart family. Argie Stewart gave more land, including the cemetery. Reverend Warren Pittman was pastor when the church had its formal dedication. The first parsonage in Carriere burned. The second was built on land given by Purvis Hall Sr. and Lucille McNeese.

WESLEY CHAPEL *(Yazoo County: 20 Hebron Church Road, Bentonia 39040).* Wesley Chapel Church was founded in 1833 on Eagle Bend Plantation, on Big Black River, about three miles southwest of the present location, the first church was called Cooks Chapel, honoring Doctor Fielding Cook, who first owned and developed the land of the plantation. In 1859, the church was renamed Wesley Chapel and moved to Phoenix. A brick building was built. One evening in 1863, a regiment of union soldiers, by order of Colonel Wood, burned that building. The brave pioneers of the community did not let this obstacle stop them. Services were held in a school in the winter and under a brush arbor in the summer. In 1873, construction on another Wesley Chapel was begun. Because of lack of funds the church was not completed until 1876. Then another Wesley Chapel building was built in 1909. The Lord provided a minister, Reverend A.

Wesley Chapel United Methodist Church, Bentonia

R. Quick, who had been a building contractor before entering the ministry. Due to his untiring efforts, as well as that of the congregation, the present building was built and completely debt free when dedicated in August 1954.

WESLEY CHAPEL *(Yazoo County: Old Highway Sixteen, Benton 39039).* The church was organized in 1881. The deed was recorded 5 September 1881. The present frame building was constructed about 1895.

WESLEYANNA *(Rankin County: 126 Wesleyanna Street, Star 39039).* Wesleyanna United Methodist Church was organized in 1847 on land donated by the organizer and first pastor, Daniel H. Loflin. The building was located two miles north of the present community of Star on old Highway Forty-nine at the location of the Wesleyanna cemetery. In 1921 the building was relocated to the heart of the

Wesleyanna United Methodist Church

West Park United Methodist Church

community of Star on a lot adjacent to the High School. On 10 August 1958 the opening service and consecration was conducted in the present building facing new Highway Forty-nine.

WEST *(Holmes County: Church Street, West 39192).* The church was organized in 1900.

WEST LAKE *(Lamar County: 1820 Oak Grove Road, Hattiesburg 39402).* The church was organized in 1972. The church met at the University of Southern Mississippi Wesley Foundation until a triple-wide trailer could be set up. The present sanctuary was completed in 1977.

WEST LAUREL *(Jones County: 523 North Fourteenth Avenue, Laurel 39440).* West Laurel was begun in 1902 as the Fifth Avenue and Kingston Charge, purchasing the property on which the present sanctuary stands on 6 June 1902. Due to growth, the Fifth Avenue and Kingston Charge was divided into two station churches on 9 December 1908, and the Fifth Avenue Church became known as the West End Methodist Episcopal Church, South, now known as West Laurel United Methodist Church. The present sanctuary was completed in 1949 under the leadership of Reverend E. E. McKeithen.

WEST PARK *(Hinds County: 220 Moss Avenue, Jackson 39209).* In January 1944, Reverend James D. Wroten Jr. began work organizing West End Methodist Church, under presiding Bishop J. L. Decell, and District Superintendent Otto Porter. The first service was held in Saint Columb's Episcopal Church on Claiborne Street in February 1944, later meetings being held in Whitfield School. The Men's Sunday School Class met at Mr. Hugh Price's home, Moss Avenue. The ladies met with Mrs. Kate Mansfield and Miss Audrey Williams at Claiborne. The formal organization of the charge was at a Quarterly Conference on 3 April 1944, held in the home of Mr. and Mrs. M. D. Cunningham, Claiborne Street, with Reverend Otto Porter, District Superintendent, presiding. The drive for building funds was launched at a banquet 29 May 1944. The new church was known as West End Methodist Church until the Fourth Quarterly Conference held 14 November 1944, when its name was officially changed to West Park Methodist Church. The initial membership was made up of thirty persons.

West Point First United Methodist Church

WEST POINT FIRST *(Clay County: Court and Broad, West Point 39773).* In the early 1800s, West Point Methodists worshipped in the Church Hill Union Church. The oldest tombstone bears the date 1842. Passing through several connectional changes, West Point First United Methodist Church, the original and present name of the West Point Charge, has been in the Aberdeen, Columbus, and Starkville District of the former North Mississippi Conference. The church was organized in 1868. The first pastor was J. P. Dancer. The church was in the Memphis Conference until 1870. In 1872, the first church was built. It was destroyed by fire and rebuilt in 1895. The present structure was started in 1920; the second addition was consecrated on 20 October 1985 by Bishop Morgan. The Child Development Center (crib through five years) opened in the fall of 1966, and now serves children in Clay County. Annual Conference of the Methodist Episcopal Church met here on 2 December 1886. The North Mississippi Conference convened on 6 December 1900. The North Mississippi Annual Conference met on 28 October 1929, at West Point again, and the fourth time it was entertained here on 3 June 1953. Recruits to the ministry from this church are: Perry Emory Duncan, 1893; Joseph L. Gerdine, 1900; Walter M. Campbell, 1903; William Henry Miller, date unknown; Elias G. Kilgore, date unknown; Paul Townsend, 1904; Amand Standifer Raper, 1910; W. H. Oyler, 1921; Archie L. Meadows, 1942; Harold Cain Vaughn, 1948; James H. Holden Jr., 1952; John Howard Millsaps Jr., 1953; William Freeman Wells, 1958; Virgil Beason Nation Jr., 1960; and Thomas Bertrand McCallister; 1963.

WHEELER *(Prentiss County: Wheeler 38880).* This church was organized in 1900.

WHITE OAK *(Copiah County: 153 New Zion Road, Crystal Springs 39059).* The exact date the church was organized is unknown, but it was in the 1800s.

WHITE PLAINS *(Harrison County: 18013 White Plains Road, Saucier 39574).* The church was organized in 1866. White Plains first appears in appointments in 1866 in Paulding District.

WHITEHALL *(Winston County: 5890 Highway Fourteen West, Louisville 39339).* The church was organized 15 September 1887. The church was once located on the old Ackerman Road, two miles northwest of the present site. The church burned in 1911, and was rebuilt at the present location. There have been three sanctuaries. The first building was a log structure built in 1887. The second frame building was constructed in 1911. The brick building was completed in 1950.

WHITE'S CHAPEL *(Wilkinson County: 2390 Whites School Road, Centreville 39631)*. The church was organized in 1900.

WHITTINGTON CHAPEL *(Amite County: Highway 567, Liberty 39645)*. The church was organized in 1954.

WIGGINS *(Leake County: Highway Sixteen, Carthage 39051)*. This church was organized in 1933.

Williamsburg United Methodist Church

Wiggins First United Methodist Church

WIGGINS FIRST *(Stone County: 520 East Pine Avenue, Wiggins 39550)*. The church was organized in 1904. There have been two sanctuaries. The first, built in 1905, was a frame structure. The second brick building was constructed in 1948, and an education annex was added in 1958. The first parsonage was deeded in 1913, the second in 1959, and the third in 1967. Additional property was acquired in 1978 and 1986.

WILLIAMS CHAPEL *(Jasper County)*. This church was organized in 1930.

WILLIAMSBURG *(Covington County: Yates Road and Sunset Road, Collins 39428)*. The Williamsburg United Methodist Church in Covington County is one of the older churches in the Mississippi Conference. It was organized in 1829, but no other known records exist until 1859, when the Williamsburg Church is listed among the records of the Methodist Protestant Church. In 1870 it is listed as a Methodist Episcopal Church South, and would remain as such until the union in 1939 at which time it became known as Williamsburg Methodist Church. Then, in 1968, at the time of the last union, it became known as Williamsburg United Methodist Church. Through the years the church has been in different districts, having been the home of the District Superintendent, then known as the presiding elder, in 1881, and the pastor of the Williamsburg congregation was listed as the presiding elder of the District. In 1880, it was in the Westville District; in 1894 to 1895, in the Enterprise District; in 1898 in the Seashore District; in 1906, in the Jackson District; and in 1914, it first came into the Hattiesburg District, in which it still remains. Apparently, it has always been a "charge," formerly called a "circuit," with more than one church sharing the same pastor. In 1997, there were two churches: Lone Star and Williamsburg. There are no available records to indicate when the first church was built, but according to older citizens, the first church building for the Methodist congregation was a small one-room building that stood in the triangle in front of the present church building and was probably built in 1885. According to Quarterly Conference reports, the building was razed in 1936, and a new church was completed in 1937 or early 1938, with some of the lumber in the older building being used in its construction. Three former members of this church have become ministers; Travis Lynwood Campbell, Kenneth Edwin Graham, and Larry C. Speed.

WILSON SPRINGS *(Jackson County: 11601 Highway Sixty-Three, Pascagoula 39581).* The church was organized in 1946. The church began meeting in a tent 16 September 1945. A wooden building was erected in 1946. A cinder block building was completed in 1961. The fellowship hall and classrooms were added in 1964.

WINBORN *(Benton County: Highway 178 East, Hickory Flat 38633).* This community was first known as Reed's Switch, but changed its name to Winborn in 1902, in honor of a sheriff of Benton County. It is the site of the state's only iron ore mine. The exact date the Methodist church here was organized has not been determined, but it was before 1900.

WINBORN CHAPEL *(George County: Lucedale 39452).* The church was organized in 1908.

WINCHESTER *(Wayne County: Winchester-Cross Road, Waynesboro 39367).* Winchester is the first Methodist church

Winchester United Methodist Church

organized in east central Mississippi. Bishop H. Y. DuBose joined the church here. The town, which was incorporated in 1818, was there before that time, and served as county seat until 1867. One Scottish family was Methodist, that of John McRae, in whose home the Annual Conference of 1822 was held and whose son was later Governor of Mississippi. Samuel Sellers visited Wayne County in 1816 in his official round of the Mississippi District, but he makes no mention of the Winchester Church. There is a tradition that the church was organized in 1816 while Ashley Hewitt and Alexander Fleming were serving the Tombigbee Circuit. Even if organized the next year when Elijah Gentry was pastor of the Chickasawhay Circuit, it would still be the oldest church in east Mississippi. In 1832 the church at Winchester went into the Alabama Conference, with all other churches in east Mississippi. In 1870 the church was returned to the Mississippi Conference as a part of the Wayne Circuit.

WOODLAND *(Amite County: 2580 Busy Corner Road, Gloster 39638).* The church was organized in 1870.

Woodville United Methodist Church

WOODVILLE *(Wilkinson County: 909 Main Street, Woodville 39669).* The Woodville Methodist Church was organized soon after the town was incorporated in 1811. Built in 1824, Woodville is the oldest Methodist church building in Mississippi and possibly several adjoining states, and still stands in an excellent state of preservation. The sanctuary has been completely redecorated and an educational unit added. Four sessions of the Mississippi Annual Conference have been held in this building. The first was in 1831, Bishop Roberts presiding, with William M. Curtiss as secretary. In 1835 the Conference met at Woodville again, with Bishop Soule in the chair and Robert D. Smith at the secretary's table. In 1843 Bishop Soule again presided with Daniel W. Speer as secretary. In 1858, Bishop Paine presided over the Conference in Woodville, with H. J. Harris, as secretary.

WRIGHTS CHAPEL *(Lowndes County: Highway Forty-Five, Columbus 39701).* This church was organized in 1878.

X-**PRAIRIE** *(Noxubee County: Prairie Point Road, Macon 39341).* The church was organized in 1842. At that time, it was located at Plum

X-Prairie United Methodist Church

Creek. There have been three buildings built in 1842, 1850, and 1990. The 1850 building was destroyed in a tornado in 1989, and was replaced a year later with the present structure.

YAZOO CITY FIRST *(Yazoo County: 203 North Washington, Yazoo City 39194).* The community was originally known as Manchester. Yazoo appears in appointments in 1829. It was the site of several Annual Conferences. The Methodists were established before 1830 with a Benton Manchester Charge, called the Yazoo Circuit, becoming a regular appointment by 1829. Prior to that time circuit riders going from Vicksburg through Mechanicsburg to Holmes County stopped along the way to preach in the rude log huts provided for the purpose, or in interested individuals' homes. Significantly, the Methodist preacher was not necessarily a resident of his charge. One individual, therefore, could serve a large area and the proliferation of Methodist

Yazoo City First United Methodist Church

groups in Yazoo County, to more than fifteen by the 1850s, was a testament to the success of the method of organization. According to tradition, the first Methodist preaching service in Yazoo City was held in 1828 by John G. Jones, a pastor of the Warren Circuit, who was passing through the area. He gathered a small handful of people together in a hut on the top of what

is now Jefferson Street for the service. In 1836 the Benton and Manchester Churches were placed on a circuit together, but the panic of 1837 caused the new charge to have financial problems so that it was returned to a circuit that covered a much larger territory. In 1842 a lot for a permanent church was purchased in Yazoo City and the group became a separate entity with a single station appointment for the preacher. Richard Abbey, who was buried here, was once known as the most prolific Methodist writer in America.

ZION CHAPEL *(Clarke County).* This church is located near the Alabama state line in eastern Clarke County.

ZION CYPRESS *(Oktibbeha County: Bradley).*

ZION FRANKLIN *(Oktibbeha County).*

ZION RIDGE *(Marion County).*

APPENDIX A

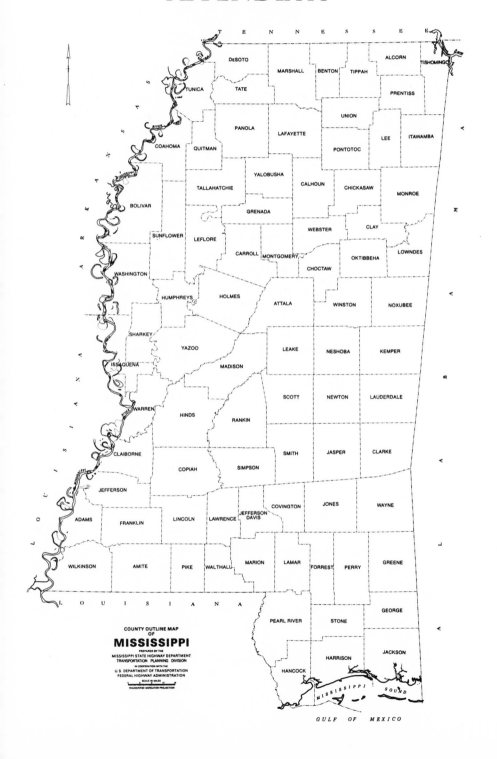

County Outline Map
OF
MISSISSIPPI

PREPARED BY THE
MISSISSIPPI STATE HIGHWAY DEPARTMENT
TRANSPORTATION PLANNING DIVISION

IN COOPERATION WITH THE
U.S. DEPARTMENT OF TRANSPORTATION
FEDERAL HIGHWAY ADMINISTRATION

SCALE IN MILES

TRANSVERSE MERCATOR PROJECTION

APPENDIX B

MISSISSIPPI UNITED METHODIST CHURCHES
BY COUNTY AND DATE OF ORGANIZATION

ADAMS

Grace	1950
Jefferson Street	1805
Kingston	1800
Lovely Lane	1951
Saint John's	1871
Washington	1799

ALCORN

Bethel	1845
Biggersville	1960
Box Chapel	1851
Christ	1906
Corinth: First	1857
Gaines Chapel	1854
Hopewell	1890
Indian Springs	1895
Kossuth	1878
Mount Carmel	1873
Mount Moriah	1866
Pleasant Hill	1881
Rienzi	1848
Shady Grove	1845

AMITE

Cedar Grove	1890
Gloster	1893
Liberty	1841-1851
Mount Vernon	1835
Union	1826
Whittington Chapel	1954
Woodland	1870

ATTALA

Barlow	1886
Bethel	1871
Buffalo	1871
Chapel Hill	1880
Ethel	1884
Friendship	1853
Kosciusko: First	1835
Liberty Chapel	1851
Liberty Hill	1857
Marvin Chapel	1876
McAdams	1926
McCool	1847
Mount Lebanon	1884
Mount Vernon	1887
Pierce Chapel	1888
Salem	
Seneasha	1828
Shady Grove	1873
Shiloh	1854
Shrock	1862

Spring Grove	1880
Tabernacle	1875
Wesley	1880

BENTON

Ashland	1860
Bethel	1872
Harris Chapel	
Hickory Flat	1851
Liberty	1835
Winborn	1800s

BOLIVAR

Benoit	1901
Boyle	1895
Cleveland: First	1870
Duncan	1890
Gunnison	1832
Litton	1914
Merigold	1902
Pac	1903
Rosedale	1877
Saint Luke	1961
Saint Mark	1972
Shaw	1889
Shelby	1888
Shipman Chapel	1893
Wesley	1887

CALHOUN

Bailey Memorial	1800s
Big Creek	1856
Bruce	1924
Derma	1890
Lewis Memorial	1906
Pittsboro	1852
Rapers Chapel	1926
Shady Grove	1881
Vardaman	1909

CARROLL

Bethel	1846
Black Hawk	1818
Carrollton	1834
Ebenezer	
Enon	1858
Good Hope	1883
Haven	1870
Longview	1889
Martin Grove	1883
McCarley	1896
Midway	1850s
North Carrollton	1902
Tillman	
Vaiden	1871
Valley Hill	1902
Vincent Chapel	1866
Wesley Chapel	1880

CHICKASAW

Boones Chapel	1890
Buena Vista	1887
Egypt	1882
Farr's Chapel	
Fosters Chapel	1887
Houlka	1883
Houston: First	1837

Macedonia	1873
McCondy	1882
Mount Olive	
Mount Pisgah	1867
New Hope	1885
New Hope (Okolona)	1866
Okolona: First	1840s
Pleasant Grove	1861
Pleasant Valley	
Prairie Mount	
Prospect	1848
Pyland	1912
Rhodes Chapel	1883
Snowtown	
Thorn	1887
Union Grove	
Van Vleet	1840
Washington	1900
Wesley Chapel	1851

CHOCTAW

Ackerman: First	1879
Antioch	1860
Lagrange	1800s
Mount Hermon	1890s
Nebo	1893
Penderville	1800s
Rockport	1880s
Salem	1873
Salem (Weir)	1873
South Union	1865
Union	1960
Weir	1880

CLAIBORNE

Brandywine	1846
Hermanville	1836
Port Gibson	1826
Rocky Springs	1805

CLARKE

Adams Chapel	1890-1916
Bethel	
Coke's Chapel	
Concord	1870
Cooper's Chapel	1916
Crandall	1921
DeSoto	1872
Enterprise	1830s
Friendship	
Goodwater	1876
Hopewell	
James Chapel	
Little Zion	1905
Magnolia	1870
McGowans Chapel	1857
Mount Jordan	1865
Mount Levy	
Mount Olive	1900
Mount Zion	
New Mount Zion	
Pachuta	1889
Quitman: First	1853
Saint John	1861
Shubuta	1843
Silver Spree	1865
Spring Hill	1880
Stonewall	1872
Sweet Pilgrim	1932
Wesley Chapel	1912
Zion Chapel	

CLAY

Cedar Bluff	1850
Christ	1960
Palestine	1856
Pheba	1890
Saint Paul	1868

Siloam	1869	Salem	1877	Bentley Chapel	1912
West Point: First	1868	Sweetwater	1824	Brooklyn	1900
		White Oak	1800s	Court Street	1900

COAHOMA

Clarksdale: First	1846			Dixie	1956

COVINGTON

Clarksdale: First	1846			Glendale	1948
Dublin	1858	Bethel	1852	Grandview	1963
Friars Point	1836	Collins	1901	Main Street	1883
Haven	1880	Eminence	1890	Maxie	1908
Jonestown	1890	Lone Star	1940	McLaurin	1880
Lula	1925	Mount Olive	1871	Parkway Heights	1949
Lyon	1890s	Saint James	1863	Petal	1908
Mattson	1913	Sanford	1906	Saint John	1921
Saint Paul's	1956	Seminary	1890	Saint Paul	1882
		Williamsburg	1829		

COPIAH

DESOTO

FRANKLIN

Beauregard	1866/79	Baker's Chapel	1852	Bethesda	1823
Bethesda	1840	Cockrum	1835	Bethlehem	
Carpenter	1901	DeSoto (New Church)	1997	Bude	1917
Centerpoint		Eudora	1860	Ebenezer	1827
Crystal Springs	1824	Faith	1978	Greendale	1912
Decell Memorial	1846	Fountain Head	1871	McNair	1813
Gallatin	1870	Getwell Road	1986	Meadville	1901
Gallman	1885	Hernando	1836	Mount Olive	1850
Georgetown	1895	Hinds Chapel	1843	New Fork	
Hazlehurst: First	1860	Horn Lake	1860	Oak Grove	1899
Little Rock		Lake Cormorant		Oak Grove (Union Ch)	1868
Little Zion	1857	Lewisburg	1879	Roxie	1876
Matthews Chapel	1889	Love	1987	Saint Paul	1897
Mount Pleasant	1847	Maples Memorial	1849	Thirkield	
Mount Sinai	1870	McDonald	1889		
New Hope	1864	Mineral Wells	1892		

GEORGE

New Zion	1864	Minor Memorial	1889	Crossroads	1826
Pleasant Ridge	1884	Pleasant Hill	1888	Lucedale: First	1899
Pleasant Valley	1845	Southaven: First	1962	Mount Pleasant	
Providence	1828			Pleasant Hill	
Rehoboth	1839			Refuge	1921

FORREST

Saint James		Asbury	1996	Saint James	
Saint Mary's	1912	Batson	1909	Salem	1818
Saint Morris					

Shipman	
Wesley Chapel	
Winborn Chapel	1908

GREENE

Antioch	1871
Bolton Chapel	
Grace	1967
Leaf	1926
Leakesville	1800s
Nebo	
New Zion	1946
Pine Grove	1837
Pleasant Ridge	
Sand Hill	1952
State Line	1876

GRENADA

Gore Springs	1892
Grace	1956
Grenada: First	1837
Holcomb	
Sparta	1835
Vincent	1866

HANCOCK

Clermont Harbor	1944
Diamondhead	1992
Holmes Chapel	1870
Main Street	1852
Pearlington	1813
Saint Rock	1908
Valena C Jones	
Waveland	1950

HARRISON

Beauvoir	1956
Biloxi: First	1842

Burton Memorial	1928
Cedar Lake	1906
Christ	1987
Coalville	1852
Epworth	
Gateway	
Gulfport: First	1896
Handsboro	1854
Haven Chapel	
Heritage	1921
Leggett Memorial	1955
Long Beach: First	1874
Mississippi City	1845
Mount Pleasant	
Mount Zion	1892
New Fayard	
Nugent	1895
Pass Christian: First	1903
Poplar Head	1879
Ramsay Memorial	1971
Riley Chapel	1880
Saint Mark	1892
Saint Paul (Biloxi)	1863
Saint Paul (Pass Chr.)	1852
Saucier	1907
Trinity	1958
White Plains	1866

HINDS

Aldersgate	1965
Alta Woods	1952
Anderson	1914
Asbury	1872
Blessed Trinity	1990
Briarwood	1956
Broadmeadow	1949
Cayuga	1828
Central	1889

Christ	1961
Clinton: First	1831
Edwards	1828
Emmanuel	1932
Epworth	1954
Forest Hill	1857
Galloway Memorial	1836
Harris Memorial	1971
Kingsley	1878
Learned	1891
Leavell Woods	1944
Lynch Chapel	1869
Memorial	1868
Mount Pleasant	1922
Mount Salem	1880
New Covenant	1995
Pratt Memorial	1897
Raymond	1837
Saint John's	1973
Saint Luke	1909
Saint Paul	1872
Seven Springs	1881
Spring Ridge	1830
Utica	1834
Van Winkle	1946
Wells Memorial	1926
West Park	1944

HOLMES

Acona	1874
Bowling Green	1840s
Durant: First	1871
Ebenezer	1828
Emory	1848
Epworth	1883
Franklin	
Galilee Treadwell	
Georgeville	1904

Goodman: First	1872	Ozark		Garlandsville	1835
Hebron	1844	Palestine		Heidelberg	1885
John Wesley	1868-1870	Shiloh		Holders	1842
Lexington: First	1836	Tremont	1892	Homewood	
Mount Zion				Hopewell	1837
Oregon Memorial		**JACKSON**		Leona	1892-1894
Pickens	1833	Big Point	1876	Louin	1906
Poplar Springs	1920	Bonnie Chapel	1928	Montrose	1857
Spring Hill	1840-1886	Caswell Springs	1875	Mount Olive	1800s
Tchula	1883	Dantzler Memorial	1853	Mount Zion	
Thornton	1887	Davis Chapel	1870	Mount Zion	1850s
Union Memorial	1886	Eastlawn	1943	Oak Bowery	
Walden Chapel	1867	Escatawpa	1858	Philadelphia	1853
West	1900	Faith	1960	Pilgrim Rest	1900
		Gautier: First	1950	Pleasant Grove	1837
HUMPHREYS		Hurley	1919	Pleasant Valley	
Belzoni: First	1884	Kreole	1924	Read's Chapel	1904
Evans Chapel	1902	Midway	1994	Rose Hill	1896
Isola	1903	Mount Pleasant	1850	Spring Hill	1900
Louise	1909	Pascagoula: First	1879	Spring Hill	1863
Silver City	1872	Red Hill	1837	Stringer	1910
		Roberts Chapel	1855	Vossburg	1867
ISSAQUENA		Rosedale	1885	Wesley Chapel	1900
Grace	1902	Saint James	1867	Williams Chapel	1930
		Saint Mark			
ITAWAMBA		Saint Paul (Moss Pt)		**JEFF DAVIS**	
Asbury	1840	Saint Paul (Ocean Spr)	1853	Carson	1903
Carolina	1840s	Saint Stephen		Good Hope	1880
Evergreen		Summerville	1800s	L. L. Roberts	1904
Friendship	1890	Tanner's Chapel	1882	Mount Zion	1817
Fulton: First	1838	Vancleave	1870	Oakdale	1936
Gilmore Chapel		Wesley	1985	Prentiss	1890
Hardins Chapel		Wilson Springs	1946	Santee	1852
Mantachie					
Mount Olive	1891	**JASPER**		**JEFFERSON**	
Mount Pleasant	1844	Bay Springs	1905	Adams Chapel	1870
New Chapel		Bethlehem	1896-1910	Belle Hill	1892
Oak Grove		Blue Ridge	1884	Blue Hill	1890

Cane Ridge	1817
Church Hill	1890
Community	1950
Crown Point	
Fayette	1827
Galatia	1859
Hickory Block	
Mount Pleasant	1876
Pine Grove	

JONES

Antioch	1875
Chapel Hill	1893
Cross Roads	1910
Dudley Chapel	
Ellisville: First	1859
Fairfield	1900
Franklin	1957
Gitano	1959
Glade	1958
Hebron	1889
Kingston	1902
Laurel: First	1884
Mallalieu	1905
Moselle	1912
Mount Olive	1902
Mount Zion	1903
New Faith	1995
Ovett	1904
Saint Paul (Laurel)	1896
Sandersville	1884
Smith Chapel	
Soules Chapel	
Wesley Chapel	1917
West Laurel	1902

KEMPER

Big Oak	1865
Binnsville	1840-1879

Blues Chapel	1868
Center Ridge	
Chapel Hill	1874
Clarkes Chapel	1914
Coy	1902
DeKalb	1835
Hopewell	1874-1879
Keys Chapel	
Liberty	
Lynville	1920
Mellen	1892
Mount Hebron	1856
Mount Pleasant	1881
New Bethlehem	1929
New Hope	
New Hope	1869
Pleasant Grove	1840-1870
Pleasant Ridge	1837
Porterville	1892
Saint Mark	
Scooba	
Spring Hill	
Tamola Bethel	
Union	1860
Union Hill	

LAFAYETTE

Abbeville	
Beverly	
Buford Chapel	1898
Burns	
Cambridge	1800s
Christ	1960
Christian Rest	
Free Springs	
Hammitt Hill	
Midway	1856
Oxford-University	1836

Paris	
Pine Flat	
Providence	1882
Saint Andrews	1962
Saint Peter	1899
Salem	1865
Taylor	
Tula	

LAMAR

Heritage	1989
Hickory Grove	1888
James Chapel	1906
Lumberton	1882
Oak Grove	1936
Purvis	1884
Saint James	1907
Saint Paul	1906
Sumrall	1903
Talowah	1917
West Lake	1972

LAUDERDALE

Andrew Chapel	1873
Bethel	1897
Bonita	1926
Central	1860
Cokers Chapel	1840
Collinsville	1910
Daleville	1889
Druid Hills	1957
East End	1891
Elizabeth	
Fifth Street	1885
Haven Chapel	1885
Hawkins Memorial	1893
Highland	1946
Lauderdale	1874

Lost Gap		Greenwood Chapel		Tupelo: First	1867
Mallalieu	1905	John Memorial	1962	Union	1858
Marion	1820	Johnson Chapel		Verona	1860
Mount Salem		Lena	1908	Wesley	1946
New Covenant	1991	Madden	1925		
Oak Grove	1875	McDonald	1942	**LEFLORE**	
Oakland Heights	1959	Singleton	1896	Barwick	1976
Pilgrim Hill	1870	Ulmer Chapel		Decell	1948
Pleasant Grove		Walnut Grove	1860	Greenwood: First	1840
Pleasant Hill	1840	Wesley Chapel		Itta Bena: First	1894
Pleasant Ridge		Wiggins	1933	Jones Chapel	1862
Poplar Springs Drive	1884			Minter City	1868
Sageville	1850	**LEE**		Saint John's	1952
Saint Elizabeth		Allens Chapel	1880	Samuel Chapel	1880
Saint Mark		Andrews Chapel	1872	Schlater	1885
Saint Matthew		Belden	1872	Sidon	1855
Saint Paul	1868	Bethel	1870	Swiftown	1920
Saint Peter	1990	Big Hill		Wesley	1870
Spring Hill	1900	Brewer	1903		
Suqualena		Guntown	1860s	**LINCOLN**	
Tabernacle	1885	Hebron	1885	Adams	1811
Wesley	1950	Lee Acres	1966	Bethel	1875
Wesley Chapel	1912	Mooreville	1850	Bogue Chitto	1882
Wesley Chapel	1956	Nettleton: First	1890	Brookhaven: First	1857
		New Chapel		Crump Chapel	1902
LAWRENCE		Oak Hill	1903	Hawkins Chapel	1903
Monticello	1810	Palestine	1880	Jackson Street	1952
New Hebron	1904	Palmetto	1854	Kynett	1873
Pleasant Grove	1886	Plantersville	1907	Macedonia	1860-1900
Tilton	1881	Pleasant Grove	1859	Mallalieu	1904
Topeka	1941	Pleasant Valley		New Hope	1860
		Saint Luke	1958		
LEAKE		Saint Mark	1932	**LOWNDES**	
Carthage: First	1848	Saint Paul		Artesia	1860
Conway	1900	Saltillo	1896	Broadacres	1961
Forest Grove	1876	Shannon	1869	Brownlee	1887
Freeny	1904	Sherman	1910	Caledonia	1908
Goshen	1848	Shiloh	1903	Central	1902

Columbus: First	1823
Crawford	1850
Flint Hill	1868
Military	1872
New Hope	1843
Piney Grove	1828
Saint James	1870
Saint Stephen	1960
Shaeffer's Chapel	1820s
Wesley	1956
Wrights Chapel	

MADISON

Camden	1831
Canton	1836
Canton: First	1836
Flora	1884
Little Zion	
Lone Pine	1867
Madison	1864
Parkway Hills	1994
Ridgeland: First	1896
Rock Hill	
Saint Johns	1939
Saint Matthews	1988
Sharon	1836
Thornton Chapel	1855

MARION

Baylis Chapel	1901
Chapel Of The Cross	1977
Columbia Valley	1960
Columbia: First	1823
Foxworth	1909
Hopewell	1846-1872
Hub Chapel	1900
Kokomo	1911
New Hope Memorial	1866

New Zion	1890
Pleasant Valley	1845
Saint Paul	1875
Sandy Hook	1909
Zion Ridge	

MARSHALL

Asbury	1866
Barton	
Bethlehem	1850s
Byhalia	1842
Calvin	
Cornersville	1874
Early Grove	1860
Holly Springs: First	1837
Mount Pleasant	1841
Potts Camp	1889
Red Banks	1886
Rice's Chapel	1849
Saint Mary	
Strickland	1871
Taylors	1896
Victoria	1848
Waterford	1949

MONROE

Aberdeen: First	1836
Amory: First	1884
Antioch	
Athens	1879
Grady's Chapel	1897
Greenbrier	1850
Greenwood Springs	1880
Hamilton	1871
Kings	1885
New Bethel	
New Hope	
New Point	

New Salem	
Paine Memorial	
Pleasant Grove	
Prairie	1876
Quincy	
Riggan Chapel	1905
Saint Andrews	1959
Saint James	1887
Saint Mark	1962
Saint Matthews	
Saint Peter	1867
Smithville	1838
Spruell	1900
Strong	1856
Tranquil	1847
Valley	1980
Wesley	

MONTGOMERY

Bethlehem	1846
Binford Chapel	1889
Columbiana	1886
Duck Hill	1850
Haven	1880
Kilmichael	1852
Moore Memorial	1871
Mount Zion	
New Hope	1899
Shady Grove	1957
Stewart	

NESHOBA

Cook's Chapel	1874
Great Spirit	1980
Green Hill	
Henry's Chapel	
Hope	1873
Hopewell	1883

Longino	
Macedonia	1928
Mars Hill	1885
Mount Zion	1880s
North Bend	1853
Philadelphia: First	1837
Prairie Chapel	
Saint Mark	1900
Sandtown	1834
Southside	1947
Stallo	
Stevens Chapel	1911

NEWTON

Chunky	1888
Conehatta	1870
Decatur	1838
Hickory	1860
Hull Memorial	
Mount Zion	1861
Newton: First	1865
Pleasant Valley	1900
Sylvester	
Thirkield	1920
Union Chapel	
Union	1864
Wesley Chapel	

NOXUBEE

Asbury	1880
Baldwin	1903
Brooksville	1829
Cooksville	1834
Drake Hill	1955
Macedonia	1854
Macon: First	1834
Mashulaville	1857
Mount Moriah	1886

Mount Nebo	
New Hope	1885-1900
Saint Michael	1900
Saint Paul	1867
Salem	1881
Salem	1850
Shuqualak	1850s
Wesley	1851
X-Prairie	1842

OKTIBBEHA

Adaton	1878
Aldersgate	1960
Bell Chapel	
Big Creek	1878
Boyd Chapel	1866
Griffin Chapel	1867
Jones Chapel	
Lindsey Chapel	
Longview	
Maben	1894
New Light	
New Prospect	
Pleasant Grove	1869
Pleasant Hill	
Pliars	
Pugh's Mill	1890
Rock Hill	
Starkville: First	1835
Sturgis	1880s
Zion Cypress	
Zion Franklin	

PANOLA

Batesville: First	1844-1872
Chapel Hill	1860
Cold Springs	1893
Como	1841

Courtland	1871
Crenshaw	1906
Davis Chapel	1850s
Eureka	1857
Fredonia	1856
Longtown	
Mount Olivet	1873
Pisgah	1854
Pleasant Grove	
Pope	1845
Saint Paul	
Sardis	1850
See's Chapel	1855
Shiloh	1874
Terza	1857
Wesley Chapel	1912

PEARL RIVER

Byrds Chapel	1820
Merrill Chapel	
Newton Chapel	1920
Picayune: First	1907
Poplarville	1883
Weems Chapel	1914
Wesley Chapel	1890s

PERRY

Beaumont	1904
Little Creek-Bolton Chapel	
McLain	
Moody's Chapel	1882
New Augusta	1904
Richton	1903

PIKE

Centenary	1873-1884
Felder	1843
Fernwood	1898

Johnston Chapel	1909
Magnolia: First	1856
Osyka	1894
Pearl River Avenue	1908
Pisgah	1893
Saint Andrews	1902
Saint James	1863
Saint Paul	
Summit	1859

PONTOTOC

Algoma	1895
Buelah Grove	
Ebenezer	1894
Ecru	1908
Fairview	1947
McDonald	1864
Mount Nebo	1876
Palestine	1857
Pleasant Grove	
Pontotoc: First	1836
Robbs	
Sand Springs	1921
Thaxton	
Troy	1882
Usher Valley	1896

PRENTISS

Asbury	1890
Baldwyn: First	1861
Blythe's Chapel	
Booneville: First	1867
Carolina	1858
Christ	
Crossroads	1840s
Grace	1953
Jumpertown	

Lebanon	
Liberty	1860
Marietta	
Meadow Creek	1943
Mount Nebo	1835
Pisgah	1852
Siloam	1870
Thrasher	
Wheeler	1900

QUITMAN

Henry Chapel	
Lambert	1902
Marks	1879
Pilgrim Rest	1913
Sledge	1901
Wesley Chapel	1950-1973

RANKIN

Andrew Chapel	1856-1899
Brandon: First	1836
Crossgates	1973
Drakes	1858
Evergreen	1869
Fannin	1871
Flowood	1948
Greenfield	1895
Greer Chapel	1935
Gulde	1876
Holly Bush	1879
Johns	1890
Little Zion	1927
Lodebar	1830
Marvin	1877
McLaurin Heights	1959
Monterey	1900
Mount Pleasant	1900

Mountain Ridge	1867
Pearl: First	1909
Pelahatchie: First	1878
Puckett	1831
Richland	1871
Saint James	1886
Saint Marks	1973
Shiloh	1826
Taylorsville	
Wesley	
Wesleyanna	1847

SCOTT

Carr	1830
Christian Banner	1896
Ebenezer	
Forest	1861
Green Grove	
Harperville	1896
High Hill	1878-1882
Homewood	1884
Independence	1867
Kalem	1928
Lake	1862
Lake Central	1903
Lynch Chapel	1868
Mars Hill	
Morton: First	1870
New Chapel	
Sebastopol	
Sherman Hill	
Sylvester	1949
Union Grove	1880

SHARKEY

Anguilla	1869
Clark's Chapel	1914

Goodman Memorial	1884
Rolling Fork	1848

SIMPSON

Bethany	1840s
Braxton	1901
D'Lo	1900
Harrisville	1849
Magee: First	1899
Mendenhall	1903
Rexford	
Rials Creek	1860

SMITH

Burns	1904
Cedar Grove	1890s
Gasque Chapel	1882
Mize	1903
Old Bay Springs	1894
Pleasant Hill	
Raleigh: First	1837
Sylvarena	1924
Taylorsville: First	1902
Unity	1905
Warren Hill	1900

STONE

Bond	1885
H. A. Brown Memorial	1993
Mount Zion	1899
Wiggins: First	1904

SUNFLOWER

Beasley	
Caile	1896
Christ	1975
Drew	1900

Hales Chapel	
Indianola: First	1888
Inverness	1901
Linn	1877
Mallalieu	1904
Moorhead	1904
Rasberry	1890s
Ruleville: First	1868
Sunflower	1899
Wallace Chapel	1945

TALLAHATCHIE

Bethel	1940
Charleston: First	1847
Glendora	
Oak Grove	1875
Rollins	
Tippo	1890s
Tutwiler	1891
Webb Sumner	1964

TATE

Arkabutla	1854
Coldwater	1886
Greenleaf	1859
Hebron	
Hunters Chapel	1878
Independence	1859
Mount Vernon	
Palestine	1877
Senatobia: First	1880
Truslow	1903
Tyro	

TIPPAH

Adkins Chapel	1896
Blue Mountain	1909

Bowers Chapel	1906
Brownfield	1895
Campground	1853
Christ	1963
Dumas	1888
Ebenezer	1836
Falkner	1854
Friendship	
Golden Hill	
Jacobs Chapel	1887
Lowry	1926
Moses Chapel	1884
Mount Pleasant	1895
New Harmony	1915
New Hope	1883
Paynes Chapel	1874
Ripley: First	1836
Saint Paul	1868
Shady Grove	1905
Union Grove	1873
Walnut	1907

TISHOMINGO

Belmont	1849
Boggs Chapel	1903
Burnsville	
Campground	1857
Dennis	1908
Golden Chapel	1967
Harmony	1885
Iuka: First	1859
Mount Evergreen	
Old Bethel	1849
Paradise	1858
Patrick	1939
Pleasant Hill	1875
Rocky Springs	1850

Rutledge	1904	Eagle Lake	1949	**WEBSTER**	
Salem	1850	Gibson Memorial	1889	Bellefontaine	1835
Snowdown	1845	Hawkins	1951	Chapel Hill	1865
Spring Hill	1909	Lynch Chapel	1866	Dumas Chapel	
Tishomingo: First	1915	Northview	1950	Eupora: First	1873
		Porter's Chapel	1830	Lebanon	1850
TUNICA		Redbone	1814	Liberty	1882
Robinsonville	1896	Redwood	1949	Mathiston	
Tunica	1890	Wesley	1858	Mount Moriah	1800s
				Nebo	1800s
UNION		**WASHINGTON**		Piney Jordan	
Bethlehem	1860	Arcola	1854-1866	Providence	1880
Calvary	1961	Avon	1902	Saint Stephen	
Ebenezer		Glen Allan	1839		
Friendship	1860	Grace	1956	**WILKINSON**	
Glenfield	1884	Greenville: First	1836-1844	Centreville	1811
Ingomar	1886	Hollandale	1864	Hopewell	1834
Liberty		Leland: First	1897	Macedonia	1860
Mallalieu		Revels	1889	Mars Hill	1859
Mount Olivet	1854	Trinity	1949	Mount Carmel	1855
Mount Zion	1854			Rosetta	1927
Myrtle	1888	**WAYNE**		White's Chapel	1900
New Albany: First	1874	Big Rock	1832-1881	Woodville	1812
Saint Mary's	1887	Boyles Chapel	1900-1901		
Salem	1840	Buckatunna	1885	**WINSTON**	
Union Hill	1860	Clara	1903	Bevil Hill	
		Hebron	1840s	Campground	1844
WALTHALL		Mamie C Weaver	1920	Center Ridge	1859
Brandon Bay		Mount Carmel	1888	Flower Ridge	1860s
New Bethel	1927	Mount Zion	1903	Hopewell	
Oak Grove	1896	New Hope	1881	Louisville: First	1835
Saint James	1924	Pleasant Grove	1870	Maple Spring	
Sartinville	1813	Poplar Springs		Middleton	1893
Tylertown	1895	Providence	1878	Mount Hebron	1887
		Saint Luke		Mount Pisgah	1882
WARREN		Salem	1893	New Hope	1870
Bovina	1873	Wayne Haven	1965	Noxapater	1875
Bradley Chapel	1888	Waynesboro: First	1858	Piney Grove	
Crawford Street	1834	Winchester	1816	Pleasant Hill	1937

Rocky Hill	1830	Oakland	1838	Holly Bluff	1889
Rural Hill	1845	Tillatoba	1892	Midway	1857
Saint Peter	1896	Water Valley: First	1845	Mount Olivet	1829
Vernon	1921			Mount Pleasant	1870s
Wesley	1874	**YAZOO**		Pleasant Hill	1896
Whitehall	1887	Benton	1829	Saint John's	1952
		Bentonia	1884	Saint Stephens	1866
YALOBUSHA		Bethany	1898	Satartia	1872
Bethlehem	1901	Couparle		Wesley Chapel	1833
Coffeeville	1828	Eden		Wesley Chapel	1881
Goshen	1854	Ellison	1842	Yazoo City: First	1829
North Main		Fletcher's Chapel	1849		

BIBLIOGRAPHY

Books

A Complete History of Methodism as Connected with the Mississippi Conference of the Methodist Episcopal Church, South (1799-1845), by John G. Jones, 1877.

A History of North Mississippi Methodism, 1820-1900, by G. R. Miller, 1966.

Hometown Mississippi, Towne Square Books, by James Brieger, 1980,1997

Methodism in the Mississippi Conference, 1846-1870, by J. B. Cain, 1939.

Methodism in the Mississippi Conference, 1871-1884, by W. B. Jones, 1951.

Methodism in the Mississippi Conference, 1884-1919, by J. A. Lindsey, 1964.

Methodism in the Mississippi Conference, 1920-1939, by J. A. Lindsey, 1980.

Mississippi Circuit Riders, 1865-1965, by John Graham, 1969.

Our Heritage, Historical Highlights of United Methodism in North Mississippi, 1986.

The Mississippi Conference of the Methodist Protestant Church, 1829-1939, by W. L.. Hamrick, 1957.

Periodicals

New Orleans Christian Advocate, 1850-1946.

Mississippi United Methodist Advocate, 1947-1998.

231

CONTRIBUTORS

Abbott, Dee Thornton
Abel, Annie Lou
Abernathy, Mac W.
Adams, Nellie M.
Adams, Ora C.
Ainsworth, Mable Virginia
Alford, Dorothy Moore
Anderson, Winston
Andrews, Betty
Arthur, Janet
Ashley, Jane
Aycock, Joyce C.
Backstrom, Elsie
Banes, Eugene
Barham, Ron
Barnes, Irene
Barton, Nona
Bell, Bernice L.
Bell, Melanie
Bell, Rogers
Bending, Willie King
Blackman, Joan
Blackwell, Sylvia
Blake, Patricia
Bohannon, Annie G.
Bostick, Lois (Mrs. O. E.)
Bourgeois, Shirley
Box, Florence

Boyd, Louise
Bridgforth, Lucie R.
Brieger, James
Brooks, Louise
Brooks, Mrs. O. B.
Brown, Thomas B.
Buchannan, Mrs. Nancy
Bucklin, Pistol
Burns, Bonnie
Burns, Sarah
Burrell, Blanche A.
Burton, Riley
Cain, Dr. J. B.
Caldwell, Irene
Campbell, Beatrice
Cantelou, Peggy
Carpenter, Van
Carr, Mable
Carrington, Katie Mae
Carroll, David W.
Carroll, Ruth M.
Carter, Sylvia
Cartwright, Laura
Cason, Wally
Chapman, Wylma
Chase, Pete
Cheroni, Joan
Clark, Barbara

Clark, Betsy
Clark, Dora D.
Clark, Lynn
Clarke, Mrs. Cornelia
Clarke, Mrs. Eugene S.
Cochran, Mitch
Coile, W.
Condia, Irma
Conger, Tom W. Jr.
Connell, Ruth M.
Conner, Mrs. L. D.
Corley, Mrs. Allene
Cotton, Jackie
Cotton, James W.
Cotton, Laura
Covington, Ruth
Cox, Lynda M.
Crabtree, Cheryl
Crawley, Jean
Crist, Alyce D.
Cupit, Barry
Cutts, Elizabeth
Daniel, Ray
Daniels, Mrs. Earl K.
Davis, Eloise A.
Davis, Louise
Davis, Willye Mary
Dean, Eleanor

Dick, Helen
Dickson-Richel, Rod
Dillard, Bobbie
Dodd, Sam
Donald, Meredith
Downey, Mrs. F. P.
Drew, Thomas M.
Duke, Margaret
Dyess, Bobbie
Eaton, Dorrence
Echols, Samuel L.
Edge, C. D.
Edwards, Deborah
Egger, Verna R.
Ehlers, William C.
Eidt, Webbie
Ellison, Bonnie A.
Elmore, Pat
Ely, Frank
Eshelberger, Vonnie
Estes, Mrs. Jap W.
Evans, Mary Rankin
Fisher, Celia Coleman
Fleming, Harold
Fleming, Hubert
Flowers, Inez
Folks, Helen
Forrest, Lena Mae
Fortner, Mrs. Pete Jr.
Franklin, Juanita Doris
Frazier, L. W.
Furr, Katherine M.
Galloway, Mrs. Charles R.
Gammill, Gerald B.
Gaughf, Rev. Keith
Gill, Rob
Givens, Roy A.

Gladney, Elizabeth
Gluver, Jack
Goodpaster, Deborah
Gordon, Hattie F.
Gray, Lucille
Gray, Sarah
Grissom, Lela S.
Groves, Colleen
Guardia, Marilyn
Hallford, Charles
Hannah, Wattine
Harden, Jean
Hardin, Doug
Harkins, Regina
Harms, Jason
Harper, Colonel Douglas
Harrell, Clell
Hart, Luther M.
Harvey, Ruth M.
Havens, Mrs. Ellen
Hawkins, Eddie
Hawks, Tom C.
Hayes, Reba
Hays, Mrs. S. D.
Henry, A. V.
Hensleigh, Kathryn Luke
Herod, Ann D.
Herrin, Mildred Mrs.
Herring, Howard
Hicks, R. Michael
Hill, D. Kenneth
Hillman, Byrd
Himebrook, Robert
Hintson, Cecille
Hobart, Rachel
Holland, Wade A.
Holloman, Mrs. Helen D.

Hollowell, Tom
Horton, Joy H.
Houston, Frenchie
Howard, Peggy
Howell, Walter G.
Hubbard, Norma
Hughley, Walter
Hunter, Homer
Hurlbert, Wanda
Ingerson, Clarence
Jackson, Martha
Jackson, Mary Jane
Jacobs, Addie W.
Johnson, Charlotte
Johnson, Claude
Johnson, Effie
Johnson, Mrs. Eunice
Johnson, Kathy
Johnson, Mary L.
Johnson, R. Wayne
Jones, Reverend John G.
Jones, Mrs. Cecil (Jewel)
Jordan, Mrs. Fay
Kaufman, Ann
King, Jimmie Lou
King, Ralph H. Sr.
Knight, Gary
Knight, Janie
Kynerd, Wilma
Landfair, Ozell Sr.
Landrum, Vicki Watkins
Latham, Albert
Lawson, Joseph R.
Lee, Marilyn
Leftwich, E. P.
Lehmann, Faye
Levy, Levora

Lewis, Harold D.

Lewis, Mrs. Peek

Lindsey, J. A.

Livingston, Rep. Richard

Loflin, Jack

Lofton, Christina

Luckett, Grace

Mabry, Mrs. Louise

Mangum, Alice

Marler, A. W. Jr.

Marler, Clyde

Marshall, Mrs. Ina T.

Martin, Elise

Mashburn, A.

Massingill, Lamar

Matthews, Ruth B.

McBryde, Betty L.

McCain, Don

McCain, Katherine

McCarty, Mrs. H. F.

McCool, Mrs. Maxine M.

McCormick, M. L.

McCormick, Richard

McCullough, Mrs. Bob

McEwen, Harriett

McIntosh, Debra

McKie, Mary Lou

McKinney, Melvin

McLain, Jo

McLean, Oliver

McMillan, Mrs. Charles D.

McRaney, Dwight

Meadors, Bishop Marshall

Miles, Barbara

Miller, Betty

Miller, Hilda

Miller, Dr. Jean

Miller, Mary K.

Mills, Eugenia

Mills, Leslie F.

Mills, William

Mingee, Barbara

Minty, Bill

Mitchell, Carolyn

Moffatt, Curtis

Money, Annie L.

Monts, Flossie

Mooney, Linda

Moore, Mrs. Ella R.

Moses, Edward

Muse, Mrs. R. C.

Nabors, Dr. Jack

Neblett, Rev. R. P.

Neely, Eloise

Nichols, Fae

Nichols, Mary

Nichols, Sophie Scott

Nimocks, Frances Lane

Norsworthy, Blanch Ellis

Oaks, Shelby

Oaks, Zenobia

Oglesby, Mary Jane

Oney, Ruth R.

Pace, Jennifer

Parker, Martha

Parr, Mrs. J. H.

Patterson, Thomas W.

Perrott, Hughlene A.

Perry, Sandra

Peters, Ruth H.

Philpot, Juanita

Pigott, Arva

Pittman, Dr. Mabel H.

Pittman, Robert

Porter, Jim

Potter, Sue

Prestage, Margaret

Price, Gerri

Price, J. E. "Sam"

Price, Mrs. O. O.

Provost, Mrs. C. N.

Purvis, Dorothy

Purvis, Lanelle

Randle, Dale

Rasberry, Henderson

Reed, Thelma H.

Reid, Joe

Rhinehart, Wilodyne M.

Rippetoe, Willie L.

Robbins, Richard

Ross, James

Rush, Fonda

Sanders, Cheerie H.

Sawyer, Sarah

Scott, Mildred M.

Seay, Robert L.

Shadwick, Leonard

Shamp, B. R.

Sharbrough, Mrs. W. C. Jr.

Shelly, Sarah

Shivers, Jo F.

Sieger, Agnes H.

Sims, Caroline

Sims, Georgia

Smith, Dr. Alice Brown

Smith, Alice R.

Smith, Mrs. Becky

Soegle, Agnes

Sparrow, Martha

Speed, Charley Sue

Spight, Bettye

Spight, F. Leon

Staggs, John H.

Stanley, Nellie Weaver

Steed, Ella

Stepney, Joyce H.

Stewart, Thomas E.

Stockett, Cary

Strachan, Wanda

Talbert, Anne

Tanner, Marie

Tate, Barbara B.

Thomas, Mary Marguerite

Thomas, Nell H.

Thompson, Emily

Thompson, Mary S.

Thompson, Timothy C. Sr.

Thoms, Doug S.

Tillman, J. D.

Tillson, Miriam A.

Tourville, Elizabeth A.

Travis, Mrs. Lela J. Gloria

Twitchell, Mary

Tyson, Linda

Vice, Michael L.

Waddell, Charles E.

Wade, Robert C.

Wadsworth, Joan

Walden, Joovis

Walley, Mrs. Alberta

Watts, Elizabeth

Watts, Everette R.

Webster, Ann L.

Weigel, Grace S.

White, Mrs. Liza

Whiteside, Smith

Whitt, Jerry

Williams, Annie F.

Williams, Hazel M.

Williams, Jester C.

Williams, Lettye Ruth

Willoughby, David

Wilson, Mrs. Byron

Windham, Ellen C.

Winstead, Anne

Winstead, Dorothy

Witherspoon, Reuben C.

Wofford, Mrs. Mary Alice

Wong, Karen

Woodall, Ed

Yates, Mrs. Joseph W. Jr.

Young, Jim

Young, Leuneil

INDEX

ABOUT THE AUTHOR

WILLIAM L. JENKINS is a native of Yazoo City, Mississippi. He earned a Bachelor of Science in Education degree from Delta State University in Cleveland, Mississippi; a Master of Divinity degree from Southern Baptist Theological Seminary in Louisville, Kentucky; and a Doctor of Ministry degree from Columbia Theological Seminary in Decatur, Georgia. He has served pastorates in Mississippi, Kentucky, Wisconsin, and Georgia. He is married to Anita Cabral, and has a stepdaughter, Deanna; stepson, Chris; and stepgrandson, Tak William Kawasaki.

Jenkins is an elder in the Mississippi Annual Conference of The United Methodist Church. He currently serves as Chair of both the Mississippi Conference and Southeastern Jurisdiction Commission on Archives and History, and is a member of the General Commission of Archives and History. He has also served as Management Information Systems Director for the Mississippi Conference. He serves as Chair of the Mississippi Conference Bicentennial Steering Committee.

Jenkins has previously written *The Resurrection of John L. Jenkins: A Genealogy* (1985); *Pearlington: Church and Community* (1991); *Mississippi Conference Appointments: 1799 to 1995* (1995); and is completing a biography on Tobias Gibson, the first Methodist missionary to Mississippi, to be published in 1998 by Providence House Publishers.

"I am a sixth generation Mississippian by birth, and a United Methodist by conviction and choice. Collecting the histories of Mississippi United Methodist Churches has been one of the great joys of my life: combining love of my native State with devotion to my chosen denomination."